APL PROGRAMMING
AND
COMPUTER TECHNIQUES

COMPUTER SCIENCE SERIES

COMPUTER SCIENCE SERIES

APL PROGRAMMING AND COMPUTER TECHNIQUES

Harry Katzan, Jr.
Pratt Institute

VNR *Van Nostrand Reinhold Company*
New York Cincinnati Toronto London Melbourne

Van Nostrand Reinhold Company Regional Offices:
New York   Cincinnati   Chicago   Millbrae   Dallas

Van Nostrand Reinhold Company Foreign Offices:
London   Toronto   Melbourne

Manufactured in the United States of America.

Published by Van Nostrand Reinhold Company
450 West 33rd Street, New York, N.Y. 10001

Published simultaneously in Canada by
Van Nostrand Reinhold, Ltd.

15 14 13 12 11 10 9 8 7 6 5 4 3 2 1

PREFACE

Recent advances in the design of computer systems and programming languages have created a need for a state-of-the-art book on programming and computer techniques. This book has two objectives. The first is to present the APL language and terminal system. APL combines the power and relevance of Iverson's programming language* with the convenience of time sharing to provide an effective system for solving small, intermediate, and large-scale problems. The second objective is to provide an introduction to computer techniques for scientists, engineers, business analysts, and managers. One of the major difficulties, initially, is a conceptual one of gaining familiarity with basic computing concepts and recognizing possible applications. A significant portion of this book is directed toward this end and toward the presentation of general information on computer systems and devices and on programming systems and languages.

The APL language can be used by people with different backgrounds and at different levels of experience. The material is organized accordingly by presenting APL fundamentals, arrays and array operations, and topics in programming as separate chapters. The user need only acquaint himself with topics that are of interest to him. Several other highlights exist:

1. A liberal number of examples are included.
2. Most of the material is summarized for review and for reference.
3. Three annotated APL terminal scripts are included to interpret the discourse between the computer and the user.
4. Five appendices, including a collection of APL programs and a *prose glossary* of APL, give an idea of the kind of problems that can be solved with the system and familiarize the reader with APL terminology.

The book is composed of eight chapters and five appendices. The first chapter provides an introduction to computation and covers: the computer environment, numbers and the coding of information, types of data errors, data organization, and operators and operations. Although most of the material is known informally, it is not usually recorded in an introductory and concise manner.

*K. E. Iverson, *A Programming Language*, New York, Wiley, 1962.

v

Chapter 2, "Programs and Algorithms," is concerned with the essentials of computing and presents the following topics: the concept of an algorithm, programs, flow charting, and decision logic tables. The information is basic to computer programming and together with Chapter 3 provides the conceptual foundation required for effective computer utilization. Chapter 3, entitled "Basic Structure of Computers," is designed to give the reader a general familiarity with the computer and answers questions which might exist in the mind of an "inquisitive" scientist or engineer at this point. Topics included are: machine fundamentals, machine operation, and arithmetic operations.

Chapters 4, 5, and 6 are the most important in the book. It is here that the *art of programming* is firmly presented. The vehicle is the APL language, and the material is organized such that APL is introduced as well. For scientists, engineers, and analysts who have been exposed to programming, these chapters along with the appendices should provide all that is needed to effectively use the APL\360 system. Chapter 4, "Fundamentals of APL Programming," includes: an introduction; arithmetic and terminal operations; numeric constants; commands, statements, and expressions; primitive operators; mathematical functions; and an annotated script of APL fundamentals. Chapter 5, "Arrays and Operations on Arrays," gently introduces the concept and use of arrays in computing. The objective is to subordinate much of the detail, ordinarily associated with programming, to the programming system itself. Topics covered are: basic concepts, vectors and vector operations, matrices and arrays of higher dimension, functions on arrays, and an annotated script of array operations. The material increases in complexity so that the reader, if he so desires, can "abort" his study once his primary goals are satisfied. Chapter 6, "Topics in Programming," presents the traditional areas into which computing is usually divided: defined functions, sequence and control, input and output, and program checkout. The chapter concludes with an appropriate annotated script.

Chapters 7 and 8 relate the basic computing techniques, introduced in earlier chapters, to the computer systems and devices available commercially and to the programming systems and languages available for using them. The subject matter reflects the most recent technological advances but is not oriented toward any particular computer manufacturer. Chapter 7, "Computer Systems and Devices," covers basic system concepts, computer systems architecture, mass storage, and input/output devices. Chapter 8, "Programming Systems and Languages," covers the concept of an operating system, operating systems architecture, and the FORTRAN language.

The five appendices are for reference purposes. Appendix A, "APL Programs," contains a sample of operational APL programs. Areas covered are: graph plotting, statistics, mathematics, and business.   The programs are intended to acquaint the reader with APL techniques and to present a body of useful knowledge.   Appendix B, "APL\360," provides detailed information on a specific implementation of the language. Appendix C, "APL Functions," is for reference and describes the wide variety of APL functions in a useful format.   Appendix D, "APL Alphabet," presents information on the alphabet and keyboard arrangement of the APL terminal system.   One of the problems with most glossaries is that many readers are not sufficiently familiar with the terminology to use them effectively.   Appendix E, "Prose Glossary of APL," presents the traditional concepts in a narrative form so that the reader can associate terminology with the context in which it can be used.

The book is organized for the professional reader and contains a liberal number of examples appropriate to the material covered.   It would also be useful as a college or industrial textbook for a *computer techniques* course in an engineering, natural science, or social science curriculum. Used as a text, a term project relating to one of the categories of APL programs might then be particularly appropriate.

Harry Katzan, Jr.

White Plains, New York
April 1970

ACKNOWLEDGMENTS

The author wishes to acknowledge numerous sources that added to the quality of the manuscript. APL-MANHATTAN, a Division of Industrial Computer Systems, Inc., served as the source of programs given in Appendix A. Special recognition is given to Messrs. K. E. Korn, J. H Lamb, and W. R. Newman, all of that company, for valuable assistance and for the necessary computer time. Several authors have given permission to list their programs: Professor K. W. Smillie and Mr. E. M. Edwards of the University of Alberta, Mr. A. D. Falkoff of IBM, and Mr W. R. Newman of APL-MANHATTAN. Their contributions are gratefully acknowledged. The authors of all programs could not be determined; however, their efforts are acknowledged as well.

Three knowledgeable people reviewed the manuscript and gave valuable comments and suggestions: Mr. M. B. Lurie of IBM and Professors T. E. Cheatham of Harvard University and G. H. Foster of Syracuse University. Mr. T. F. Epley, Professional and Reference Editor of the Van Nostrand Reinhold Company, served as a continual source of administrative support.

Lastly, but of prime importance, special thanks are given to my wife Margaret, who typed the manuscript, and who did a notable job of providing inspiration and moral support.

Harry Katzan, Jr.

CONTENTS

APL PROGRAMMING
AND
COMPUTER TECHNIQUES

1 | INTRODUCTION

1.1 THE COMPUTER ENVIRONMENT

The processing of information involves some well-defined functions, regardless of whether the processing is performed by manual, mechanical, or electronic methods.

Information must initially be recorded. The information, or data, can originate in many ways, such as the reading of a dial, the recording of an event, or the extraction of a value from a table. The information can be recorded on a medium such as punched cards or tape by a human operator or be collected on an electromechanical device, such as a magnetic tape, which is part of the experimental apparatus. If the information is recorded in a coded form, then a hard copy, such as a typewritten sheet, is usually produced for human use.

Information must be transmitted to other locations. In most cases, information is processed in a different location from that in which it was recorded. Traditionally, manual methods were used for transporting documents and records. Modern telecommunications facilities have reduced the need for manual methods and have provided the user with direct access to the processing facility.

Information must be stored. It may be stored temporarily during processing or be stored permanently. The storage may involve a variety of forms and several transactions. The information may be stored in the same form as originally recorded or it may pass through several devices

3

during processing and eventually reside permanently on a direct-access mechanism. For example, input data may be typed in at a remote terminal, stored in a computer during processing, and then saved permanently on a disc storage volume. Results of the processing may be stored in a coded form and presented to the user as a typed report.

Information is eventually processed and results are obtained. In some cases, a small amount of data is entered into the computer, a large number of calculations are performed, and a small but significant amount of output is obtained. In other cases, a large amount of data is reduced to a few meaningful statistics. In yet other cases, information is stored for later retrieval.

Processed information must be made available to the ultimate users. The processed information may take the form of a printed report, an updated file, or the control of a physical process.

Later, it will become evident that a computer is organized in somewhat the same fashion, with devices for input-output, arithmetic, control, and storage.

Conceptual Description of a Digital Computer

Essentially, the electronic computer is a system for accepting, judging, and otherwise processing or usefully modifying information. Thus, it extends our brainpower as other man-machines enlarge muscle power.

Somewhat like its human inventor, the computer operates on *symbols*. That is, it operates on symbolic representations of physical or abstract information, which can take the form of numeric data or a coded representation of characters or events. The computer is said to operate on operands which are usually regarded as sequences of digits. The primary arithmetic operations are addition, subtraction, multiplication, and division for which the operands are interpreted as numeric data. Operands are also regarded as numeric for certain comparison and logical operations. Most computers include nonarithmetic operations for processing coded information, for control and decision making, and for input and output.

In general, the operations provided by digital computers are elementary and do not directly represent complex operations such as differentiation, integration, or even summation. Thus, complex operations must be synthesized from sequences of elementary operations. The great speed of modern computers has enabled increasingly sophisticated sequences of elementary operations to be constructed and has created a need for a new type of human activity, *computer programming*. This book endeavors to put the power of the computer into the hands of the scientist and engineer through programming.

Major Computer Applications

From space flight to data analysis, computers have become involved in the everyday life of most scientists and engineers. In spite of a wide range of diversity, the vast majority of computer applications can be placed into some well-defined classes. The classifications tend to be independent of how the computer is accessed, that is, whether the scientist or engineer uses the machine via a. remote terminal, whether he submits his work locally on punched cards or tape, or whether the computer is intimately involved with the physical apparatus of an experiment or process. The classifications tend to be more conceptual than actual, and a given problem could conceivably be placed in two distinct categories by different investigators.

Descriptive Computing. This type of computing provides the user with more information on a subject, such as the area under a curve, the trajectory of a space vehicle, or the design parameters of an airplane or road. The object under consideration is usually defined mathematically and the formulae are normally used in the computer calculations.

Data Analysis. This type of computing often involves statistics and permits the scientist or engineer to draw conclusions from actual or experimental data. This category also draws heavily upon mathematics; however, the calculations frequently involve simple comparison operations, for checking tolerance conditions, and logical operations, for determining combinations of events.

Simulation. This category concerns mathematical or procedural models of physical processes or events involving the interrelationship of independent variables. The use of simulation models permits decision makers to evaluate alternatives without having to implement real-life systems.

Optimization. This category involves finding the best solution to a problem of a given type. Research in mathematics and operations research has uncovered a collection of prototype problems, for which solutions are known. Thus optimization amounts to determining which of the prototype problems applies to a given situation and using the techniques inherent therein.

Experimental Process Control. The operation of many physical processes and laboratory experiments can be aided by using a computer to collect data or provide real-time control of the process. In applications of this type, one of the input or output functions is usually a sensory or control device.

Data Processing. Like its business counterpart, scientific data processing involves the creation and updating of files of information and the generation of reports from these data. The files usually contain numerical data from which summary calculations are made and with which data analysis is performed.

Information Retrieval. Many applications in science and engineering require that case histories be maintained or results stored such that they can be retrieved on a demand basis. Mass storage devices are used to store the data to which the user has access with remote terminals or by using traditional batch processing techniques.

Obviously, other applications of computers exist that cannot be classed into the categories given above. It follows that any problem which can be defined can be programmed. The word "defined" is important here and means that the solution to the problem can be broken down into a series of steps that can be represented as a sequence of computer instructions.

The Capabilities and Limitations of Computers

Computers have some well-defined characteristics which make them useful for certain applications and not for others. A computer performs repetitive operations very rapidly and with great reliability. Yet, it requires that all steps in the solution of a problem be stated explicitly. Thus, applications requiring intuitive and adaptive behavior are not generally amenable to computer programming. Recent advances in machine intelligence have widened the scope of computers considerably, and as computer technology evolves as a science, it is likely that more intuitive and adaptive behavior can be programmed.

1.2   NUMBERS AND THE CODING OF INFORMATION

In the outside world, symbolic information can be conveniently recorded by the digits 0 through 9, the letters of the alphabet, and special characters such as the parenthesis, the dollar sign, and the decimal point. The computer, by design, stores the same characters in a form chosen for the internal representation of data. In some machines, the internal coding scheme is binary, and in others it is a form of binary coded decimal. Although the scientist or engineer need not necessarily be aware of the internal coding scheme, he must be familiar with the forms and properties of decimal numbers and how they are coded in punched cards or tape.

Number Representation

In performing ordinary arithmetic, most people deal with sequences of decimal digits, a decimal point, and possibly an algebraic sign. Actual arithmetic is performed using well-defined rules for signs and decimal points and by using digit-by-digit operations on the numbers. Numbers of this type are termed *fixed-point* or *decimal* numbers. Thus, a fixed-point number x is represented by an expression of the form

$$x = n + 0.d_1 d_2 d_3 \ldots$$

where n is a whole number and each d_i is a digit between 0 and 9. An *integer* is a fixed-point number with no fractional part and is treated as a specific type of operand in some programming systems. Integer arithmetic has some properties of interest here. When integers are added, subtracted, or multiplied, the result is a whole number. The same holds true for division. If the division of integer a by integer b is defined by

$$a = q \cdot b + r, \qquad \text{with } r < b$$

then the result is the quotient q and the remainder r is lost. Thus, in integer arithmetic

$$(3 \div 2) \times 4 = 4$$

Clearly, the rule applies to expressions on an operation-by-operation basis. With the APL programming system, the user need not be concerned with integer arithmetic; with other systems, such as FORTRAN, integers are regarded as a specific type of operand.

Although fixed-point arithmetic is satisfactory for some calculations, it is not convenient for representing very large or very small numbers. For example, Young's modulus, which is 30,000,000 pounds per square inch, is frequently written as 0.3×10^8 to facilitate computation. A similar situation exists in handling the range of numbers from large to small in a computer. To avoid carrying a great many digits and to eliminate the effort of keeping track of the location of the decimal point for these numbers, a *floating-point* representation is used. A common procedure is to maintain the seven or eight most significant digits of a number plus a two- or three-digit *exponent* or *characteristic* to indicate the proper position of the decimal point. The fractional part of a floating-point number is frequently called the *mantissa*. For example, the number

$$-.00000061957533$$

can be expressed as

$$-.61957533 \times 10^{-6}$$

However, this representation requires carrying two signs: one for the exponent and one for the fraction. This is inconvenient for computers which have only one sign associated with a storage location. Therefore, a common practice is to *bias* the exponent by adding a positive base value. Using a base value of 50, the exponent in the preceding example becomes $50 + (-06) = 44$ and the internal representation of the number becomes

| $-$ | 44 | 61957533 |

Normally, as implied here, the exponent and fraction are each represented by a sequence of digits in the same computer storage location; the circuitry of the machine makes whatever adjustments are necessary during the execution of numeric operations.

The ordinary user of computers need not be concerned with the internal form of numbers and is aware only of their external representation. The subject of *numeric constants* is covered in detail in Section 4.3.

The Accuracy of Floating-Point Numbers

In preceding examples, numbers to the base ten were used. It should be recognized that in many machines, the internal representation of data is not to the base ten but to another base such as two or sixteen. Using a base b, a floating-point number is written as

$$N = n \times b^e$$

where n is the fraction and e is the exponent. Most computations are performed with the fraction in *normalized* format which implies that the base point is considered to be immediately to the left of the first nonzero digit.

In computers, only a finite number of digits can be used to represent numbers that are directly usable as operands by the circuitry of the machine. Thus, all numbers are restricted to a fixed range of values and most numbers contain a round-off error in their low-order positions. For example, the six-digit sequence .666666 more accurately represents the fraction $\frac{2}{3}$ than does the four-digit sequence .6666. Internal to the computer, the accuracy and range of values is determined by the number of digits allocated to the exponent and to the fraction. The number of digits in the exponent determines the range of values and the number of digits in the fraction determines the accuracy of the values. The following basic relationships can now be stated:

1. If k digit positions are used to represent the fraction, then the normalized fraction n satisfies the condition

$$b^{-1} \leq |n| \leq 1 - b^{-k}$$

   or is zero.

2. If l digit positions are used to represent the exponent e, then

$$|e| \leq b^l - 1$$

3. All floating-point values N are restricted to the range

$$b^{-1} b^{(1-b^l)} \leq |N| \leq (1 - b^{-k}) b^{(b^l - 1)}$$

In a decimal machine, for example, where $b = 10$, $k = 10$, and $l = 2$,

$$.1 \leq |n| \leq .9999999999$$
$$e \leq 99$$
$$10^{-100} \leq |N| \leq (1 - 10^{-10})10^{99}$$

Coding of Information

It was mentioned earlier in this section that a computer operates on symbolic representations of actual data and that these data may exist in a coded form. For entry into the computer, data and programs, as well, must be coded in a medium of some kind, such as punched cards or paper tape, or be typed in at a remote terminal. In the latter case encoding takes place during the transmission of information, but it is transparent to the user. During the input process, the external representation is converted to internal representation, whether it be a numeric form or a coded form. The conversion is done by a combination of hardware and software facilities. For output, the process is reversed.

Figures 1.1 and 1.2 give an example of a punched card and a segment

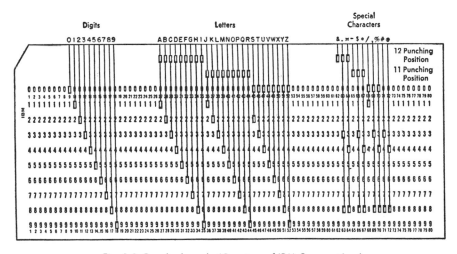

Fig. 1.1 Punched card. (Courtesy of IBM Corporation.)

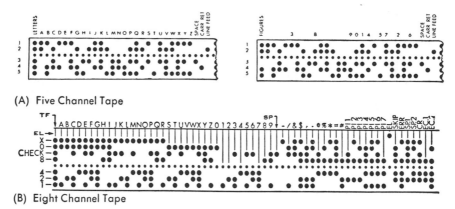

(A) Five Channel Tape

(B) Eight Channel Tape

Fig. 1.2 Punched tape. (Courtesy of IBM Corporation.)

of punched tape; Figure 1.3 pictures a communications terminal. As described in Table 1.1, punched cards come in two forms: Binary Coded Decimal (BCD), often called Hollerith cards, and Extended Binary Coded Decimal Interchange Code (EBCDIC). The codes are quite similar and are produced by the IBM 026 and IBM 029 card punches, respectively, as well as a variety of on-line card punches. Table 1.1 also contains the American Standard Code for Information Interchange (ASCII), which is authorized by The United States of America Standards Association. Binary and hexadecimal equivalents are given for EBCDIC and ASCII; a representative set of binary and octal equivalents are given for BCD.

Fig. 1.3 Computer terminal device. (Courtesy of IBM Corporation.)

TABLE 1.1   CODED INFORMATION[a]

Symbol	BCD Card[b]	BCD Code[c]	Octal[d]	Binary	Symbol	EBCDIC Card	EBCDIC Hexadecimal	EBCDIC Binary	ASCII Binary (7-bit code)
A	12-1	BA1	61	110001	A		C1	11000001	1000001
B	12-2	BA2	62	110010	B		C2	11000010	1000010
C	12-3	BA21	63	110011	C		C3	11000011	1000011
D	12-4	BA4	64	110100	D		C4	11000100	1000100
E	12-5	BA41	65	110101	E		C5	11000101	1000101
F	12-6	BA42	66	110110	F		C6	11000110	1000110
G	12-7	BA421	67	110111	G		C7	11000111	1000111
H	12-8	BA8	70	111000	H		C8	11001000	1001000
I	12-9	BA81	71	111001	I		C9	11001001	1001001
J	11-1	B1	41	100001	J		D1	11010001	1001010
K	11-2	B2	42	100010	K		D2	11010010	1001011
L	11-3	B21	43	100011	L		D3	11010011	1001100
M	11-4	B4	44	100100	M		D4	11010100	1001101
N	11-5	B41	45	100101	N		D5	11010101	1001110
O	11-6	B42	46	100110	O		D6	11010110	1001111
P	11-7	B421	47	100111	P		D7	11010111	1010000
Q	11-8	B8	50	101000	Q		D8	11011000	1010001
R	11-9	B81	51	101001	R		D9	11011001	1010010
S	0-2	A2	22	010010	S		E2	11100010	1010011
T	0-3	A21	23	010011	T		E3	11100011	1010100
U	0-4	A4	24	010100	U		E4	11100100	1010101
V	0-5	A41	25	010101	V		E5	11100101	1010110
W	0-6	A42	26	010110	W		E6	11100110	1010111
X	0-7	A421	27	010111	X		E7	11100111	1011000
Y	0-8	A8	30	011000	Y		E8	11101000	1011001

TABLE 1.1 (continued)

Symbol	BCD Card[b]	BCD Code[c]	Octal[d]	Binary	Symbol	EBCDIC Card	EBCDIC Hexadecimal	EBCDIC Binary	ASCII Binary (7-bit code)
Z	0-9	A81	31	011001	Z		E9	11101001	1011010
$	11-3-8	B821	53	101011	$		5B	01011011	0100100
@	4-8	84	14	001100	@		7C	01111100	
#	3-8	821	13	001011	#		7B	01111011	0100011
0	0	82	12	001010	0		F0	11110000	0110000
1	1	1	01	000001	1		F1	11110001	0110001
2	2	2	02	000010	2		F2	11110010	0110010
3	3	21	03	000011	3		F3	11110011	0110011
4	4	4	04	000100	4		F4	11110100	0110100
5	5	41	05	000101	5		F5	11110101	0110101
6	6	42	06	000110	6		F6	11110110	0110110
7	7	421	07	000111	7		F7	11110111	0110111
8	8	8	10	001000	8		F8	11111000	0111000
9	9	81	11	001001	9		F9	11111001	0111001
(space)	(no punches)	(no code)	00	000000	(space)	(no punches)	40	01000000	0100000
=	3,8	821	13	001011	=	6-8	7E	01111110	0111101
+	12	BA	60	110000	+	12-6-8	4E	01001110	0101011
-	11	B	40	100000	-	11	60	01100000	0101101
*	11-4-8	B84	54	101100	*	11-4-8	5C	01011100	0101010
/	0-1	A1	21	010001	/	0-1	61	01100001	0101111
(	0-4-8	A84	34	011100	(	12-5-8	4D	01001101	0101000
)	12-4-8	BA84	74	111100	)	11-5-8	5D	01011101	0101001
,	0-3-8	A821	33	011011	,	0-3-8	6B	01101011	0101100
.	12-3-8	BA821	73	111011	.	0-5-8	4B	01001011	0101110

Symbol	Card code	BCD	Octal	Binary	Symbol	Card code	Hex	Binary	Binary
'(quote)	4-8	84	14	001100	'	5-8	7D	01111101	0100111
°	0-4-8	A84	34	011100	%	0-4-8	6C	01101100	0100101
;	11-6-8	B842	56	101110	;	11-6-8	5E	01011110	0111011
:	5-8	841	15	001101	:	2-8	7A	01111010	0111010
⌐	—	—	—	—		11-7-8	5F	01011111	—
¢	12	BA	60	110000	&	12	50	01010000	0100110
¬	—	—	—	—	-	11-7-8	4F	01001111	—
>	6-8	842	16	001110	>	0-6-8	6E	01101110	0111110
<	12-6-8	BA842	76	111110	<	12-4-8	4C	01001100	0111100
—(break)	—	—	—	—		0-5-8	6D	01101101	1011111
?	12-0	BA82	72	111010	?	0-7-8	6F	01101111	0111111

a Some codes are duplicated indicating that in one set, both symbols are not permitted.

b The numbers represent a punch in the indicated row for a given column of the card. For example, the letter A is represented by a punch in the 12 row and the 1 row; all other rows are left unpunched.

c In BCD code, a character of data is represented by a combination of the positional symbol BA8421, which can be recorded magnetically or by some physical means.

d Octal and binary codes correspond to the BCD codes and differ from system to system.

Punched tape comes in five-, seven-, or eight-channel varieties, and several coding schemes are used. A standard BA8421 weighted code is given. Only the characters most frequently used in scientific or engineering computations are listed, although with ASCII and EBCDIC codes, 2^7 (or 128) and 2^8 (or 256) different characters can be represented, respectively.

1.3 TYPES OF DATA ERRORS

The subject of data errors is of great concern in arithmetic computations for several reasons, which are not always obvious to the occasional user. First, as mentioned in previous sections, arithmetic is performed on a fixed number of digits. Thus, when the partial results exceed the size of arithmetic registers, values must be rounded or truncated. Next, small errors tend to snowball. Because of the speed of most computers, extremely long sequences of calculations can be performed. Small initial errors may significantly affect final results. Lastly, logical decisions in computers are effectively made on the relative values of numbers, stored internally. When the possibility of errors in data is not considered, the actual flow of a computer program can be altered   perhaps by a few meaningless digits.

Absolute and Relative Error

Most estimates, measurements, and calculations involve errors of some kind. They are usually classed as being absolute or relative. The sources of errors are considered in subsequent paragraphs.

Consider a number x approximated† by the number x^*. The difference $E = x - x^*$ is termed the *absolute error* and the ratio $E \div x$ is referred to as the *relative error*. In general, there is no prior knowledge whether E will be positive or negative, so the absolute value must be used. A realistic example might be to test if the absolute value of the absolute error is less than a prescribed amount e; if so, then a specified procedure should be performed. If not, then an alternate procedure is invoked. More specified, the example could be expressed as:

> if $\mid E \mid >e$ then do *procedure-1*
> otherwise do *procedure-2*

In many practical cases, the relative error is a better measure of the significance of an error than is the absolute error. A relative error test applied to the above example would be stated as:

> if $\mid E \div x \mid >e$ then do *procedure-1*
> otherwise do *procedure-2*

†In this context, the words *represented* or *estimated* would serve equally well.

Sources of Error

Data errors can arise in a variety of ways and deserve consideration in any numerical problem. Ordinarily, errors originate from some human activity such as measurement or programming, although in some cases they are caused by the nature of the computing hardware itself.

Initial Error. This type of error is the most frequent and results from variations in data recording or in taking measurements. If x is the true value of a data reading and x^* is the reading used in computation, perhaps reflecting an error in measurement, then the initial error is $x - x^*$. Initial errors are significant since they affect computed results regardless of how sophisticated the computer program might be.

Rounding Error. This type of error results when the less significant digits of a quantity are deleted and a rule of correction is applied to the remaining part. For example, pi, 3.14159265..., rounded to five significant digits, is 3.1416. An accepted rounding procedure is as follows: If rounding is to take place in the nth digit, then add 5 to the $(n+1)$st digit and truncate after the nth digit. Truncation is covered next.

Truncation Error. Truncation is the gentle art of chopping off a number after a certain number of digits; the resulting error is a truncation error. Truncating pi, in the preceding example, after five significant digits would yield 3.1415. Another common source of truncation error results from chopping off all terms in an infinite series expansion after a particular term. For example, cutting the series for e^x at

$$e^x = 1 + x + \frac{x^2}{2!} + \frac{x^3}{3!}$$

gives a truncation error—sometimes called a *residual error*—for series approximations.

Propagated Error. Errors accumulate or build up during computation. If x is the true value of a variable and x^* is used during computation, then $f(x) - f(x^*)$ is the propagated error.

Floating-point arithmetic with fixed length registers contains many pitfalls for the unwary programmer. By its very nature, floating-point arithmetic is inexact. Most applications require only limited precision, so the vast majority of users are not concerned with the problem. One of the major problems of numerical analysis, on the other hand, is to determine the accuracy of computed results. A good rule of thumb is that floating-point multiplication and division do not significantly affect the relative error but floating-point addition and subtraction do, especially when x is nearly equal to $-y$ for $x + y$ and x is nearly equal to y for $x - y$. In fact, the *associative law:*

$$x + (y + z) = (x + y) + z$$

does not hold for certain values of x, y, and z. When rounding to four digits after each operation, for example, it is easily shown that:

$$(31.58+88.43)+9.348 \neq 31.58+(88.43+9.348)$$

1.4   DATA ORGANIZATION

As a general rule, mathematics deals with symbolic quantities. The concept has enabled basic principles to be developed which apply to both theoretical and practical applications and which exist independently of a particular problem under consideration. The practice of representing quantities symbolically has found its way into everyday language, and the use of A, B, C's and x, y, z's has become an everyday occurence. Natural language is frequently inadequate for expressing a complex idea, whereas a symbol or a mathematical expression can often summarize what would take many qualifying phrases. This is an application of what is called *discursive mathematics*, an area which utilizes the notation but not the underlying theory of modern mathematics.

The idea of referring to operations and operands symbolically (i.e., by name) is also useful in computing and is a significant feature in most computer languages. Symbolic programming, as it is sometimes called, has contributed to the generality with which programs can be written and has made it easier to do so.

In programming, a symbolic name is most frequently used to denote a variable or a parameter, although in some cases it is used additionally to name a constituent of a computer language itself. The discussion here concerns data and how they are named and organized. Constituents of computer languages are covered in later chapters.

Scalars and Variables

A single item of data is known as a *scalar*. It can be expressed as a constant, in either a fixed-point or floating-point form, or as a variable. In computing, a *variable* names a data element, the value of which can change during execution of a program. Thus, a variable which names a scalar is termed a *scalar variable*. Most systems for programming contain facilities for defining and using variables and also provide for a variety of data types.

Arrays, Subscripts, and Indexing

It is often convenient to group data elements with the same characteristics and treat them as a single entity. Familiar examples are ordinary vectors and matrices. In general, the concept is extended to an *n*-dimensional ordered collection of elements which is termed an *array*. Only the array itself is given a name, and an individual data element is selected by giving its relative position in the array.

Consider, for example, the array A defined as follows:

$$
\begin{array}{ccccc}
a_{1,-2} & a_{1,-1} & a_{1,0} & a_{1,1} & a_{1,2} \\
a_{2,-2} & a_{2,-1} & a_{2,0} & a_{2,1} & a_{2,2} \\
a_{3,-2} & a_{3,-1} & a_{3,0} & a_{3,1} & a_{3,2} \\
a_{4,-2} & a_{4,-1} & a_{4,0} & a_{4,1} & a_{4,2}
\end{array}
$$

It has several properties of interest.   The first is the *number of dimensions*, of which it has two: a row dimension and a column dimension.   Each dimension is further characterized by a bounds and an extent.   The *bounds* of a dimension are the beginning and end of that dimension and determine the manner in which elements are referenced.   The *extent* is the number of elements in a dimension, independent of how they are referenced.   Thus in the array A, the row bounds are (1:4) and the column bounds are (-2:2). The row extent is 4 while the column extent is 5.

A *subscript* is a quantity used to select a data element of an array.   In ordinary mathematics, a subscript usually assumes its literal definition (e.g., a_{i+1}) although superscripts are frequently used.   Computer input is restricted to linear sequences of characters so that a substitutive convention is required.   The most widely accepted convention is to enclose subscripts, separated by a punctuation character, in parentheses or brackets. Thus, $A_{-2,1}$ would be represented as $A(-2,1)$ or $A[-2;1]$.   Ordinarily, a subscript may be a constant, a variable, or an expression; in either case, the accepted practice is to reduce its value to an integer before the selection of an element of an array takes place.

Very closely related in concept to that of subscripting is the notion of *indexing*.   It is frequently desired to count the number of times that a given portion of a program has been executed and to maintain the counter as an *index variable*, which can additionally be used as a subscript when necessary.   It is customary to use a subscript (or index) in both ways, giving it significance as a spacewise indicator and a timewise indicator, as well.

A great many programming problems can be greatly simplified if the data are organized as an array.   One of the outstanding features of the APL* programming system is that it permits operations to be performed on entire arrays thereby subordinating much of the detail usually associated with computer programming.   APL is considered in Chapter 4.

1.5   OPERATORS AND OPERATIONS

The concept of a function is basic to mathematics and is frequently used in everyday discourse.   It is customary to hear, for example, that the cost

---

*APL is an acronym for A Programming Language, based on: K. E. Iverson, *A Programming Language*, New York, John Wiley & Sons, Inc., 1962.

of a certain product is a function of its weight or its volume. A great many values are a function of several variables, similar to the way in which the cost of living is a function of the cost of money, the level of unemployment, the amount of government spending, etc.

In computer programming, an elementary function (such as addition) is termed an *operator*. It is elementary in the sense that it cannot be constructed from other elementary operators. The term *function* is reserved for a well-defined sequence of calculations composed of operators and other functions.

Monadic and Dyadic Operators

The ordinary operations of arithmetic, such as addition and multiplication, require two operands (e.g., $x+y$) and are classed as *dyadic operators*. Dyadic operators are further characterized by the fact that the operator separates the operands, as in $x+y$. Thus if $\lceil$ denotes the dyadic maximum operator, then $\max(x,y)$ would be expressed as $x \lceil y$.

It is possible to define, on the other hand, operators, such as negation, which require only one operand. For example, negation, which is frequently defined as*

$$-x \equiv 0-x$$

is a *monadic operator* and is characterized by the fact that it requires one operand which is preceded by the operator symbol. Similarly, the monadic absolute value operator, ordinarily represented by double bars (i.e., $|x|$), can also be denoted by a single verticle stroke; it is written and defined as

$$|x \equiv x \lceil (-x)$$

Arithmetic Operations and Expressions

Mathematical notation permits several operators to be combined in the same expression; for example

$$a \times b + 13 \div c$$

The concept has been included in most computer programming languages and permits the specification of complex sequences of calculations in a notation familiar to the user. The order in which operations are executed is of particular interest. First, parentheses are usually permitted and indicate groupings such that expressions within parentheses are executed before the expressions of which they are a constituent part. The concept is obviously extended to as many levels as necessary. The case where

---

*The symbol $\equiv$ should be read "is defined as."

parentheses are not used requires a second convention.   One of two methods is ordinarily chosen.   One method assigns a hierarchy to the operators so that the operators with the greatest hierarchy are executed first.   If, for example, multiplication takes precedence over addition, then

$$10 \equiv 2 \times 3 + 4$$

The other method involves executing the operators from right to left or left to right in a sequential manner.   Thus if right-to-left execution is selected, then

$$14 \equiv 2 \times 3 + 4$$

A choice between the two methods requires a study of basic concepts. APL permits monadic and dyadic operators to be defined in a context where the assignment of hierarchy is not feasible and has adopted a right-to-left rule for the execution of operators.

Comparison Operators

A familiar example of a dyadic operator is the comparison operator,* which compares the two operands algebraically.   The result of a comparison operation is a truth value with 1 representing *true* and 0 representing *false* in most systems.   Thus if $x = -4$ and $y = 6$, then

$$x < y \equiv 1$$
$$x \leq y \equiv 1$$
$$x = y \equiv 0$$
$$x > y \equiv 0$$
$$x > y \equiv 0$$
$$x \neq y \equiv 1$$

where the operators are defined as

$<$ less than
$\leq$ less than or equal to
$=$ equal to
$\geq$ greater than or equal to
$>$ greater than
$\neq$ not equal to

Logical Operators

Logical operations are frequently used to determine the truth of two or more assertions and can be combined with comparison operations to form expressions in much the same way that arithmetic expressions are formed.

*Frequently called a relational operator.

Two dyadic operators, *and* (denoted by ∧) and *or* (denoted by ∧), and one monadic operator, *not* (denoted by ∼) are generally used and are defined as follows:

1. A∨B is *true* if either A is *true* or B is *true* or both; thus
   A∨B = 1 if and only if A = 1 or B = 1.
2. A∧B is *true* if both A and B are *true*; thus
   A∧B = 1 if and only if A = 1 and B = 1.
3. ∼ A is *true* if A is *false*; thus
   ∼ A = 1 if and only if A = 0.

The following logical expression combines logical and comparison operators in the manner stated:

$$((x > y) \wedge (z = w)) \wedge u$$

and would assume the value *true* (e.g., the numerical value 1), for example, when $x = 4$, $y = 3$, $z = 10$, $w = 10$, and $u = 1$. Obviously, a whole family of values for the given variables would also give the expression a *true* value.

1.6   SUMMARY

Although advanced programming and operating systems have made it easier for the professional programmer and the occasional user to effectively utilize the digital computer, there still remains some introductory material which must be reviewed. The need for an introduction is more the result of a changing emphasis than a lack of basic knowledge on the part of the reader. As in any other field, technological advances create an interest in more subtle problems yet eliminate many of the details which previously shielded them.

In developing a system or simply a program, it is important to recognize the basic functions which are usually involved: recording, transmission, storage, processing, and reporting. Even though the same functions are involved in manual processing, it is necessary to relate them to the digital computer and to the major classes of applications: descriptive computing, data analysis, simulation, optimization, experimental and process control, data processing, and information retrieval. Obviously, the major applications exploit the capabilities of computers but implicitly indicate their limitations, as well.

Computers manipulate information which is represented numerically, and the internal and external forms that these data can assume must be defined. A study of data also requires that the various types of error be given and related to the source of these errors: initial error, rounding error, truncation error, and propagated error.

Most programming systems rely specifically on the manner in which data are organized and the operations that can be performed on them. The capability for organizing data over a large repetoire of operators facilitates programming and reduces one of the major problems in computers—the man-machine interface.

After this brief introduction, the experienced user may go directly to Chapter 4 and the APL programming system. The curious reader may wish to explore Chapters 2 and 3 to gain an intuitive feeling for programs, algorithms, and computers.

2 | PROGRAMS AND ALGORITHMS

2.1 THE CONCEPT OF AN ALGORITHM

One of the concepts fundamental to computing is that of an algorithm. The term is used in a variety of contexts but is rarely defined—even though the idea is deeply rooted in mathematics and the origin of the word stems from the time of the ancient Arabic author al-Khowârizmî (c.825).* It is conveniently defined as follows:

> An *algorithm* is a list of instructions specifying a sequence of operations which will give the answer to any problem of a given type.

Thus, by definition, the notion of an algorithm seems particularly appropriate for expressing numerical problems, which are characterized by the fact that most instructions which need be executed can be constructed entirely of elementary arithmetic and logical operations.

The General Nature of an Algorithm

Generally speaking, an algorithm is a sequence of steps leading to the solution of a given problem; however, one feature distinguishes it from an ordinary procedure or list of instructions. The distinguishing feature is that an algorithm is designed to operate on data that are not known beforehand. In fact, the input of data may be a part of the algorithm itself.

*See Knuth (19), p. 1.

As an example, consider the familiar *Euclidean Algorithm* that is stated as follows:

Given two positive integers a and b, find their greatest common divisor.

There are, of course, as many different problems of this type as there are different pairs of positive integers a and b. Any of the problems can be solved by constructing a descending sequence of numbers, the first of which is the larger of the two numbers and the second the smaller. The third number is the remainder from dividing the first by the second. The fourth number is the remainder from dividing the second by the third, etc. When one of the divisions leaves no remainder, the divisor in the last division is then the required number. The above procedure can be summarized in the following list of instructions: (although the steps differ for computational reasons)

Instruction 1
   Consider (or obtain) the numbers a and b. Proceed to the next instruction.
Instruction 2
   Compare the two numbers (i.e., determine whether the first is greater than, equals, or is less than the second number). Proceed to the next instruction.
Instruction 3
   If the numbers are equal, each of them is the required result and the calculation stops. Otherwise, proceed to the next instruction.
Instruction 4
   If the first number is smaller than the second, exchange them and proceed to the next instruction.
Instruction 5
   Subtract the second number from the first and replace the two numbers under consideration by the subtrahend and remainder, respectively. Proceed to instruction 2.

From this example, it can be seen that the number of actual instructions that must be executed in solving a particular problem is not known beforehand and is dependent upon the input data (in this case a and b). The number is discovered only during the course of computation.

Characteristics of an Algorithm

By its very nature, an algorithm implies a set of specific properties. They are conveniently summarized in two defining characteristics: the deterministic nature and generality of algorithms.

The deterministic nature of an algorithm. An algorithm must be given in the form of a finite list of instructions giving the exact procedure to be followed at each step of the calculation. Thus, the calculation does not depend on the calculator; it is a deterministic process which can be repeated successfully at any time and by anyone.

The generality of an algorithm. An algorithm is a single list of instructions defining a calculation which may be carried out on any initial data and which, in each case, gives the correct result. In other words, an algorithm tells how to solve not just one particular problem, but a whole class of similar problems.

2.2 PROGRAMS

The design of modern computing machines parallels the algorithmic nature of most applications. The computer operates under control of a series of instructions which are stored in high-speed internal storage, along with data, and are interpreted and executed by the circuitry of the machine. The instructions are usually primitive in nature, each being composed essentially of an operation and one or more operands or modifiers, and exist in a form chosen for the representation of data. Machine instructions which exist in this form are said to be in *machine language* since they are numerically coded and directly executable by a specific computer.

The Nature of a Program

A computer program* is similar in concept to an algorithm or to a sequence of machine language instructions; it is defined as follows:

A *program* is a meaningful sequence of statements, possessing an implicit or explicit order of execution, and specifying a computer-oriented representation of an algorithmic process.

A statement, in turn, is a string of symbols from a given *alphabet*, composed of letters, digits, and special characters. The form of each statement adheres to a set of rules (*syntax*), and implies an operational meaning (*semantics*). Collectively, the alphabet, syntax, and semantics are termed a *language*. Thus a machine language instruction, synthesized from the alphabet of internal machine codes, adhering to a primitive syntax of operation codes, operands, and modifiers, and possessing an operational meaning determined by the circuitry of the machine, satisfies the definition of a statement even though the set of basic operations is not directly suited to the execution of commonly needed procedures, and the representation of operands, that is, numeric addresses, affords little mnemonic advantage.

---

*Usually referred to as simply a *program*

Programming Languages

Since machine languages, in general, are not suitable for human use, it is necessary and feasible to define languages which are and then translate programs written in these languages to machine language for subsequent execution on a computer, or to interpretively execute the programs without going through a translation phase.

Languages of this sort are often termed *programming languages* and come in a variety of forms. The most primitive form of programming language is closely akin to machine language except that operations, operands, and modifiers are replaced by symbolic equivalents. A language of this type is called *assembler language*, a simple example of which follows:

```
              .
              .
              .

LOOP          READ      X
              LOAD      X
              MULT      FACTOR
              ADD       E
              STORE     ANS
              PRINT     ANS
              BR        LOOP
              .
              .
              .
```

Although assembler language negates the principal disadvantage of machine language (i.e., the necessity of manipulating internal machine codes), it is obvious that basic machine operations (or their symbolic equivalents) are not convenient for representing most algorithmic processes.

A *procedure-oriented language* is a form of programming language that is related, in a sense, to a class of programs under consideration. Procedure-oriented languages are usually classed as to whether they are scientifically oriented or commercially oriented or whether they are amenable to applications programming or to a form of systems programming. The following statements:

$$SUM = SUM + A(I)*Y**2$$

MOVE NAME TO REPORT-FIELD.

$$N \leftarrow (10* - N) \times \llcorner 0.5 + X \times 10*N$$

are examples of the FORTRAN, COBOL, and APL languages, respectively, and are typical of the general form of most programming languages.

Basic Functions

Although programming languages differ widely in scope, form, and content, the various statements can be grouped into five well-defined classes which perform distinct basic functions. The classes of statements are: data manipulation, program control, input and output, declarative, and subprogram.

Data manipulation statements perform the calculations, data movement, list processing, or string editing required by a particular application. As a result of data manipulation, computation is performed and/or a data variable is replaced.

Program control statements provide a facility for altering the sequential flow of execution in a program. Control statements are divided into four categories: unconditional branches, conditional statements, looping, and execution control. Statements in the latter category halt or terminate program execution or supply the computer with compile-time information.

Input and output statements are the facilities with which a program communicates with the outside world. A variety of device types is usually supported and sets of data can be organized in any of several ways.

Declarative statements specify problem and execution-control data, establish storage requirements, define file types, inform the compiler of hardware configurations, and specify the manner in which execution-time conditions are processed.

Subprogram statements permit a program to be structured into functionally distinct and efficient subprograms. Function or subroutine type procedures can be defined by the programmer or retrieved from a personal or installation-based library of programs.

Program Structure

In its simplest form, an executable program is composed of a collection of machine instructions and data (whether it be initial data, intermediate values, or intermediate results) stored in contiguous locations in computer storage. However, very few programs are actually executed in this form. The reason is that common ordinary functions, such as the trigonometric sine or the square root, need to be used, and it would not be feasible, from an efficiency standpoint, for each programmer to prepare his own version. This leads, generally, to the notion of a subprogram, a concept which permits the execution of identical kinds of computation with different data.

Thus, most executable programs are composed of a *main program* and a collection of subprograms, where a *subprogram* is defined informally as a segment of coding that is prepared in a general fashion for use at multiple points in a program.

Subprograms exist in two forms: functions and subroutines. A *function* has an explicit result and assumes a value as a constituent of a mathematical expression. The trigonometric functions (*SIN, COS, TAN*), the square root (*SQRT*), and the absolute value (*ABS*) are common examples of functions. A *subroutine* does not have an explicit result and is usually invoked by a special statement in the programming language.*   As described below, a subroutine is classed as a closed subprogram. A function, on the other hand, can be an open or closed subprogram.

In some cases, the number of machine instructions required to invoke a subprogram is not justified by time and space savings. For these cases, it is convenient simply to insert the necessary instructions directly into the machine language program at each place where it is used. A subprogram of this type is called an *open* subprogram and is contrasted to a *closed* subprogram for which only one copy exists per program and standard linkage is made to it each time it is referenced.† The two types are depicted as follows:

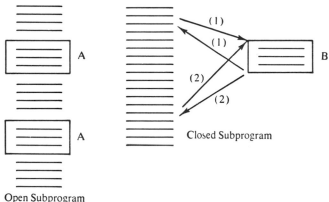

Open Subprogram

2.3 FLOW CHARTING

The old cliche, "a picture is worth a thousand words," has particular truth for the person preparing a program for computer processing or designing a data processing system that uses a computer for one or more of its functions. A *flow chart* is a picture of the steps which must be performed to accomplish a given job; it is useful during the planning stage and serves as a guideline for implementation as well. A flow chart is also an important part of the documentation of a program or system. The logic of data processing systems and computer programs tends to become very complicated, especially after a few changes have been made. It is

*The most familiar example is the *CALL* statement used in COBOL, FORTRAN, and PL/I.

†Other common names for open and closed subprograms are *in-line* and *out-of-line*, respectively.

usually difficult to grasp the overall flow of a system from its outward appearances. Similarly, it is equally difficult to grasp the logic of a program from a perusal of its statements. A flow chart is useful in both cases for indicating the sequences of operations and for clarifying what must be done as the result of each decision that is made.

Types of Flow Charts

The amount of detail included in a flow chart is usually left to the originator and is dependent upon the application to be described. Two different types are identified: system flow charts and program flow charts. Each type can be further classified as to whether it is a macro flow chart or a micro flow chart. No formal distinction is made between the two levels of detail, although the word *macro* is generally used when only the overall flow of a system or program is included, whereas the word *micro* is used to indicate a flow chart in which most essential details are recorded.

A *system flow chart* describes the flow of data and the operational procedures in a data processing application. Normally, the following elements are defined: the origin of data, manual operations, storage devices, data transmission procedures, data processing functions, and input/output operations. Figure 2.1 depicts a typical system flow chart. The various symbols are defined in the following section.

A *program flow chart*, often called a logic diagram or block diagram, depicts the sequence of operations and decisions in a program, subroutine, or function. Because of the sophisticated logic in most computer programs, flow charts are extremely important during the coding stage of program preparation and for documentation as well. In the latter use, a good flow chart greatly aids recall in the event the program needs modification at a later date. Figure 2.2 provides a sample program flow chart, the symbols of which are introduced next.

Flow Charting Symbols

It is clear from the previous examples that different symbols (or boxes) are used for different purposes. Flow charting conventions, regardless of their specific content, facilitate understanding and decrease the effort required to develop an effective diagram.

Flow charting symbols are divided into three categories: basic symbols, programming symbols, and system symbols. No explicit rules for using the symbols exist, and programming symbols are frequently used in system flow charts and vice versa. The *basic symbols* (Figure 2.3) form a minimum subset and apply, in general, when a more specialized symbol does not exist. The *programming symbols* (Figure 2.4), with the exception of the decision box, apply mainly to computer programs and are exten-

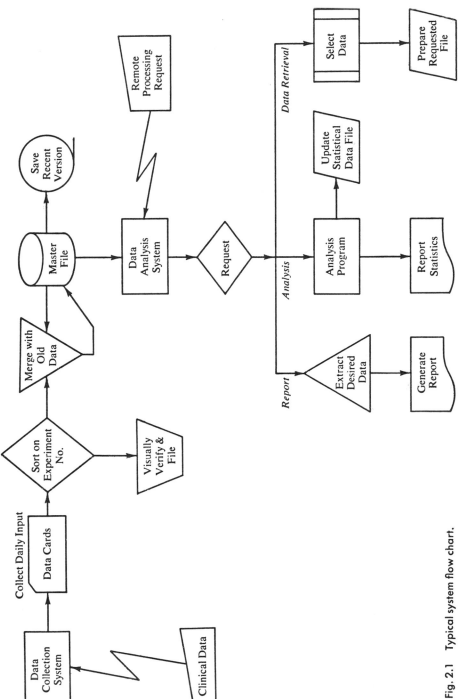

Fig. 2.1 Typical system flow chart.

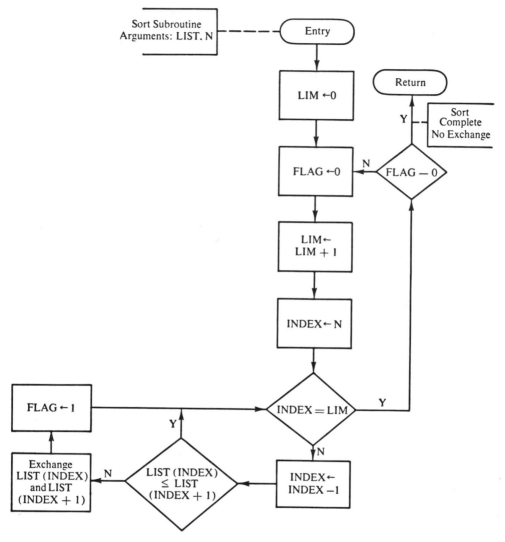

Fig. 2.2 Typical program flow chart.

sions to the basic symbols. The *system symbols* (Figure 2.5) are the largest collection and are divided into: input/output media, input/output devices and device types, and processing operations.

Information is represented in a flow chart in two ways: by the symbol chosen and by descriptive terms placed within the symbol. Use of the *decision symbol*, for example, would further indicate whether the basis of decision is a comparison, the checking of a switch, or the testing of a hardware indicator.

The *process* symbol is defined as the symbol used to represent an operation or group of operations not represented
by other operations. These operations are concerned with
the actual functions performed by a system or program.

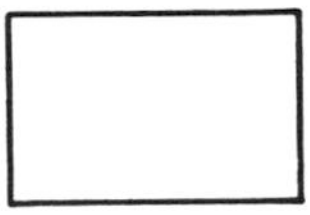

The *input/output* symbol is used to denote any function
of an I/O device. Making information available for
processing is an input function; recording processing
information is an output function. Included in the I/O
category are reading, writing, backspace, rewind, etc., of
magnetic tape, I/O functions of card readers, card
punches, and printers, as well as those operations involving communication between random access storage
units and the main storage.

The *flow direction* symbol is the basic element of a flow
chart. It represents the direction of processing flow:
general flow is top to bottom, left to right. It is inherent
in most programs and systems that many decisions are involved   that is, tests to determine which of two or more
paths should be taken. This leads to complex flow charts
and hence to the requirement that flow lines be drawn
with an arrowhead whenever the direction is not immediately clear. Looping   that is, repeating a sequence
of operations   is also a common occurrence and in some
cases leads to violation of the basic rule of the processing
flow. Flow lines may cross indicating no logical interrelationship. Arrowheads may appear on all lines; when
used, they should be placed at the point of entry to a
connector or functional symbol.

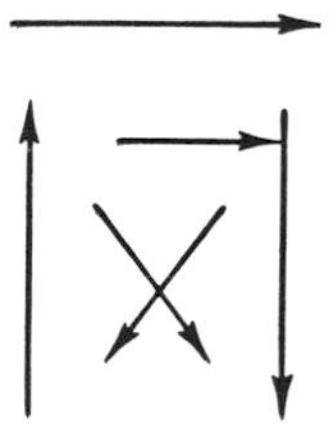

The *connector* symbol represents an entry form, or an
exit to, another part of the flow chart. A set of two
connector symbols is used to indicate a continued flow
when the use of a line is precluded by the physical or
esthetic limitations of the flow chart. Identification
information should be placed within the symbol.

The *annotation* symbol provides a means of adding
descriptive information to a flow chart. It is connected
to the flow chart where meaningful.

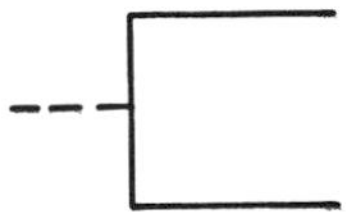

Fig. 2.3   Basic flow charting symbols.

The *decision* symbol is used to depict a point at which a branch to one of two or more alternate paths is possible. The basis for the decision should be clearly indicated and all possible conditions should be accounted for.

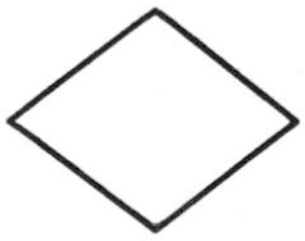

The *predefined process* symbol represents a group of operations not detailed on the particular flow chart—for example, a library subroutine.

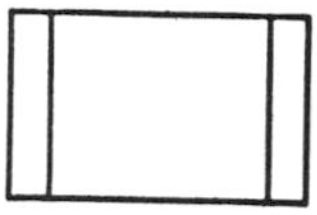

The *preparation* symbol indicates that an operation or group of operations changes the program itself—for example, initialization, address modification, loading of an index register, or the setting of a switch.

The *terminal* symbol represents any point at which a program originates or terminates.

The *parallel mode* symbol indicates the beginning or end of two or more simultaneous operations.

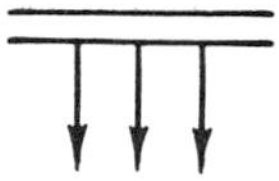

Fig. 2.4   Program flow charting symbols.

Input/Output Media

Input/output using punched cards.

Input/output using magnetic tape.

Input/output using punched paper tape.

Input/output using a document.

Input entered manually on keyboards, switches, dials, etc.

Output displayed on a display device, console typewriter, etc.

I/O Devices and Device Types

I O Devices and Device Types

Input/output using direct access storage devices such as drums, discs, magnetic strips, etc.

Storage not directly accessible by a computer.

Magnetic disc storage.

Magnetic drum storage.

Auxiliary core storage.

Data Processing Operations

Data Processing Operations

The *merge* symbol represents the operation of combining two or more sets of data into one set.

The *extract* symbol represents the removal of specific data items from a set of data.

The *sort* symbol represents the arrangement of data items in a given sequence.

The *collate* symbol indicates that two or more sets of data are formed from two or more other sets using the merge and extract operations.

The *auxiliary operation* symbol represents an off-line process which is not limited by operator speed.

The *manual operation* symbol represents an off-line process limited by operator speed.

The *communication link* symbol represents data transmitted by a telecommunications link.

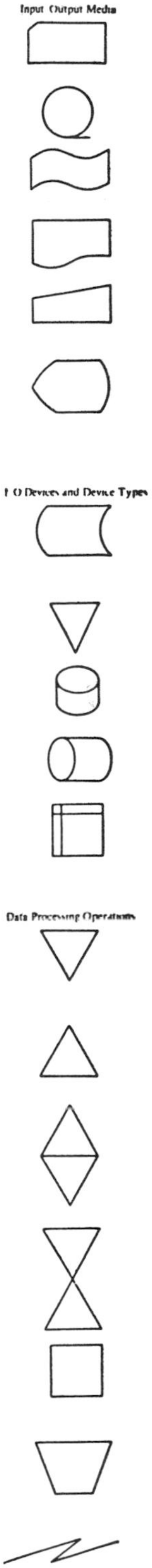

Fig. 2.5   System flow charting symbols.

The Robot Problem

The robot problem is one of the classic problems in the theory of flow charting and is included for the amusement of the reader.

Write a flow chart to tell a robot how to find a door in an L-shaped room and open it. The starting point and the position of the door(s) are not known. Initially, the robot faces parallel to some wall. The doors slide open to the left. The computer in the robot has a stored program. The robot can accept the following commands:
1. *Move* straight ahead until you either bump something or sense the crack on the right of a door. The crack cannot be sensed unless the wall is directly to the robot's right, and the sensing mechanism is unreliable and should be given three chances to find a crack.
2. *Turn* 90° to the left.
3. *Insert* hand in crack.
4. *Ring* buzzer—to be done if crack cannot be found.

The computer receives the following feedback:
1. Whether the robot has stopped moving.
2. Whether it was stopped by a wall or a crack.
3. Whether there is a wall on the robot's right.

2.4 DECISION LOGIC TABLES

Decision logic tables provide a means of describing complex decision processes for which flow charts tend to become quite lengthy. Whereas flow charting requires that the analyst describe his problem and develop his system or program in the same operation, use of a decision logic table permits the logic of a decision process to be stated independently of how it is to be implemented.

Basic Concepts

A decision logic table is a tabular display of all pertinent aspects of a problem situation. The table contains all relevant conditions, relationships, and actions to be taken under each set of circumstances. For example, consider the following decision process: "If credit is OK, approve order; if credit is not OK, but payment record is favorable, approve order; if credit is not OK, payment record is not favorable, but special approval has been obtained, approve order; otherwise, return order to sales." The process would normally be flow charted as shown in Figure 2.6. A decision logic table to represent the same procedure would appear as Table 2.1.

In a decision logic table, a set of conditions and its related set of actions is presented as a verticle *rule*. Whereas a flow chart depicts a decision

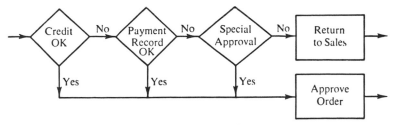

Fig. 2.6   Credit approval flow chart.

TABLE 2.1.   DECISION LOGIC TABLE FOR CREDIT APPROVAL

	Rule 1	Rule 2	Rule 3	Rule 4
Credit OK?	Y	N	N	N
Payment record favorable?		Y	N	N
Special approval obtained?			Y	N
Approve order.	X	X	X	
Return to sales.	—	—	—	X

process serially, a decision logic table represents the same process in parallel.

A decision logic table has four major sections, described in Table 2.2, and listed as follows: conditions stub, action stub, condition entry, action entry.

TABLE 2.2.   SKELETON OF A LIMITED-
ENTRY DECISION LOGIC
TABLE

Condition Stub	Condition Entry
Action Stub	Action Entry

The *condition stub* is the upper left quadrant and contains descriptions of conditions on which decisions are to be based. Conditions are usually represented as questions. The *action stub* occupies the lower left quadrant and supplies all possible actions for the conditions listed above. The *condition entry* section is found in the upper right quadrant and answers the questions found in the condition stub. All feasible combinations of answers to the questions are formed here where the responses are restricted to Y to indicate yes and N to indicate no. If no response is indicated, then the response need not be checked for that particular question. The *action entry* is the remaining quadrant of the table and indicates the appropriate actions resulting from the conditions above. The only permissible entry here is the X to indicate, "Take this action." One or more actions may be designated for each combination of responses.

Types of Decision Logic Tables

The decision logic table used in the previous example is named a limited-entry decision logic table. Two other varieties are in general use: extended-entry tables and mixed-entry tables.

The *limited-entry decision logic table* (*LEDT*) is the most widely used type and is readily identified by the fact that the condition entries are restricted to Y, N, or are irrelevant (represented by —) and the action entries are restricted to the character X. As an additional example, an LEDT for a personnel classification problem is given as Table 2.3.

TABLE 2.3.   LEDT FOR PERSONNEL CLASSIFICATION PROBLEM

	1	2	3	4	5	6	7	8
Bachelor's Degree					Y	Y	N	N
Master's Degree			Y	Y	N	N	N	N
Ph.D.	Y	Y	N	N	N	N	N	N
Less than 5 Years Experience	Y	N	Y	N	Y	N	Y	N
Greater than or Equal to 5 Years Experience	N	Y	N	Y	N	Y	N	Y
Assign-grade 4							X	
Assign-grade 8					X			X
Assign-grade 12				X		X		
Assign-grade 16	X			X				
Assign-grade 20		X						

In an *extended-entry decision logic table*, the condition and action stubs serve only to identify the variables to be tested and the actions to be taken respectively. The condition entries must then contain a value or condition to be tested. Similarly, the action entries must contain specific procedures or data for the actions to be taken. The number of entries in the condition and action stubs tend to be less in this form compared to limited-entry tables; however, in many cases extended-entry tables must be converted to their LEDT counterparts before computer processing can be attempted.

Features characteristic of both limited-entry and extended-entry tables may be combined into a single table called a *mixed-entry decision logic table*. In any one horizontal row, however, entries are limited to one of the two types, exclusively. Mixed-entry tables have one major advantage. Conditions that can be appropriately expressed by binary values (i.e., Y or N) may be represented in that fashion and conditions that must be expressed by relational expressions may be written in that manner.

Because of the relative simplicity of decision table methods and their ease of understanding, they are especially suitable for documentation and for communicating ideas among people. For computer applications, several subsidiary topics exist: equivalent LEDTs, conversion of decision tables to computer programs, and the generation of optimal sequential testing procedures. The reader is referred to Katzan (18) for more information on these and related topics.

2.5 SUMMARY

The notion of an algorithm, defined as a list of instructions specifying a sequence of operations that give the answer to any problem of a given type, is a key concept in mathematics and in computing and characterizes many existing computer applications. A program is defined accordingly and is expressed in an appropriate language; some familiar languages are machine language, assembler language, and procedure-oriented language. The meaning of a program is frequently difficult to grasp from a perusal of the statements contained in it, so more explicit ways of describing the overall logic are required. A flow chart is a picture of the overall flow of a program and uses well-defined symbols to facilitate development and understanding. A decision logic table is a tabular display of the pertinent conditions and actions in a complex procedure. The principle advantage of decision logic tables is for describing sophisticated decision processes for which flow charts would become exceedingly lengthy and difficult to follow.

3 | BASIC STRUCTURE OF COMPUTERS

3.1 MACHINE FUNDAMENTALS

Even though a practical algorithm is usually based on subtle and complicated arguments and its construction requires a certain amount of ingenuity, it can be used by a person who does not even know its purpose. He need only follow instructions and is thus able to solve any problem from the class for which the algorithm was constructed. In a sense, the person is behaving as a numerical transformation machine which can be depicted as follows:

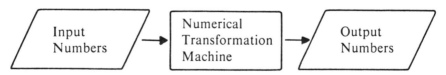

The process involved in performing numerical transformations is of particular interest. The steps performed by a human calculator are described as an introduction to machine fundamentals. In following an algorithm, a person receives, processes, and stores various data. Usually he writes these data on paper and performs the operation either mentally or mechanically. The process can be summarized as follows:

The storage of information is usually accomplished by writing down all data, including the instructions for solving the problem (the algorithm), on a piece of paper. In practice, of course, the calculator does not write down everything. Some things he remembers (stores in his brain rather than on paper), while some he looks up in charts or tables. However, this must not obscure the basic fact that some means is provided for storing all necessary information.

Processing the information involves performing the elementary operations required by the algorithm. This may be done by using computing devices; for example, arithmetic operations may be done on an adding machine, a slide rule, or by using a remote terminal system. Each step of the calculation consists of taking certain information (e.g., numbers) from the paper, performing a specified operation on it, and recording the result at another place on the paper.

Control of the process, that is, the determination of what step is to be performed next, is carried out by the calculator by referring to his instructions and by carrying out comparison and logical operations.

In an automatic computer, analogous physical devices exist, that is, a *storage unit* plays the role of the piece of paper and a *processing unit* controls and performs the necessary operations. This concept can be expressed schematically as follows:

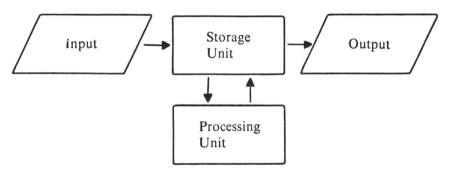

For controlling and performing the necessary operations, the processing unit contains two functional units: a control unit and an arithmetic unit. These units, along with the storage unit, are the subject of the remainder of this section. Two other types of devices that are obviously necessary in an automatic computer have been omitted here: input units and output units. They are treated in detail in Chapter 7, "Computer Systems and Devices."

Storage

The function of the *storage unit* of the computer is to hold instructions, initial values, input data, intermediate values, and final results before output. Each of the preceding quantities (i.e., a data item) is located at a specific place in computer storage and that location is termed its *storage address*. As mentioned previously, both numbers and computer instructions are represented internally as sequences of digits with the essential difference being in how the quantities are interpreted by the circuitry of the computer.

The manner in which storage is organized determines to a great extent how a specific location is addressed. In early computers, storage was organized on a *word* basis with each word being composed of a finite number of digits. *Each word was assigned a physical address.* Thus, a word could represent an instruction, a numerical value, or a series of characters. Two significant problems existed: (1) Before a specific character could be processed, a series of shifting or masking operations was necessary. (2) Special considerations were necessary for processing character operands which occupied more than one computer word. This basic difficulty led to the facility, in some computers, of addressing *variable-length words*, with the smallest addressable unit being a character.* Variable-word computers also had their limitations in that quantities requiring more than one character, such as a number, had to be terminated with a special symbol, or a length attribute had to be given with the machine instruction itself.

The inadequacies in both systems led to the facility in some recent computers† that allows both fixed and variable word lengths to be used in the same computer. This is achieved by having a *byte-addressable* storage organization. A *byte* is a group of digits‡ which form a subunit of a computer word and which has a physical address in storage. In the example of Figure 3.1, two bytes make up a half word, four bytes make up a full computer word, and eight bytes compose a double-length word. When a computer instruction references§ a full word, the computer automatically fetches or stores four bytes. Other instructions use half words and double words, and two or eight bytes are referenced, respectively. Instructions which operate on variable-length operands specify the address of the first byte and the length of the field, which can represent a string of characters or decimal digits in a coded form.

Control

It has been implied thus far that in the modern version of an automatic computer, instructions are stored internally, that is, in computer storage,

---

*A character is referred to as a *byte* on some computers. The facility of addressing characters directly is particularly useful for applications that primarily involve the manipulation of nonnumerical data.

†For example, the IBM System/360 and the RCA Spectra/70.

‡Usually taken to be binary digits.

§A word is referenced by the address of its high-order (leftmost) byte.

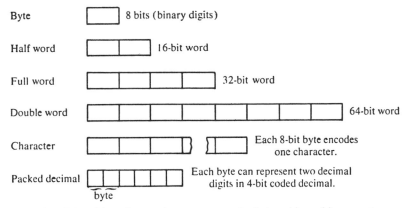

Fig. 3.1 Address formats in a representative byte-addressable computer.

and that the computer executes instructions sequentially, that is, one after another, until it is instructed to do otherwise. The *control unit* governs the operation of the overall system. It fetches an instruction from storage, interprets it, and generates sequences of internal signals to have it executed. The control unit also synchronizes the timing of internal signals with the operational speed of the functional units.

The functions of the control unit can be summarized as follows: (1) keeping track of the program address; (2) addressing storage; (3) interpreting instructions; and (4) generating internal signals to synchronize and execute basic machine operations. In performing the above functions, the control unit requires and utilizes several internal registers. They are described in a succeeding section on *machine registers and their functions*.

Arithmetic

The *arithmetic unit* contains the registers and circuitry necessary to execute the fixed-point, floating-point, logical,* and variable-length instructions of the computer. To some extent, the level of sophistication of the computer is reflected in the arithmetic unit. For example, some high-performance systems contain multiple subunits for fixed, floating, and logical operations. Some arithmetic units perform addition and subtraction serially on a digit-by-digit basis whereas others perform the operations in parallel using high-speed registers. Ordinarily, a multiplication is performed as a repeated addition by the computer hardware and a division is performed similarly as a repeated subtraction,† although on some machines, the process is speeded up with special circuits.

---

*Including shifting and related instructions.
†See Section 3.3, "Register Operations."

The basic design of the computer is also reflected in the addressable registers used to hold intermediate values during data manipulation and to utilize index values during addressing. Three general methods exist: (1) Have *no* addressable registers and require that all operations operate from storage to storage. This method is frequently used with variable word length computers. (2) Include one or more *accumulators*, which can hold either a fixed, a floating, or a logical operand. Indexing is then performed with special *index registers*. This philosophy is usually associated with fixed word length computers. (3) Include separate registers for fixed-point and for floating-point operands. This philosophy reduces the number of "stores" to memory and allows fixed-point registers to be used for indexing, as well. This latter technique is used with byte-addressable computers.

Machine Registers and Their Functions

A register is a storage mechanism for holding fixed-length computer words. It differs from ordinary storage in that it is synthesized from expensive components and is capable of operating at relatively high speeds. Most registers are used to hold data or instructions temporarily and may or may not be addressable by the programmer. As pictured in Figure 3.2, an addressable register may be loaded, may be used as an operand for arithmetic and logical operations, and its contents may be placed in storage. In spite of the wide variety of computer designs, a basic subset of registers is found in most machines. They are listed as follows:

1. *Current Address Register* (Control Unit)
    contains the address, in storage, of the current computer instruction.

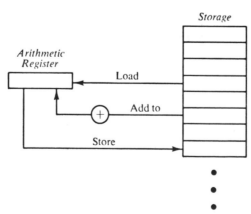

Fig. 3.2 Use of an addressable register.

2. *Instruction Register* (Control Unit)—
    holds the current instruction during execution.
3. *Address Register* (Control Unit)—
    holds the address portion or operand of an instruction during execution.
4. *Accumulator* (Arithmetic Unit)—
    the high-speed register in which arithmetic is performed.
5. *Multiplier-Quotient Register* (Arithmetic Unit)—
    the MQ register, frequently referred to as the X register, holds the multiplier during multiplication and the quotient during division and is considered as a right-hand extension to the accumulator.
6. *Index Register* (Arithmetic Unit)—
    high-speed register used for indexing.
7. *Storage Register* (Arithmetic Unit)—
    a temporary storage register internal to the arithmetic unit, not directly addressable by the programmer, and which forms a data buffer between storage and the processing unit.

3.2 MACHINE OPERATION

Similar to the manner in which a user synthesizes complex operations from elementary machine instructions, the processing unit must perform a series of internal *micro* operations to effectively execute a machine instruction. This section gives a functional description of how the processing unit of an automatic computer operates.

Machine Instructions

All computer operations take place in fixed intervals of time, measured by pulses emitted from an electronic clock at frequencies as high as a billion per second. A fixed number of pulses is termed a *machine cycle*. Within a machine cycle, the computer can perform one or more specific micro operations, which can be combined with other micro operations to form machine instructions. Thus, the number of micro operations in an instruction is variable and depends on the particular instruction. In a variable-length instruction, the required number of micro operations is additionally dependent upon the length of the operand(s).

A machine instruction consists basically of two parts: an operation and an operand. The *operation* tells the machine which function to perform. The *operand* augments the operation by providing: the location(s) of data or an instruction which the operation references; the physical address of a hardware device, such as an input/output unit, which the operation uses; or a modifier for a control function, such as the number of places that a register should be shifted. Examples of machine instructions which address locations in storage are the ordinary ADD, SUB, and MOVE. A READ or WRITE instruction would ordinarily address a hardware device whereas a SHIFT instruction would indicate the number of places to be shifted.

The processing unit must operate in a prescribed sequence to perform its main functions of fetching, interpreting, and executing instructions. Two major cycles are identified: the instruction cycle and the execution cycle. Collectively, they determine the manner in which a machine instruction is processed.

Instruction Cycle

The first major cycle involved in executing an instruction is termed the *instruction cycle*, often referred to as the I-cycle. During an I-cycle, the control unit performs the following functions (see Figure 3.3):

1. The instruction is fetched from storage and placed in the storage register.
2. The operation part is routed to the instruction register to determine what function must be performed.

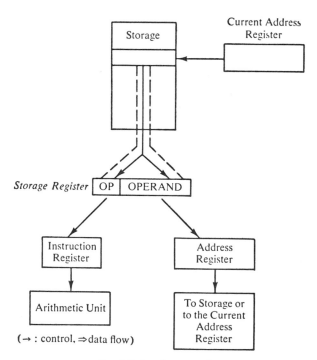

Fig. 3.3 I-cycle processing.

3. The operand part is routed to the address register to obtain the information to be used in the operation.*
4. The current address register is updated to the location in storage of the next instruction.

During the execution of a program, the current address register is set initially to the address of the first executable instruction in the program. The instruction is fetched from storage, and while it is being decoded and interpreted, the current address register is updated by the length attribute of the current instruction to point to the address of the next instruction in sequence. Normally, a program is executed serially and the automatic updating of the current address register is a sound design tradeoff. In some cases, however, it is desired to continue execution from another portion of the program as the result of a program decision or to repeat an entire block of instructions. Branching instructions are thus included in most instruction repertoires and effectively allow the contents of the current address register to be altered.

Execution Cycle

The instruction cycle is usually followed by an *execution cycle* (E-cycle) to execute the decoded instruction. The operand is fetched from storage, and control signals are sent to the arithmetic unit to activate the proper arithmetic, logical, or control circuits. For a variable-length instruction, the arithmetic unit is provided the addresses of operands in storage rather than actual data values in the arithmetic and storage registers. Figure 3.4 depicts a typical E-cycle. The address register frequently contains information other than storage addresses. The operation part of an instruction indicates how the contents of the address register should be interpreted—that is, as an address for data, the location of the next instruction for branching, the number of places in a shifting operation, or the identity of an input/output device. The actual length of the execution cycle varies depending upon the instruction to be executed. For example, a floating-point multiply usually requires more machine cycles than does a fixed-point addition.

Stored Program Concept

It was mentioned earlier that in most modern computers, the program, in the form of machine instructions, is stored internally and the processing unit has access to it at electronic speeds. Since the program is stored along with its data, instructions are available to the processing unit as data. Thus, a computer can be programmed to alter its own instructions,

---

*At this point, indexing of addresses to form effective addresses takes place.

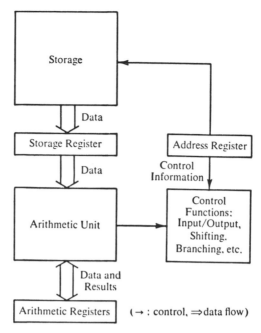

Fig. 3.4 E-cycle processing.

providing a great amount of flexibility and the widely heralded logical capability of modern machines.

Usually, there are no specific areas of storage for programs and for data, although each type is frequently grouped together for convenience and for operating efficiency. To the computer, the only difference between an instruction and a data item is the time when it is brought into the processing unit. If information is fetched from storage during the I-cycle, then it is processed as an instruction. If it is brought into the processing unit or returned to storage during the E-cycle, then it is regarded as data. In spite of the potential danger of generating invalid and inappropriate instructions, program modification has become one of the marvels of the computer age.

3.3   ARITHMETIC OPERATIONS

As in the case of the automobile and the airplane, a person need not be capable of designing and building a computer to effectively use one. Yet, a fundamental knowledge of how operations are performed is intellectually satisfying and gives the occasional user an intuitive feeling for practical limitations.

Fixed-Point Operations

One of the objectives of the computer designer is to simplify the circuitry of the computer. The standard approach has been to use the same circuitry for more than one function, with the most frequent candidate being the subtraction operation. One often hears the phrase, "Subtraction can be performed by the addition of complements." As shown below, this is precisely true:

$$m - n = m + (100 - n) \quad \text{(modulus 100)}$$

For example:

$$71 - 44 = 71 + (100 - 44) = 71 + 56 = 27 \quad \text{(modulus 100)}$$

As shown later, the hardware necessary to perform complementation is relatively simple to implement. Now, multiplication is essentially repeated additions and division is repeated subtractions; thus all fixed-point arithmetic can be reduced to forms of addition.

The preceding example used the ten's complement. The *ten's complement* of a number N is defined as $10^n - N$ where n is the number of digit positions in N. It should be recalled that 10^n is one more than the largest decimal number that can be formed with n decimal digit positions. The ten's complement is easily formed: Subtract all of the digit positions from 9 and add 1 to the result. The ten's complement of 44, for example, can be formed as $(99 - 44) + 1 = 56$. Complements can be formed of numbers to any base. The *base complement* of a number N occupying n digit positions in the base b is computed as $b^n - N$. Thus, the two's complement of the binary number 110010 is 001110. It can be formed by changing all 1's to 0's and all 0's to 1's and adding one. The simplicity of the process for binary numbers is obvious and is the determining factor in the use of complement arithmetic in binary computers.

Consider a fixed-point number represented in computer storage as follows:

S	integer

S refers to the sign (either $+$ or $-$) of the number and the integer part represents its magnitude. Assume for simplicity that the integer part occupies three positions and that the sign position is offset to distinguish it from an overflow position; then the number -723 might be pictured as follows:

$-$		
7	2	3

Clearly, the ten's complement of -723 would be represented similarly:

+		
2	7	7

A three-position computer word will be used in subsequent examples. Terminology may be recalled as follows:

m	(addend)	m	(minuend)
$+n$	(augend)	$-n$	(subtrahend)
$m+n$	(sum)	$m-n$	(remainder)
m	(multiplier)	m	(dividend)
$\times n$	(multiplicand)	$\div n$	(divisor)
$m \times n$	(product)	$m \div n$	(quotient)

Addition and subtraction can now be performed in a *signed-magnitude* representation by applying well-defined rules:

1. If the operation is subtraction, change the sign of the subtrahend.
2. If the numbers have the same sign, add the magnitudes and assign that sign to the result.
3. If the numbers have different signs, subtract the smaller number from the larger number and affix the sign of the larger number.

A *decision tree* for addition is given in Figure 3.5. A flow diagram for both operations is given as Figure 3.6.

The use of complement arithmetic is so convenient that in some computers, all negative fixed-point numbers are stored in complement form. This design philosophy permits the elimination of an explicit sign position and further simplifies the arithmetic circuitry.

Fixed-point multiplication and division are performed by repeated additions and subtractions, respectively. Both make explicit use of addressable registers in the arithmetic unit, named the *accumulator* register (AC) and the *multiplier-quotient* (MQ) register and a word in storage called the *memory register*. They are defined as follows:

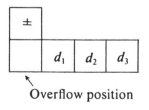

Overflow position

Accumulator— AC register
(high-speed register where arithmetic is performed)

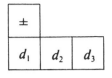

Accumulator Extension—MQ register
(contains pertinent data during arithmetic
computation)

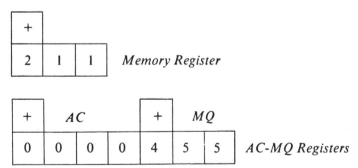

Memory Register
(contains multiplicand during multiplication;
contains divisor during division)

Multiplication and division are introduced in the following examples.

Description of multiplication: The number in the specified *memory register* is algebraically multiplied by the number in the *MQ* register forming a six-digit product in the combined *AC-MQ* registers.

Example: Multiply the number 211 by the number 455.

Initially, the second number would be placed in the *MQ* register and the location of the first number would be specified as the memory register. Pictorially, this would look as follows:

+		
2	1	1

Memory Register

+	AC			+	MQ	
0	0	0	0	4	5	5

AC-MQ Registers

The memory register will not change and will always be the multiplicand.

The contents of the memory register are added to the *AC* as many times as the value of the last digit (third position) of the *MQ* register, so that the *AC-MQ* would look as follows:

+	AC			+	MQ	
1	0	5	5	4	5	5

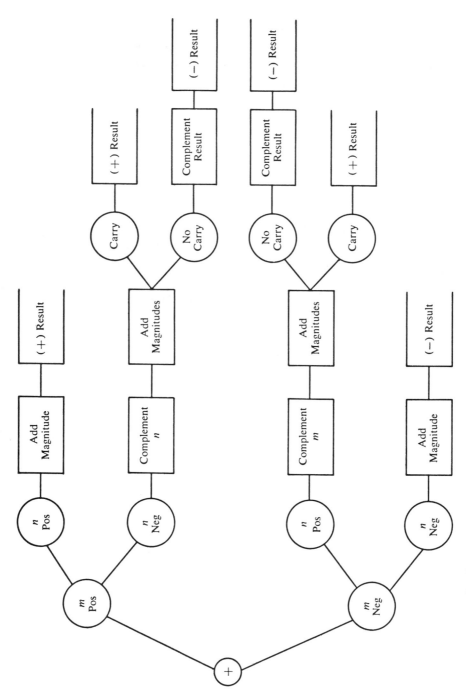

Fig. 3.5 Decision tree for algebraic addition for operands in signed-magnitude representation.

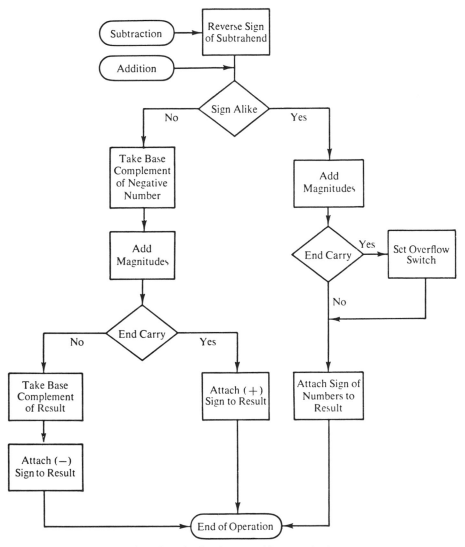

Fig. 3.6 Flow chart for fixed-point addition and subtraction.

The combined contents of the AC-MQ registers are shifted right one place, that is,

+	AC			+	MQ	
0	1	0	5	5	4	5

The contents of the memory register are again added to the AC register as many times as the value of the last digit of the MQ, which is again 5, that is,

+	AC			+	MQ	
1	1	6	0	5	4	5

Again shift right one place, that is,

+	AC			+	MQ	
0	1	1	6	0	5	4

The contents of the memory register (i.e., the multiplicand) are again added to the AC, this time only four times because the last position of the MQ contains a 4, that is,

+	AC			+	MQ	
0	9	6	0	0	5	4

Shift once and the multiplication is complete,

+	AC			+	MQ	
0	0	9	6	0	0	5

Note that the process of adding a number of times and then shifting was executed three times. If the registers were ten digits in length, the operations would have been executed ten times.

Description of division: The number in the AC-MQ registers (combined) is algebraically divided by the number in the memory register. The result appears in the MQ register.

Example: Divide the number 56088 by the number 456.

Initially,

+		
4	5	6

Memory Register (does not change)

+	AC			+	MQ	
0	0	5	6	0	8	8

AC-MQ Registers

If the contents of AC (alone) are greater than those of the memory register, the division stops. Otherwise, AC-MQ is shifted *left* one place, that is,

+	AC			+	MQ	
0	5	6	0	8	8	0

The contents of the memory register are subtracted from the AC register as many times as possible without changing the sign of the AC register; the number of subtractions is placed in the low-order position of the MQ register, that is,

+	AC			+	MQ	
0	1	0	4	8	8	1

The AC-MQ registers are again shifted left one place, that is,

+	AC			+	MQ	
1	0	4	8	8	1	0

The contents of the memory register are again subtracted as many times as possible without changing the sign of the AC register; the count (number of subtractions) is put in the last position of the MQ, that is,

+	AC			+	MQ	
0	1	3	6	8	1	2

The AC-MQ registers are again shifted left one place (for the last time— count = 3), that is,

+	AC			+	MQ	
1	3	6	8	1	2	0

The repeated subtraction is again performed, that is

+		AC		+		MQ
0	0	0	0	1	2	3

The quotient is in the MQ register and the remainder is in the AC register.

Floating-Point Operations

In Chapter 1, a floating-point number was defined as having three component parts: a sign, an exponent, and a fraction. Moreover, the exponent was said to be *biased* so that the sign position represented the sign of the number and not the exponent. A floating-point number can be pictured as follows:

S	exponent	fraction

Although floating-point numbers are represented in a manner slightly different from fixed-point numbers, addition and subtraction reduce to similar operations after decimal points have been aligned. Consider the two numbers, 70 and 8, in scientific notation, that is, $.7 \times 10^2$ and $.8 \times 10^1$, respectively. To align the decimal points, the number with the smallest exponent is shifted right until the exponents agree, that is,

$$.7 \times 10^2 = .7 \times 10^2$$
$$.8 \times 10^1 = .08 \times 10^2$$

Then, disregarding the exponents, the fractions can be added or subtracted as in fixed-point arithmetic. After the operation is complete, the fraction is shifted left or right until the first nonzero digit appears immediately to the right of the implied decimal point and the exponent is updated accordingly. The last shifting of the fraction is termed *normalization*. For example, consider the operation: $.102 \times 10^3 - .94 \times 10^2$. The actual subtraction would progress as follows:

1. Equalize exponents

$$.102 \times 10^3 - .094 \times 10^3$$

2. Subtract

$$.102 \times 10^3 - .094 \times 10^3 = .008 \times 10^3$$

3. Normalize

$$.008 \times 10^3 = .8 \times 10^1$$

Floating-point multiplication and division require no more circuitry than is required for floating-point addition and subtraction and for fixed-point multiplication and division. In fact, floating-point multiplication or division is actually less complex than floating-point addition or subtraction since the exponents do not have to be compared. Consider a floating-point number of the form $N = n \times b^e$. The multiplication of two floating-point numbers requires a multiplication of fractions and an addition of exponents:

$$(n_1 \times b^{e_1}) \times (n_2 \times b^{e_2}) = (n_1 \times n_2) \times b^{(e_1 + e_2)}$$

Similarly, the division of two floating-point numbers requires a division of fractions and a subtraction of exponents:

$$(n_1 \times b^{e_1}) \div (n_2 \times b^{e_2}) = (n_1 \div n_2) \times b^{(e_1 - e_2)}$$

After either operation, normalization may be required, depending upon the characteristics of the result and of the specific operation. All of the constituent operations in floating-point multiplication and division can utilize the corresponding fixed-point operation—thus, no additional arithmetic circuits are specifically required except for those that control the process and normalize the result.

The multiplication of $(.2 \times 10^2)$ by $(.1 \times 10^1)$ would progress as follows:

1. Add exponents and multiply fractions

$$(.2 \times 10^2) \times (.1 \times 10^1) = .02 \times 10^3$$

2. Normalize result

$$.02 \times 10^3 = .2 \times 10^2$$

Similarly, the division of $(.72 \times 10^2)$ by $(.8 \times 10^1)$ would involve the following steps:

1. Subtract exponents and divide fractions

$$(.72 \times 10^2) \div (.8 \times 10^1) = .9 \times 10^1$$

2. No normalization is required as is often the case in floating-point multiplication and division.

Floating-point arithmetic provides a variety of interesting problems. One of them was alluded to in Chapter 1 and involved cases where the associative law of addition fails in some cases. Another problem is concerned with the rounding of floating-point results. Whereas in a fixed-point multiplication, a double-length product is formed, in a floating-point multiply, a single-length fraction is formed. Thus, the technique for rounding and the time when it takes place are of great importance.

Yet another problem questions the feasibility of normalizing results at all, since the process tends to imply more accuracy than actually exists.

3.4 SUMMARY

Conceptually, the functioning of an automatic computer is not far removed from the process performed by humans when doing calculations. Three essential units are found in computers: storage, control, and arithmetic. The storage unit holds the instructions, data, intermediate results, and final results of a program. The control unit initiates the execution of machine instructions and provides for the automatic mode of execution. The arithmetic unit performs the fixed and floating-point operations required by a particular application. The basic operation in the arithmetic unit is fixed-point addition, from which other operations can be synthesized. Input and output units are also of importance but are covered in a later chapter.

4 | FUNDAMENTALS OF APL PROGRAMMING

4.1 INTRODUCTION

From the notched stick of the ancient cave man, through the Chinese abacus and the calculations of Pascal and Leibniz, past the analytical engine of Babbage, to modern times, man has always had a need for calculating devices and a means of storing information. As more complex instruments were developed, more glamorous applications were found. Today, technological man views with pride his large computer systems with complex programs such as those for tracing neutrons, making airline reservations, controlling space flights, and predicting weather. Notwithstanding, everyday problem solving and data processing are taken for granted—although they constitute the primary work load of most computing devices. As a programming system, APL* is oriented towards the last category. As a descriptive and an analytic tool, it serves as a valuable vehicle in synthesizing systems in the first group. In general, APL is a system with which the digital computer can be used, conveniently, as an integral part of problem solving, in teaching, in algorithm design, and in some forms of data processing and information retrieval.

Desk Calculators and Automatic Computers

The ordinary desk calculator provides a means of simplifying calculations and achieves its greatest value from compactness, mobility, simplicity of

---

*Which stands for *A Programming Language* (K. E. Iverson, New York, John Wiley & Sons, Inc., 1962).

use, and *relevance*. In this context, relevance generally refers to the fact that the human factors problems in using most calculators for arithmetic computations are minimal. Although an automatic computer is often likened to a desk calculator, its attributes are much different. It can be characterized as a fairly large and structurally sophisticated instrument which is generally immobile, operationally complex, and provides for considerable generality of use. The flexibility of an automatic computer is almost beyond question yet it is not applicable to many problems because operational procedures are often excessively complicated and response is frequently inadequate. In fact, the complexity of many computer programs is a result of a poor man-machine interface and limited access. APL combines the simplicity and relevance of a desk calculator with the power and flexibility of an automatic computer. It utilizes a recent technique called time sharing and the richness of Iverson's programming language to provide a system which can be used for both simple and complex problems and which is relevant to mathematical description and natural for human use.

Time Sharing, Interactive Computing, and Remote Terminals

The user has access to the APL system via a remote terminal, which may be located miles from the computer installation. The connection is made with ordinary telephone lines and transmission is practically instantaneous. The *remote terminal* is a keyboard type device which can be located in any convenient place where a telephone outlet is available. The user types the information that he wants sent to the computer and the computer responds normally within a few seconds with appropriate results. The discourse between user and computer is termed *interactive computing*. An obvious question might be, "What is the computer doing while the user is scratching his head?" The answer is that the computer is time sharing. *Time sharing* is a technique whereby a central computer can service several users by giving each a "slice" of computer time on a periodic basis. Thus, the user has the operational advantage of having the machine to himself. Because of the ultra-high speed of most modern computers, control can be switched between users without an appreciable delay in response time.

Time sharing would be useful without Iverson's language. It will become evident later, however, that a substantial amount of computation can be specified in each interaction with the APL system—making APL relevant to most problems being studied and to the experience level of most users. As a result, the user is provided a system with the simplicity and mobility of a desk calculator and the flexibility of an automatic computer.

Principle Areas of Application

It has been said that APL possesses simplicity and power.* In the sense that large complicated programs and small elementary calculations can be handled with ease, this is certainly true. It is also true that APL does not require complicated constructions, as in some programming languages, and that calculations can be specified succinctly and without ambiguity.

The notation of APL is based on the primitive and well-defined notation of mathematics. Yet, it is not correct to say that APL is limited to mathematical applications. As in computing in general, a substantial amount of APL use is mathematical in nature. In addition, the concise notation and interactive mode of operation make it useful in teaching for drill exercises and for experimentation with functions. It has been used to store and retrieve information, for text editing, for logical analysis and simulation, and for recreation.

One of the most significant advantages of using APL has yet to be stated. It is that APL provides a concise means of describing an algorithmic, physical, or logical process and that the description can be verified on a digital computer for later use in a variety of ways. In this light, APL is one of the more significant advances in computer technology.

4.2 ARITHMETIC AND TERMINAL OPERATIONS

In using any terminal-oriented programming language, certain conventions exist which apply to the physical facilities as well as to the procedures for using the system. In the description given here, an attempt is made to make the presentation independent of a particular implementation. Although the material contained here is patterned after the APL\360 system implemented by Falkoff and Iverson (9) at the IBM Watson Research Center, specific operating procedures, characteristic of that implementation, are omitted and included for reference purposes as Appendix B. Thus, this presentation is concerned with general operating procedures and the APL language.

The Concept and Use of a Remote Terminal

The practice of using ordinary telephone lines constitutes a state-of-the-art concept in information processing. Although the user needs only a typewriter-like device to use APL, some "black boxes" are needed to convert digital signals to telephone signals and telephone signals to digital signals on either end of the telephone line (See Figure 4.1). The black boxes take two forms: a dataset and an acoustical coupler. A *dataset* is

*See reference (1), p. 4.

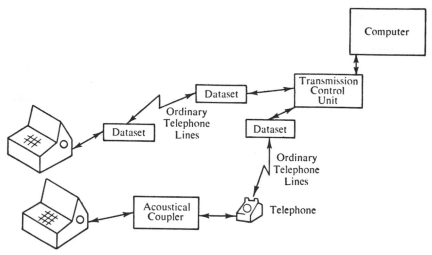

Fig. 4.1 Remote terminals.

supplied by the Telephone Company and establishes a fixed connection between one terminal and one telephone line. The dataset contains facilities for dialing and for establishing a "data" connection. The dataset on the computer end of the connection is answered automatically by the transmission controller of the computer system. An *acoustical coupler* is a mobile device attached to a terminal but *not* to any specific telephone. A terminal equipped with an acoustical coupler is connected to the computer by establishing an ordinary telephone connection and then clamping the receiver into the coupler mechanism. The coupler converts digital signals to acoustical signals and achieves the same results as the dataset described above. The reference manual for any terminal-oriented system normally contains detailed procedures for establishing a telephone connection.

It is desirable to establish well-defined procedures for setting up a telephone link to the APL system. A basic set is given here:

1. *Prepare the terminal for operation.* This not only involves turning the device on but also setting the dials and switches to operate in the communications mode rather than the local (or typewriter) mode.
2. *Dial the APL computer.* With a dataset connection, push the TALK button and dial. With an acoustical coupler, simply dial. After the telephone rings, you will hear a high-pitched sound.
3. *Make the connection.* With a dataset, push DATA and cradle the telephone. With an acoustical coupler, clamp the receiver into the coupler mechanism.

4. *Sign on.* Identify yourself to the APL system as a valid user by typing an established sequence of characters. See Appendix B for the sign-on procedures used with the APL\360 system.

After the sign-on has been completed, the user can enter into a dialogue with the APL system using a combination of *system commands* and *APL language statements*, typed in at the terminal. Commands and statements are formed from the letters, digits, operators, and punctuation characters of the APL alphabetic. The alphabet, type styles, and keyboard arrangement are designed to facilitate human use in an interactive mode of operation.

The APL Typeface and Keyboard Arrangement

The APL alphabet and keyboard arrangement are given in Figure 4.2. The letters are capitalized italics and the digits are upright, allowing sim-

Fig. 4.2 APL alphabet and keyboard arrangement.

ilar characters to be readily distinguished. The special symbols of the APL language are primarily included as uppercase characters and generally have some apparent relationship to their alphabetic or numeric correspondents. For example, ω is over W, ϵ over E, ρ (rho) over R, $*$ (for power) over P, $\circ$ (circle symbol) over O, α over A, $\lceil$ (for ceiling) over S, and $'$ (for Kwote) over K.

The meanings of the various operator symbols will become apparent as the respective operations are introduced.

Operators

As in ordinary mathematics and in most programming languages, operations are represented by special symbols. In APL, the most frequently used operations have corresponding operator symbols that are widely known. The ordinary operations of arithmetic are used in subsequent examples and are denoted as follows:

+ for *addition*
− for *subtraction*
× for *multiplication*
÷ for *division*
∗ for *power* or *exponentiation*

Thus,

$$2+3=5$$
$$10-8=2$$
$$4\times4=16$$
$$6\div2=3$$
$$8*2=64$$

Most operators have two interpretations—one as a monadic operator and the other as a dyadic operator. Usually, this facility is available only with the negation operation. The *degree* of an operator is easily determined. If the operator is preceded by a variable, a constant, or a parenthesized expression, it is dyadic. Otherwise, it is a monadic operator. Variables, constants, expressions, and the significance of monadic and dyadic operators are discussed in subsequent sections.

Discourse with the APL System

When APL is used, the terminal serves as an input device and an output device, depending upon whether it is the user's turn or the computer's turn to type. If the keyboard is unlocked, the user may enter a statement. When the user has finished typing his information, the RETURN key is pushed so the computer knows that the statement is complete. Only then does the computer interpret and execute the operations contained therein. Three events take place when the RETURN key is pushed; they are listed as follows:

1. The carriage returns to the left margin and the paper moves up one position—similar to an electric typewriter.
2. The keyboard is locked.
3. The computer recognizes that the statement has been completed and that it may initiate processing it.

When the computer is processing one statement, additional statements cannot be entered. Not only is the keyboard locked, but the computer is simply not ready to accept another statement. When the required calculations have been completed, the computer responds by unlocking the keyboard and by initiating the typing of the result (if any) beginning in the left-hand margin. When typing is complete, the carriage is returned, the paper is moved up one position, and the carriage is indented six spaces. The keyboard is then unlocked for the user's next statement.

The user's input and the computer's output are easily distinguished. The computer output begins in the left-hand margin while the input is indented six spaces. In this book, the left-hand margin and the six-space indention will be denoted as follows:

c *u*

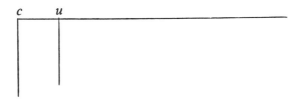

where *c* denotes the computer and *u* the user. Normally, the *c* and *u* will be omitted. A blank line, which sometimes gets typed, is denoted by the character *b̸* in column one. The following simple examples are given for clarification:

```
      5×4.2
21
      10+20-1
29
      3+8÷2
7
      2.5*2
6.25
```

When a statement is typed in the APL language, spaces (or blanks) may appear anywhere except within a constant or a name, which names a constituent of the language. Thus, spaces can be included, almost at will, to improve readability. However, an APL statement cannot be continued on another line. The conciseness of APL notation makes this a minor restriction.

Two typing conventions are of special importance:

1. Several APL symbols are composed from two characters of the APL alphabet by backspacing and overstriking. For example, the character ⌽ is formed by typing ○ followed by BACKSPACE followed by |. Similarly, the factorial symbol (!) is formed from a quote symbol (') and a decimal point (.). Therefore backspacing and overstriking are not permitted unless specifically intended. Although this method is frequently used with some terminal systems for correcting typing errors, it is an invalid practice with APL.

2. Typing mistakes may be corrected by implementation-defined procedures. See Appendix B for procedures that have been established for APL\360.

Error Messages

Most sequences of operators, operands, and punctuation characters have a meaning in APL. This is partly the result of allowing operators to assume different interpretations depending upon whether the context is monadic or dyadic. Thus, the lack of an error message for a particular statement does not automatically guarantee that it serves its intended purpose. On the other hand, a great many serious errors can be diagnosed by the APL interpreter. A frequent example is the use of a variable* which has not been defined. Assume the user types $AB + 12$, where AB has not been defined. The terminal sheet would look as follows:

The error message is followed by the invalid statement followed by a caret typed under the constituent that was in error. The error messages included with the APL\360 system are included in Appendix B for reference purposes.

The Workspace Concept

A terminal connected to the APL system is said to be *active*. Associated with each active terminal is a block of storage in the central computer called a *workspace*. Contained in each user's workspace is working storage and control information for the current terminal session along with *variables* (data values and their names) and *defined functions* (programs and subroutines) used during the calculations. The size of the workspace is fixed for each APL system and an inactive workspace can be saved in a library designed for this purpose. System commands exist for loading, saving, and modifying the contents of a user's workspace.

4.3 NUMERIC CONSTANTS

Basic to all numerical computations is a means of representing numbers. Although numbers are stored in a coded form internally to the computer, the user of APL need not be concerned with this. He may enter his num-

*See Section 4.4

bers in one of two convenient forms: decimal or exponential. Clearly, both systems use digits to the base ten, although decimal notation is probably more familiar to the average reader.

Characters Used in the Representation of Numbers

The thirteen characters 0 1 2 3 4 5 6 7 8 9 .⁻ E can be used to represent numeric data. The digits are ordinary keyboard digits; the decimal point is used interchangeably with the period; the negative sign should be distinguished from the minus sign which denotes subtraction—close observation will detect that the negative sign is raised to a superior position;* and the E, which denotes an *exponent*, is the same letter E frequently used for constructing words. No embedded blanks, commas, or other punctuation characters are permitted in APL numeric constants.

Decimal Form

Practically, any number can be entered in the decimal form, with the limit being the size of an APL line. Twelve of the above characters (the E is omitted here) can be used, and only those parts of a number that are actually required need be written. For example, the number five may be written 005, or 5, or 05.000, or even 5.00. Leading zeros and trailing blanks are ignored. Additional examples are:

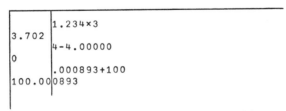

```
        1.234×3
3.702
        4-4.00000
0
        .000893+100
100.00  0893
```

On output, however, APL picks whatever form would represent a number in the simplest manner (see the following section on accuracy).

Use of the Negative Sign

The character ⁻, called the negative sign, is used to specify a negative number. As mentioned above, it should be distinguished from the minus sign. For example:

```
      ⁻2+4
2
      ⁻2-⁻5
3
```

*On the APL keyboard, the negative sign is found over the digit 2; the minus sign is found over the + character; and another similar character, the underscore, is found over the letter F.

The negative sign may also be applied to an exponent in the exponential form as described below.

Exponential Representation

It is frequently convenient to express numbers in a (fraction, exponent) form called *exponential form* or scientific notation. For example, 30000000 is more succinctly written as $.3 \times 10^8$ or as 3.0×10^7. Similarly, .000000123 would likely be expressed as $.123 \times 10^{-6}$ or 1.23×10^{-7}. Although it is true that in APL 30000000 could be entered as 3.0×10*7, the operation requires a multiplication and an exponentiation. Therefore, APL permits constants to be entered in exponential form without requiring explicit calculations by the computer. In exponential form, the letter *E* is used to denote an exponent to the base ten; the remainder of the number follows the same conventions as with decimal form. The following list gives several examples:

Scientific Notation	*APL Exponential Form*
$.3 \times 10^8$	$.3E8$
$.123 \times 10^{-6}$	$.123E^-6$
-1×10^{10}	$^-1E10$
-1.0×10^{-13}	$^-1.0E^-13$ same as $^-1E^-13$

Accuracy

The number of digits of internal precision carried by APL for a numeric value is of casual interest to most users and of particular concern to those working on precise calculations. Although the exact precision is implementation-dependent, the APL\360 system at IBM Research carried 16 decimal digits* with the number being stored internally in the most convenient form.

On output, the user has some control over the number of significant digits that are printed. Ordinarily, the 10 most significant digits are printed and trailing zeroes after the decimal point are suppressed.

```
       1÷9
0.1111111111
       5÷4
1.25
       1E6÷9
111111.1111
```

The system command)*DIGITS* (see Appendix B) enables the user to alter the number of significant digits printed, with the number ranging from one to sixteen.

*See reference (9).

Although the user may enter a numeric constant in whatever form he chooses, that is, either decimal or exponential form, the computer must choose one of the two when printing results. The following rules are applied:

1. A fractional number is displayed with one leading zero regardless of how it was entered.

```
          2.5E¯1
   0.25
          .55555
   0.5555|5
          1÷3
   0.3333|333333
          00.007
   0.007
          2÷4
   0.5
          .1
   0.1
```

2. If a number is less than $1E^-5$, greater than $1EN$ (where N is the number of significant digits displayed—usually 10), or an integer greater than $2^{31}-1$, then exponential form is used (note that the value $2^{31}-1$ is APL\360 implementation-dependent). Otherwise, decimal form is used. Exponential form always prints a number whose magnitude is between one and ten followed by an appropriate exponent.

```
          2E5
   200000
          2E11
   2E11
          .000000123
   1.23E¯7
```

Two additional precautions are in order: (1) The number of digits retained by the system may be less than the number of digits entered; and (2) the APL system *usually* retains more digits than are printed. The latter comment is particularly significant in tests for equality.

4.4 COMMANDS, STATEMENTS, AND EXPRESSIONS

One of the significant advantages of a programming language is the facility by which data, conditions, the state of physical devices, and constituents of the language itself can be assigned meaningful names and later be referenced, conveniently, using the given names. In APL, names are used most frequently in three ways:

1. To store information or the results of computation, either temporarily or permanently, for later recall using the assigned name.
2. To identify a user-defined function.
3. To name a workspace so that it can be saved and subsequently reloaded.

A statement may also be named by what is known as a statement label, and groups of names may be collected and given a group name for reference purposes. In this section, names used to identify data items and workspaces are considered. Data items are then used as constituents of statements and expressions, and workspace names are used with some of the system commands. The presentation of function names and statement labels is postponed until Chapter 6. By then, all of the necessary requisite material will have been covered. Group names are considered in the appendix on APL\360.

Basic Input to APL—Statements and Commands

Thus far, discourse between the user and the computer has been limited to examples involving one or two operations and only a few characters. Each line of input, which is typed at the terminal and transmitted to the computer with the RETURN key, can take one of three forms:

1. An APL statement.
2. A system command.
3. A response to a request for input from a statement containing one of the input operations (see Section 6.4).

An APL statement is the means by which computations are performed by the computer. A statement may specify one or more mathematical operations, branching, input/output, or a combination of them. Other statements are available for defining functions and for tracing or stopping their execution. The following examples are APL statements:

$$2 \times 3$$
$$M \leftarrow 2 \quad 3 \rho \iota 12$$
$$T \Delta DOIT \leftarrow 3 \quad 4 \quad 7 \quad 8$$
$$\rightarrow (K > 13) / LOOP$$
$$\nabla R \leftarrow A \ PLUS \ B$$
$$\rightarrow 0$$

The meaning of each of these statements will be made clear as the language is developed. It should be noted in the preceding example, however, that no attempt has been made to indicate a computer response to the statements, as was previously the case. The reason is that the APL system has two modes of operation: the execution mode and the definition mode. When the system is in the *execution* mode, statements are executed immediately after they are entered. The *definition* mode is used to define a user function. In this mode, a statement is not executed* as it is entered but serves to compose a function. A defined function must eventually be invoked by an executable statement, and it is then that statements from the function are selected for execution. Defined functions may invoke other defined functions, etc. This process can be extended to as many levels as are necessary. In the example which follows, the function *PLUS* is defined which adds two numbers.

```
      ∇R←X PLUS Y                     (1)
[1]   R←X+Y                           (2)
[2]   ∇                               (3)

      10 PLUS 20                      (4)
30
      10 PLUS ¯20                     (5)
¯10
```

Statement (1) establishes the function *PLUS* and puts the system into the definition mode. Statement (2) enters a statement into the function being defined. Statement (3) terminates the function definition and takes the system out of the definition mode. Statements (4) and (5) are entered in the execution mode and utilize the defined function, *PLUS*. All computations, regardless of whether they are defined functions, are initiated in the execution mode.

Statements, as discussed, are part of the APL language and indicate what operations the computer is to perform. There are times when the user wishes to communicate with the computer system itself. For this reason, *system commands* are defined which deal with the mechanical aspects of using a computer, such as signing on or off or for saving, loading, or copying a workspace. A system command may be entered only when the system is in the execution mode of operation and begins with the right parenthesis followed by appropriate letters or digits. The following examples give some sample commands:

>)*OFF*
>
>)*LIB*
>
>)*CLEAR*

---

*In fact, a statement entered into a function is not checked for errors until the execution of *that* statement is attempted.

Although system commands are implementation-dependent (and treated fully in Appendix B on APL\360), they can be generally classed as follows:

1. *Terminal control* (TC) commands which are used for initiating and terminating a work session.
2. *Workspace control* (WC) commands which allow the user to modify the state of his active workspace.
3. *Library control* (LC) commands which provide facilities for saving, loading, and deleting a workspace.
4. *Inquiry* (IQ) commands which provide information on the status of the active system.
5. *Communications* (CM) commands which permit the user to correspond with other terminals.

System commands supplement the APL language by providing operational facilities which are primarily dependent upon the method of implementation.

Identifiers, Simple Variables, and Workspace Names

In APL, an identifier is used to name a variable, a workspace, a function, a statement label, or a group. An *identifier* is a sequence of the letters *A* through *Z*, the digits 0 through 9, or the Δ character. A letter may additionally be underscored for clarity or to indicate a data value of special interest to the user. The first character of an identifier must not be a digit, and the beginning sequences *S*Δ and *T*Δ are not permitted. Operators, punctuation characters, and spaces delimit identifiers so that the use of an embedded space specifies a different construct than the identifier intended. Theoretically, an identifier may be of any length although APL\360 limits variable and function names to 77 characters and workspace names to 11 characters (see Appendix B). The following list gives some valid and invalid examples:

Valid Identifiers	Invalid Identifiers
*AB*12	1*B*18
X	*M__N*
*M*44	*S*Δ*ABC*
PRIME	*T*Δ*X*2
*YPLUS*Δ *Y*	*AB.CD*
SUMOFIMPORTANTVALUES	*X,Y*
*XT*Δ*T*	
Δ*Z*	

A *simple variable* (usually called a *variable*) refers to the name given to a scalar value by the operation of specification, covered in the next section. Thus, a variable has two components—a name and a value. The correspondence is established in the user's active workspace for subsequent use.

A *workspace name* is the identifier assigned to an active workspace when it is saved using one of the system commands. For example, the command:

$$)SAVE\ ASPACE$$

stores the active workspace under the name *ASPACE*. At a later time, an exact copy of that workspace may be recalled with the $)LOAD\ ASPACE$ command.*

The Specification Operation

The specification† operator, that is, the left-pointing arrow, is used to assign a value to a variable. For example, the first statement causes the

```
        DENSITY←11.4
        DENSITY
11.4
```

value 11.4 to be stored in the active workspace with the name *DENSITY*, which is said to be specified as 11.4. In this statement, the specification operation is executed, the carriage is indented six spaces, and the keyboard is unlocked for the user's next input. Once the variable, *DENSITY* in this case, is assigned a value, then it can be used as an operand in other calculations. Thus, complex calculations can be programmed using variables such as this. Actual results obtained from the calculations would reflect the latest values assigned to the variables used.

The criteria used by the computer for deciding whether or not to print a result are of particular interest. Recall that in the multiplication operation, 5×4.2, the answer 21 is printed; but in the specification operation, $DENSITY \leftarrow 11.4$, nothing is printed. After a calculation or series of calculations, three possibilities exist‡ for printing or storing the result: (1)

---

*It should be noted, here, that the $)SAVE$ command does not change the status of the active workspace; that is, it is still available for use. Similarly, the $)LOAD$ command does not alter the saved workspace in computer storage. It may be reloaded as many times as necessary.

†In other programming languages, the specification operator may be referred to as the *replacement* operation, and the statement as a whole is called the *assignment statement*.

‡The possibilities are not necessarily mutually exclusive.

The specification operation is specified as the last operation to be executed.
The result is assigned to the specified variable and no printing takes place.
(2) *The specification operation is not specified as the last operation to be performed.* The computer assumes that the user would like to see the result
and types it at the terminal. (3) *The specification operation may be embedded in a more complex statement.* In this case, the assignment is made
and the result is used as an operand in another operation. This last case
is treated more fully in a following section on the order of execution. Examples of the preceding cases are:

```
           5×12
60
           SQUARE←25.039*2
           SQUARE
626.951521
           A←1
           25*A←A+1
625
           A
2
```

Using the Value of a Variable

A variable can be used in any context that a constant can be used. However, as mentioned earlier, a variable must be assigned a value before
any operations can be satisfactorily completed. If the)ERASE command
deletes its referents from the active workspace, then the following examples exhibit the manner in which variables can be used:

```
           X←2
           X+1
3
           )ERASE X
           X+1
VALUE ERROR
           X+1
           ^
           X←10
           X*2
100
           Y←2
           X*Y
100
```

A variable may be respecified. That is, a variable which has been defined through a specification operation may be assigned another value by placing that variable to the left of the specification operator in an APL statement. For example:

```
        RADIUS←2
        AREA←3.14159×RADIUS*2
        AREA
12.56636
        RADIUS←1
        AREA←3.14159×RADIUS*2
        AREA
3.14159
```

In the first series of calculations, *RADIUS* is assigned the value 2 and *AREA* is computed and specified as 12.56636. In the second instance, *RADIUS* is respecified as 1. Thus, the first value for *RADIUS*, which was 2, is replaced by the value 1 and only the latter value is retained. Similarly, *AREA* is respecified as 3.14159. If it were desired to retain the first value of either variable, then a sequence of statements of the form:

```
        RADIUS←2
        AREA←3.14159×RADIUS*2
        TEMPR←RADIUS
        TEMPAREA←AREA
```

would be required.

One of the most frequent uses of a variable is to keep a count of the number of occurrences of a particular event. Each time the event occurs, the counter is increased or decreased by one. For example, assume that *TIMESREMAINING* initially contains a value corresponding to the number of times a particular operation should be executed. Each time an operation is performed, the variable is decreased in value. Similarly, assume that *I* operates in a positive direction and is increased by one. The following examples depict use of these variables under the given circumstances.

```
TIMESREMAINING←LIMIT
I←0
    .
    .
    .
I←I+1
    .
    .
    .
TIMESREMAINING←TIMESREMAINING-1
    .
    .
    .
```

Both statements, excluding the initialization, exhibit a situation where the same variable appears on either side of the specification operation. In each case, the calculation is executed and then the specification is performed. That is:

```
        COUNT←1
        COUNT
1
        COUNT←COUNT+2
        COUNT
3
        COUNT←COUNT-1
        COUNT
2
```

These examples have implied that the specification operation is always the leftmost operation in a statement. This is not necessarily true. It will become evident later that the specification is a dyadic operator, of the ordinary variety, and that it may be embedded within a mathematical expression.

Introductory Example—The Right Triangle Problem

The essence of computer programming is the synthesis of meaningful calculations from a sequence of ordinary statements. With APL, an attempt has been made to simplify the programming process as much as possible by providing a programming language closely related to ordinary mathematics. Yet, differences do exist and it is wise to mention them explicitly, even though most readers either know them or have suspected them by now. The vehicle is a simple right triangle problem, shown as follows:

$$d = \sqrt{h^2 + b^2}$$
$$p = h + b + d$$
$$a = \tfrac{1}{2}bh$$

When $h=3$ and $b=4$, the problem is ordinarily stated as:

$$h = 3$$
$$b = 4$$
$$d = \sqrt{3^2 + 4^2} = 5$$
$$p = 3 + 4 + 5 = 12$$
$$a = \tfrac{1}{2}(4)(3) = 6$$

In APL, the same problem would be stated as follows:

```
         H←3
         B←4
         D←((H*2)+B*2)*.5
         P←H+B+D
         A←.5×B×H
         D
5
         P
12
         A
6
```

It is customary to refer to the preceding series of statements as a *program*, even though the operational procedures were executed manually. This leads to a more precise formulation of the two basic modes of operation. In the *execution mode*, as evidenced above, statements are executed by the computer as they are entered by the user. Responses, when appropriate, are returned immediately to the terminal. In the *definition mode*, statements are entered by the user and saved by the computer as a part of a function definition. Later, when that function is executed by the computer, statements are selected from the defined function automatically as

execution progresses. In the *automatic mode*, printed results may be specified as part of the statement. These results are transmitted to the terminal
as the particular statement is executed, even though the user makes no
explicit interaction with the computer.

Returning to the example above, some deviations from ordinary mathematical notation should be mentioned. First, every operator has a symbol, and that operation must never be specified by implication alone.
Thus, implied multiplication, as in the statement

$$a = \tfrac{1}{2}bh$$

must be made explicit with the appropriate operator, that is,

$$A \leftarrow .5 \times B \times H$$

Next, the keyboard/terminal arrangement restricts the line of input to a
linear sequence of characters. Therefore, operations such as the power
functions usually denoted by a raised or lowered argument must be indicated by an appropriate symbol. In the example, the mathematical
statement:

$$d = \sqrt{h^2 + b^2}$$

was given in APL as:

$$D \leftarrow ((H*2) + B*2)*.5$$

Lastly, the equals sign (=) used in

$$h = 3$$

to *set* a variable equal to a value is replaced by the left-pointing arrow:

$$H \leftarrow 3$$

This convention allows the equals sign to be used as a test of strict
equality.

The Concept of a Program in APL

The notion of exactly what constitutes a program in the APL language is
frequently of concern, particularly to those readers familiar with other
programming systems. First, it is obvious that APL can be used as a desk
calculator, and as the remainder of the language is unfolded, other facilities, amenable to the *execution mode* of operation, are presented. Next,
statements can be entered by the user and are executed immediately by the
computer. Since a program is nothing more than a sequence of state-

ments, possessing an implicit or explicit order of execution, and specifying a computer-oriented representation of an algorithmic process, statements entered and executed in the *execution mode* satisfy the basic definition even though the sequence in which statements are processed is determined explicitly by the user. However, most computer users regard a program as something that, once initiated, is executed automatically with no intervention. This facility is also permitted in APL through *defined functions*. In a general sense, an APL defined function may be similar in concept to a mathematical operator or it may be a program (i.e., a series of statements) which has been assigned a name. In the former case, a function defined as an operator is used in a mathematical expression. In the latter case, a function defined as a program is invoked by typing the name of that function as a single statement. This leads to an important point. When APL is used, all computations by the computer are initiated from the terminal, through either an executable statement or a defined function.

Compound Expressions, Parentheses, and Order of Execution

In ordinary mathematics, complex expressions that imply a series of operations can be specified in one statement. In most of the APL examples given thus far, only one or two operations were denoted. The reason, obviously, was to avoid problems relating to the structure of expressions and to the order in which operations are executed.

The structure of an operation in APL has two general forms, appropriately termed monadic and dyadic. If m denotes a monadic operator and d denotes a dyadic operator, then the structure of the two forms is depicted as follows:

$$\text{Monadic Operation} \qquad \text{Dyadic Operation}$$
$$mR \qquad\qquad\qquad LdR$$

Here, L represents a constant, a variable, or an expression in parentheses. R represents a constant, a variable, or an expression either enclosed in parentheses or not. The precise meaning of this latter statement relates to the order of execution, which is covered next.

The distinction between a monadic and a dyadic operation is obvious. Given an operator that can represent either a monadic or a dyadic operation, such as the minus sign, which can indicate subtraction or unary minus, the monadic interpretation is assumed if the symbol to its immediate left is another operator symbol. Consider the following expressions:

$$A + - B \qquad (1)$$
$$A - B \qquad (2)$$

In expression (1), the minus sign denotes a monadic operator since the symbol to its immediate left is another operator. In expression (2), the minus sign indicates a dyadic operator because it is preceded by an operand. The following examples give valid and invalid *dyadic* operations:

Valid	*Invalid*
$A+B$	$5X$
$(A+1)\times2$	$(^-10+N)T$
$-Z*W$	$X+\wedge Y$

In textbook mathematics, familiar conventions exist for determining the order in which operations are applied in a mathematical statement. In the expression

$$ax+b$$

for example, the implicit multiplication of a times x is assumed to precede the addition of b to the product. Ordinarily, conventions of this sort cause little difficulty in spite of the facts that:

1. Multiplication may be denoted as ax, $a{\cdot}x$, $a\times x$.

2. Division is commonly specified as $a\div x$, a/x, or $\dfrac{a}{x}$.

3. The power function $a^{b^{c^d}}$ is frequently interpreted as $\left(\left(a^b\right)^c\right)^d$ or as $a^{(b(c^d))}$.

In a programming language, such as APL, with a multiplicity of operators and with facilities for defining functions, the assignment and use of precedence relations among the operators and functions can be tedious, cumbersome, and a potentially unmanageable situation. APL uses no precedence relations and interprets and executes all expressions in a strict right-to-left order.* Thus, any operator, function, or specification symbol assumes as its rightmost operand the entire expression to its right. In the following script:

---

*Iverson has a very interesting discussion as well as some sound arguments for the choice of right-to-left execution in his book on *Elementary Functions* (16).

the product of 2 and the sum of 3 and 4 are formed. Similarly:

```
             A←11
             B←6
             100÷B-A
  ¯20
             C←2
             A-B-C
  7
             8÷4÷2
  4
             2*3*2
  512
             2*3×2
  64
             A×B←B÷2
  33
             B
  3
             C←-A-B
             C
  ¯8
```

The right-to-left convention is not without disadvantages since most expressions are read from left to right and since most readers are familiar with some conventions for the precedence of operators. As additional operators are introduced for scalars as well as for arrays, it will become increasingly evident that any inconvenience is certainly worthwhile.

How, then, is it possible to deviate from the right-to-left rule for execution? The answer is through judicious use of parentheses, which are interpreted in the usual manner. That is, expressions within parentheses are evaluated before the expressions of which they are a part. The use of parentheses is extended to as many levels as is necessary. Several additional examples exhibit the use of parentheses:

```
             (2×3)+4
  10
             A←5+B←2×3
             A, B
  11   6
             (99÷A)-B
  3
             Z←(2×X)+Y←1+X←-W←¯2
             X, Y, Z, W
  2    3     7  ¯2
             (X+Y)×Z+W
  25
             (X×((3×X)+2))+1
  17
             3×X*2+2×X+1
  768
```

Since an expression within parentheses is normally used as a constituent part of other expressions, it must have an explicit result (or value). Thus an expression enclosed in parentheses must be well formed and adhere to the structure for monadic and dyadic operators given above. The following script depicts some well-formed and some ill-formed expressions within parentheses:

```
             A←15
             (A)
      15
             (-A)
    ¯15
             (A+)
  SYNTAX ERROR
             (A+)
               ^
             (+)
  SYNTAX ERROR
             (+)
               ^
```

In several of the examples, more than one specification operator was included in a single statement. This is termed *multiple specification*, which also adheres to the strict right-to-left rule. Extreme care should be exercised when using multiple specification, especially in cases where a variable is a constituent part of an expression and is also multiply-specified therein. Given the following examples:

```
             A←2
             B←(A←3)×A
             B
       9

             A←2
             B←(A←3)×-A
             B
     ¯6
```

In the first case, the specification within parentheses is executed first and *B* assumes the value 9. In the second case, the unary operation $(-A)$ is executed prior to the multiple specification and *B* is specified as ¯6. In general, it is best to avoid expressions of this type.

4.5 PRIMITIVE OPERATORS

A *primitive operator* is an operator that is defined as a constituent of the APL programming language and is available to the user without having to define it. Addition (+), subtraction (−), multiplication (×), and division (÷) are common examples. A primitive operator is denoted by a special symbol or composite symbol* in the character set and requires either one or two scalar values as operands. A primitive scalar operation always yields a result which is a scalar value. Appendix C contains a condensed summary of the primitive operation in APL. After the reader has become familiar with the APL language, Appendix C will serve as a valuable reference.

One of the powerful features of APL is that scalar operations are extended to arrays on an element-by-element basis. *Extensions to arrays* are covered in the next chapter after the most widely used primitive operations and mathematical functions are introduced.

Monadic Arithmetic Operations

The monadic *negation operation* was introduced earlier as a means of changing the sign of an operand. For example:

```
              A←-B←2
              A
  ¯2
              B
   2
              +B
   2
              -B
  ¯2
              ¯B
SYNTAX ERROR
              ¯B
             ^
```

Formally, the result R of the negation operation applied to an argument B is defined as:

$$R \equiv 0 - B$$

---

*That is, an operator formed by overstriking one symbol with another. For example, the quote symbol (') followed by a BACKSPACE, and overstruck by the period (.) forms the *composite symbol* !.

At this point, the reader is probably wondering if +, ×, ÷, and even *
have monadic interpretations. Well, they do and are introduced here
except for * which is covered in the section on exponentials.

The monadic operator + is termed the *identity operator* which returns
the value of the given operand. For example:

```
        +10
10
        A←-5
        +A
 ¯5
        +¯15
¯15
```

Formally, the result R of the identity operation applied to an argument
B is defined as:

$$R \equiv 0 + B$$

The monadic operator × is termed the *signum operator* and returns
the value -1, 0, or 1 depending upon whether the operand is negative,
zero, or positive, respectively. For example:

```
        A←¯5
        ×A
¯1
        ×5
1
        ×A+5
0
```

Formally, the result R of the signum operation applied to an operand B
is defined as: *

$$R \equiv (0 < B) - 0 > B$$

*At this point, it should be noted that formal definitions use other operators in the
language. Formal definitions are normally used for reference purposes, and the reader, in
his first reading of the material, could effectively branch around them.

The monadic operator ÷ is a convenient way of finding the reciprocal of a value and is more convenient than using a division into 1. It is appropriately named the *reciprocal operator* and is exhibited as follows:

```
        ÷5
0.2
        ÷÷5
5
        1÷÷5
5
```

Formally, the result R of the reciprocal operation applied to an argument B is defined as:

$$R \equiv 1 \div B$$

As evidenced by the formal definitions, the monadic arithmetic operations are a convenience rather than a necessity. However, the relevance of a terminal-oriented system is directly related to the amount of typing required to get the job done.

Exponentiation

The dyadic *exponentiation operation* is commonly regarded as raising a number to a given power. The operation uses the power operator * and the operands are not restricted to integers, so exponentiation can be used for taking square roots, cube roots, etc. For example:

```
        5*2
25
        25*.5
5
        25*÷2
5
        (3*3)*÷3
3
```

Formally, the result R of the exponentiation operation applied to operands A and B is defined as:

$$R \equiv A^{B}$$

The definition holds for the following cases:

1. $A > 0$ and B any value.
2. $A = 0$ and $B \geq 0$.
3. $A < 0$ and B equivalent to an expression of the form $M \div N$ where M is an integer and N is an odd integer.

Moreover, $(A*0) = 1$ and $(0*0) = 1$ but $(0*B) = 0$, when $B \neq 0$. For example,

```
        |FIVE←5
        |ZERO←0
        |0*FIVE
0       |
        |ZERO*ZERO
1       |
        |FIVE*0
1       |
        |5*¯2
0.04    |
        |0*5-FIVE
1       |
        |
```

Exponential

The monadic *exponential* operator * raises the mathematical value e to a given power and thus eliminates inaccuracies resulting from entering that value at different times. For example:

```
          |*1
2.71828182|8
          |*¯1
0.36787944|12
          |
```

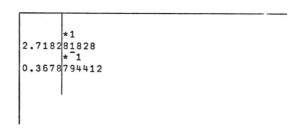

Formally, the result R of the exponential operation applied to an argument B is defined as:

$$R \equiv e^{B}$$

where e is stored as 2.718281828459045.

Maximum and Minimum

Many algorithmic procedures require that the maximum or the minimum of two values be selected. APL includes, as primitive operations, two dyadic operators which perform these functions. The *maximum* operator ⌈

selects the algebraic largest of two operands while the *minimum* operator L selects the algebraic smallest of its operands. For example:

```
            A←.25
            B←.3
            AΓB
0.3
            (÷A)L÷B
3.333333333
            (÷A)Γ÷B
4
            AL-B
⁻0.3
            -BLA
⁻0.25
```

Formally, the result R of the maximum operation applied to the operands A and B is defined as:

$$R \equiv A, \quad \text{if } A > B$$
$$R \equiv B, \quad \text{if } A \leq B$$

Similarly, the result R of the minimum operation applied to the operands A and B is defined as:

$$R \equiv A, \quad \text{if } A \leq B$$
$$R \equiv B, \quad \text{if } A > B$$

Floor, Ceiling, and Rounding

Many computer applications involve computations in the neighborhood of a given value. In addition, it is frequently desirable to limit the resulting values to integers. The monadic operator L is termed the *floor operation* and gives the largest integer not exceeding the single operand. Similarly, the monadic operator Γ is termed the *ceiling operation* and provides the smallest integer not exceeded by the given operand. For example:

```
      L3.14
3
      L⁻3.14
⁻4
      Γ3.14
4
      Γ⁻3.14
⁻3
      L5
5
      Γ5
5
```

Formally, the result R of the floor operation applied to the operand B is defined as: *

$$R \equiv B - 1 | B$$

Similarly, the result R of the ceiling operation applied to the operand B is defined as:

$$R \equiv B + 1 | - B$$

The floor operation can be used to conveniently round a number to the nearest integer or to a given number of decimal places. The accepted practice for rounding a number to the nearest integer is to add one half and to retain only the integral part of the result. In APL, this process applied to the value B is expressed as:

$$\lfloor B + .5$$

A similar expression for rounding the value B to N decimal places is given as:

$$(10 * - N) \times \lfloor 0.5 + (10 * N) \times B$$

For example:

```
        B←33.3
       ⌊B+.5
33
        C←77.7
       ⌊C+.5
78
        N←3
        B←2÷3
        B
0.6666666667
       (10*-N)×⌊0.5+(10*N)×B
0.667
       (10*-N)×⌊0.5+(10*N)×1÷3
0.333
```

Absolute Value

The absolute value function in mathematics is identified by vertical strokes enclosing a single argument. For example, the expression

$$| x |$$

---

*The meaning of the | operator is given later; formal definitions are included for reference purposes.

denotes the magnitude of *x*, regardless of its original sign. In APL, the absolute value operation is indicated by the monadic operator $|$, placed in its usual position, and is defined on the expression to its right   such as any other monadic operator. For example:

```
          D←¯5
          |D
5
          |¯8*÷3
2
          |÷¯3
0.3333333333
```

Formally, the result *R* of the absolute value operation on an operand B is defined as:

$$R \equiv B\lceil - B$$

or as

$$R \equiv B \times \times B$$

Comparison Operations

When the values of *A* and *B* are known and posed with the question, "Is *A* greater than *B*?" one can usually respond with the answer *yes* or *no*. In a computer, the truth values *true* for yes and *false* for no must be represented by symbolic values, and the values chosen can be of major significance. In APL, the truth value *true* is represented by the scalar value 1 and the truth value *false* is represented by the scalar value 0. Thus, the result of a comparison can be used in arithmetic calculations much like any other numeric value. Six comparison operations are incorporated into APL as primitive dyadic operators:

Operator	Meaning
<	less than
≤	less than or equal to
=	equal to
≥	greater than or equal to
>	greater than
≠	not equal to

In fact, the six operators are conveniently located, in sequence, over the numeric characters 3 through 8 on the APL keyboard. The six comparison operators are further defined in Table 4.1. Like any other dyadic

TABLE 4.1   COMPARISON OPERATIONS

Expression	Truth value if A is less than B	Truth value if A is equal to B	Truth value if A is greater than B
$A < B$	1	0	0
$A \leq B$	1	1	0
$A = B$	0	1	0
$A \geq B$	0	1	1
$A > B$	0	0	1
$A \neq B$	1	0	1

operator, a comparison operator adheres to the right-to-left convention for arithmetic. For example:

```
      5>4
1
      5<4
0
      A←6
      B←5
      C←4
      A>B+C
0
      (2×B)=A+C
1
      C>A>B
1
      0=A=B
1
```

(Note that in the last two interactions with the computer, the right-to-left rule significantly affects the result.)

When dealing with floating-point numbers, the question of how close is equal is of importance. The *comparison operations* as well as *floor* and *ceiling* are dependent, to some extent, on how close in magnitude numeric values have to be before they are regarded as equal. This tolerance is termed *fuzz*, and in APL\360 it is set, approximately, to $1.0E^-13$. When computing is done with only a few significant digits, as in integer arithmetic, tests of equality are of little concern. On the other hand, the following examples indicate cases where equality can be of concern:

```
        0.3333333333333333=0.33333333333333334
    1
        ⌈5+10*¯12
    6
        ⌈5+10*¯13
    5
```

Fuzz is used in the formal definition of the comparison operations.

Formally, the result R of a comparison applied to Operands A and B is defined as:

	$R \equiv 1$ if	$R \equiv 0$ if
$A < B$	$(A-B) \leq -FUZZ \times \mid B$	otherwise
$A \leq B$	$(A-B) \leq FUZZ \times \mid B$	otherwise
$A - B$	$(\mid A-B) \leq FUZZ \times \mid B$	otherwise[a]
$A \geq B$	$(A-B) > -FUZZ \times \mid B$	otherwise
$A > B$	$(\mid A-B) > FUZZ \times \mid B$	otherwise
$A \neq B$	$(\mid A-B) > FUZZ \times \mid B$	otherwise[a]

$$FUZZ \leftarrow 1.0E^-13$$

[a] If operands A and B are characters (see Section 5.2), then $R = 1$ if the relationship holds; otherwise $R = 0$.

Logical Operations

Logical operations are ordinarily used to form complex expressions from the truth values of one or more logical events. In APL, a logical event can take the form of a scalar data item which has the value 0 or 1 or it can be the result of an operation. A 0 or 1 truth value can additionally result from arithmetic computation. The APL language contains five logical operations: *and*, *or*, *not*, *nand*, and *nor*. *And*, *or*, *nand*, and *nor* are frequently referred to as *connectives* and are dyadic operators. *Not* is a monadic operator.

The connective *and* is represented by the symbol ∧ and returns the value 1 if both operands are 1. For example:

```
        1∧1
    1
        1∧0
    0
        (3<2)∧5>4
    0
```

The connective *or* is represented by the symbol ∨ and returns the value 1 if either or both of the operands is 1. For example:

```
      │0∨0
0     │
      │1∨0
1     │
      │(3<2)∨5>4
1     │
```

The unary operator ~ (tilde symbol) is termed the *not operation* and returns the value 0 if its operand is 1 and returns 1 if its operand is 0. For example:

```
      │~1
0     │
      │~0
1     │
      │~(3<2)∨5>4
0     │
      │~(3<2)∧5>4
1     │
```

The *nand operation* is a composite operation commonly referred to as *not and*. Accordingly, it uses the dyadic operator ⍲, formed from a ∧, a backspace, and a ~. *Nand* returns the value 0 if both operands are 0 and returns 1 otherwise. For example:

```
      │(3<2)⍲5>4
1     │
      │1⍲1
0     │
      │(100<1)⍲2>200
1     │
```

The *nor operation* is a composite operation commonly referred to as *not or*. It uses the dyadic operator ⍱, formed from a ∨, a backspace, and a ~. *Nor* returns the value 1 if both operands are 0 and returns a 0 otherwise. For example:

```
                0∨0
         1
                (3<2)∨5>4
         0
                (100<1)∨2>200
         1
```

Since the operands of logical operations are limited to the values 0 and 1, the result of the dyadic operations can be formally defined by truth tables. They are given as follows:

∧	0	1		∨	0	1		⍲	0	1		⍱	0	1
0	0	0		0	0	1		0	1	1		0	1	0
1	0	1		1	1	1		1	1	0		1	0	0

The result R of the not operation applied to operand B is defined as:

$$R \equiv 1 \ne B$$

where B must be a 0 or a 1.

Operands are restricted to 0 or 1 values as depicted in the following script:

```
                (3<2)∨1-2
         DOMAIN ERROR
                (3<2)∨1-2
                ∧
                2∨1
         DOMAIN ERROR
                2∨1
                ∧
                1∧1∨1∧1∧0
         1
```

Residue

In many computational procedures, it is necessary to compute the residue R of a numeric value B modulus another value A; that is:

$$R \equiv B \pmod{A}$$

If A and B are both integers, then R is the remainder after dividing B by A. APL extends this facility by allowing the arguments to be nonintegral and nonnegative. The residue operation uses the dyadic operator symbol $|$, the vertical stroke, and has the following form:

$$A \mid B$$

the letters A and B correspond to those in the above definition. For example:

```
        A←2
        B←7
        A|B
1
        A|6
0
        A|13.4
1.4
        5|¯13.4
1.6
        1.5|3.4
0.4
```

As evidenced in the above examples and described in the formal definitions, below, the result of the residue operation is always *positive*. The order of the operands is of particular interest. Because of the right-to-left rule and the fact that an operator interprets the expression to its right as its rightmost operand, the residue operation can be applied to a compound expression without requiring parentheses. The value of the following statements is 1 (for true) if the value of the expression to the right of the residue operator is divisible by 2:

```
        X←3
        0=2|1+X*3
1
        X←2
        0=2|1+X*3
0
```

Formally, the result R of the expression $A \mid B$ is defined as follows:

$$R \equiv B - (\mid A) \times \lfloor B \div \mid A, \quad \text{if } A \neq 0$$
$$R \equiv B, \qquad\qquad\qquad \text{if } A = 0 \text{ and } B \geq 0$$
$$R \text{ is undefined}, \qquad\quad \text{if } A = 0 \text{ and } B < 0$$

TABLE 4.2   PRIMITIVE OPERATIONS

Symbol	Name	Monadic Interpretation — Meaning or Example	Dyadic Interpretation — Name[a]	Meaning or Example	Identity Elements	Example
+	Identity	$+B \approx 0+B^b$	Plus	$2+3\approx 5$	0	$B+0\approx 0+B\approx B$
−	Negative	$-B \approx 0-B$	Minus	$5-2\approx 3$	0	$B-0\approx B$
×	Signum	$\times B \approx (B>0)-(B<0)$	Times	$2\times 3\approx 6$	1	$1\times B\approx B\times 1\approx B$
÷	Reciprocal	$\div B \approx 1\div B$	Divide	$5\div 2\approx 2.5$	1	$B\div 1\approx B$
*	Exponential	$*B \approx (2.71828\ldots)*B$	Power	$5*2\approx 25$	1	$B*1\approx B$
⌈	Ceiling	$\lceil B \approx B\lfloor -B$	Maximum	$5\lceil 2\approx 5$	ℓ	$B\lceil \ell \approx \ell\lceil B\approx B^c$
⌊	Floor		Minimum	$5\lfloor 2\approx 2$	γ	$B\lfloor \gamma\approx\gamma\lfloor B\approx B^d$
|	Absolute value	$\lvert B \approx B\lceil -B$	Residue	$2\lvert 5\approx 1$	0	$0\lvert B\approx B$
~	Not	$\sim B \approx 1\neq B$				
∧			And		1	$B\wedge 1\approx 1\wedge B\approx B$
∨			Or		0	$B\vee 0\approx 0\vee B\approx B$
⍲			Nand			
⍱			Nor			
<			Less than		0	$0<B\approx B$
≤			Less than or equal to		1	$1\leq B\approx B$
=			Equal to		1	$1=B\approx B=1\approx B$
≥			Greater than or equal to		1	$B\geq 1\approx B$
>			Greater than		0	$B>0\approx B$
≠			Not equal to		0	$B\neq 0\approx 0\neq B\approx B$

[e] (Logical arguments block)

A	B	$A\wedge B$	$A\vee B$	$A⍲B$	$A⍱B$
0	0	0	0	1	1
0	1	0	1	1	0
1	0	0	1	1	0
1	1	1	1	0	0

$ArB\approx 1$ if the relation r holds, 0 otherwise

a See definition in Chapter 4.   b $\approx$ equivalent to.   c ℓ lowest value represented in computer.   d γ greatest value represented in computer.   e Logical arguments only.

Summary of Primitive Operators

The primitive operators are the basis of the computational capability in APL. Specifically they include the monadic and dyadic arithmetic operations, the comparison and logical operations, residue and absolute value, maximum and minimum, and floor and ceiling. The primitive operators are listed in Table 4.2.

4.6 MATHEMATICAL FUNCTIONS

The mathematical functions in APL supplement the primitive operators by supplying resources frequently needed in numeric computations. Clearly, all of the mathematical functions utilize the primitive operations, presented in Section 4.5, and could be effectively programmed using some ingenuity and mathematical expertise   which was obviously done in the early days of computer programming. Yet, routines included within the programming system provide accuracy and precision and relieve the user of the chore of doing everything himself. From a cost-effectiveness standpoint, prewritten functions are far superior. APL goes one step further than most programming systems. Not only are the routines included in the APL system, but operator symbols have been selected for them as well. Both monadic and dyadic functions exist, and they are used in a similar fashion to the primitive operations.

Generalized Combination and Factorial

One of the fundamental identities in mathematics and statistics is the binomial theorem, frequently expressed as:

$$(a+b)^n = \sum_{k=0}^{n} \frac{n!}{k!(n-k)!} a^k b^{n-k}$$

The coefficient $n!/k!(n-k)!$ is commonly known as the binomial coefficient and is usually abbreviated as $\binom{n}{k}$ or C_k^n. In the latter case, C_k^n is usually interpreted as the number of combinations of n things taken k at a time. For example, $C_2^3 = 3$. In mathematics, n is not restricted to integers and the function is known as the complete beta function. APL contains a mathematical function to compute the binomial coefficient* which uses the dyadic operator !, a composite symbol formed from the quote symbol, a backspace, and a period. Thus, the binomial coefficient $\binom{N}{k}$ is represented in APL as $K!N$. For example,

---

*Called the *generalized combination* because of its extension to nonintegral values.

```
        N←6
        3!N
20
        (7-2)!10-2
56
        1.3!8.9
14.3627854
        4!¯7
0
```

Formally, the result R of the generalized combination of N things taken K at a time is defined as:

$$R \equiv (!N) \div (!K) \times !N - K$$

and is related to the complete beta function as follows:

$$\text{Beta } (K,N) = \div N \times (K-1)!K+N-1$$

The definition of the generalized combination function uses another mathematical function, which is also widely known. Usually called the *factorial*, it gives the number of arrangements of n distinct objects in a row. In APL, the factorial function uses the monadic operator ! and gives the product of the first N positive integers, that is, $N \times (N-1) \times (N-2)...1$. For a nonintegral operand, the factorial function is equivalent to the gamma function of $N+1$. The following examples also demonstrate an obvious restriction:

```
        !3
6
        !2×5
3628800
        !1.5
1.329340308
        !¯1.5
¯3.544907702
        !¯2
DOMAIN ERROR
        !¯2
        ∧
```

Formally, the result R of the factorial function on operand N is defined as:

$R \equiv N \times (N-1) \times (N-2)...2 \times 1$, for $0=1 \mid N$;
$R \equiv$ undefined, for $(0=1 \mid N) \wedge (^-1 = \times N)$; and
$R \equiv \Gamma N+1$, otherwise.

Random Number Generation

APL contains two built-in functions for generating pseudo-random numbers. Both appropriately use the question symbol, ?. The monadic interpretation, called *roll*, that is, *?N*, selects an integer pseudo-randomly from the first *N* positive integers. The dyadic version called *deal*, that is, *M?N*, creates a vector of *M* components selected pseudo-randomly from the first *N* positive integers without replacement. A discussion of the *deal* function, which uses the concept of a vector, is postponed until Chapter 5. With the monadic roll function, any integer in the range 1 to *N* has an equal chance of being selected. For example:

```
        ?5
1
        ?10
8
        ?7
4
```

The roll function uses a starting number for generating the random result. In APL\360, it is initially set to 16807 or 7*5 and is modified each time a random number is generated. The starting number is termed the *seed*, which is stored along with a workspace. The seed for a clear workspace is always the initial value given above.

Logarithms

The age-old definition, "A logarithm is an exponent," is useful for remembering the operator symbol for the logarithm functions, which is the composite symbol ⊛ formed from the circle ○ and the exponentiation (or power) operator *.*

The monadic form of the operator is defined as the *natural logarithm*. It is written as ⊛ *N* and computes the expression: $\log_e N$. The dyadic version of the operator computes the *common logarithm* so that *M⊛N* is defined as the $\log_M N$. For example:

```
        ⊛2
0.6931471806
        ⊛*1
1
        (*1)⊛2
0.6931471806
        10⊛1
0
        10⊛2
0.3010299957
        10⊛2×3
0.7781512504
```

*The circle ○ is found above the O on the APL keyboard.

Antilogarithms can be computed by exponentiation using the familiar relations:

1. If $L = \ln N$, then $\text{antilog}_e(L) = e^L = N$.
2. If $L = \log_b N$, then $\text{antilog}_b(L) = b^L = N$.

For example:

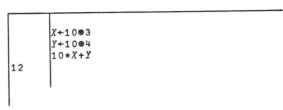

```
     |X←10⊛3
     |Y←10⊛4
     |10*X+Y
 12  |
```

Formally, the result R of the natural logarithm applied to operand N is defined as:

$$R \equiv \ln N$$

or

$$N = *R$$

Similarly, the result R of the common logarithm applied to operands M and N is defined as:

$$R \equiv \log_M N$$

or

$$R \equiv (\circledast N) \div \circledast M$$

Pi

A familiar problem to most computer users doing scientific work involves the exact value of π. The first problem usually requires a secondary decision regarding how many places to include once the value has been looked up in a table. APL contains a monadic function, which uses the operator $\bigcirc$, and is defined as pi times the operand; that is, $\pi \times N$ is written $\bigcirc N$. For example:

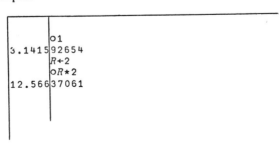

```
            |○1
 3.1415|92654
            |R←2
            |○R*2
12.566|37061
```

TABLE 4.3   MATHEMATICAL FUNCTIONS

Symbol	Monadic Interpretation		Dyadic Interpretation	
	Name	Meaning or Example	Name	Meaning or Example
!	Factorial	$!N \approx N \times (N-1)...2 \times 1$ $24 \approx !4$	Combination	$K!N \approx (!N) \div (!K) \times !N-K$ $20 \approx 3!5$
?	Roll	$?N \approx$ random choice from $1,2,...,N$	Deal	$M?N \approx$ vector of M components selected randomly from $1,2,...,N$ without replacement.
⊛	Natural logarithm	$\circledast N \approx \ln N$	Common logarithm	$M \circledast N \approx \log_M N$
○	Pi times	$\circ N \approx \pi \times N$	Circular function	

Domain of N	$(-M) \circ N$	M	$M \circ N$
$N \leq 1$	$(1-N*2)*.5$	0	$(1-N*2)*.5$
$1 \geq \lvert N$	arcsine N	1	sine N
$1 \geq \lvert N$	arccos N	2	cosine N
$1 \geq \lvert N$	arctan N	3	tangent N
$N \geq 1$	$(^{-}1+N*2)*.5$	4	$(1+N*2)*.5$
	arcsinh N	5	sinh N
$N \geq 1$	arccosh N	6	cosh N
$1 > \lvert N$	arctanh N	7	tanh N

Formally, the result R of the monadic pi function applied to operand N is defined as:

$$R \equiv \pi \times N$$

where

$$\pi \approx 3.141592653589793$$

Circular Functions

The circular functions, commonly known as the trigonometric functions, are defined in APL as the dyadic interpretation of the operator ○. Each of the circular functions, defined in terms of radian measure, is assigned an identifying number which serves as the left operand. The right operand is the value to which the function is applied. The functions are identified in Table 4.3. Thus, 1○÷6 is the sine of $\pi/6$ radians, which is one half. For example:

```
              THIRTY←○(1÷6)
              1○THIRTY
      0.5
              FORTY5←○÷4
              1○FORTY5
      0.7071067812
              X←(100÷4)÷200÷4
              X
      1
              Y←¯3○X
              (○1)÷Y
      4
```

The following list presents the frequently used circular functions:

sin X: 1○X	arcsin X: ¯1○X
cos X: 2○X	arccos X: ¯2○X
tan X: 3○X	arctan X: ¯3○X

4.7 ANNOTATED SCRIPT OF APL FUNDAMENTALS

If there is any truth to the saying that a picture is worth a thousand words, then an annotated APL script is probably worth much more. Therein lies the subject of this section. First, some important comments regarding the order of operands is required.

A Comment on the Order of Operands

In spite of the fact that operations in a statement are executed in a right-to-left sequence, the established *order of operands* is maintained in most cases. For operations that are commutative, such as addition and multiplication, the order is not significant. In noncommutative operations, such as division or exponentiation, the defined order must be maintained; for example,

$$A \div B \text{ means } A \text{ divided by } B$$

and

$$A * B \text{ means } A \text{ raised to the power } B.$$

In other operations, such as residue and the circular functions, no formal order of operands has been established. In fact, $B(\text{mod } A)$ is expressed in APL as $A \mid B$. It is here that the right-to-left order of execution is of prime significance. Clearly, an operator, regardless if it is monadic or dyadic, is defined on the entire expression to its right, except when grouping indicates a departure from the established order of execution. In the residue operation, denoted as $A \mid B$, the operand B is more likely to be the result of a series of computations than the left operand A. Similarly, with the circular functions, for example sin X written as $1 \circ X$, the argument X is more likely to be the result of an expression than the function designated 1. Thus, the convention of placing the operand that is more likely to be computed on the right is consistent with the right-to-left order of execution.

Script of Primitive Operations and Mathematical Functions

● Terminal preparation and dial up

```
)1234567
004)   01.02.03 01/01/70JSMITH
     APL\360
```

Initiating a
Terminal Session

	`2+2`	Simple operation input line is indented.
`4`		Computer response not indented.
	`3*2`	Exponentiation is denoted by an asterisk.
`9`		
	`25÷2`	Division—numbers expressed in standard form.
`12.5`		Computer suppresses trailing zeros for printing.
	`11.89-2`	
`9.89`		
	`X←5×4`	Assignment of the value of the expression to X.
	`X+1`	Add 1 to X and print result.
`21`		
	`)ERASE X`	Delete variable X from workspace.
	`X`	
`VALUE`	`ERROR`	X is no longer defined.
	`X`	The statement in error is printed.
	`∧`	Caret denotes the error.
	`X123T←5*⁻2`	Multicharacter name for variable—power operation—negative
	`X123T`	constant.
`0.04`		
	`(÷X123T)*.5`	Monadic operator ÷ denoting reciprocation.
`5`		
	`Y←4×3+X←2`	Right-to-left rule and multiple specification.
	`Y`	Display Y.
`20`		
	`X`	Display X.
`2`		
	`Z←.00000123E6`	Exponential form of numeric constant.
	`Z`	
`1.23`		Computer chooses how result is displayed.
	`A←⁻75.1`	Negative constant.
	`×A`	Signum function (monadic).
`⁻1`		Result is ⁻1 if operand is negative.
	`A←0`	Respecification of A.
	`×A`	
`0`		Result is 0 if operand is zero.
	`×13`	
`1`		Result is 1 if operand is positive.

	`A←2`	
	`3A`	Implied multiplication?
`SYNTAX ERROR`		No! Not permitted.
	`3  A`	
	`  ∧`	
	`3×A`	Every operation requires an operator.
`6`		
	`---¯5`	Monadic operators have no left operand.
`5`		
	`*1`	Power of the mathematical constant *e*.
`2.718281828`		
	`⌈3.14`	Ceiling– the smallest integer which exceeds the operand.
`4`		
	`⌊3.14`	Floor the largest integer not exceeding the operand.
`3`		
	`10⌈5`	Maximum (dyadic form).
`10`		
	`10⌊5`	Minimum (dyadic form).
`5`		
	`5×10⌊5`	
`25`		Compound expression (right-to-left rule).
	`A←¯10`	
	`A⌈-A`	Expression for the absolute value of *A*.
`10`		
	`A←|A`	Monadic absolute value operation.
	`A`	*A* assumes a new value.
`10`		
	`B←3`	
	`B|A`	*A* (modulus *B*).
`1`		
	`B<A`	Comparison operation gives a 1(true) or 0(false) result.
`1`		
	`(A>0)-A<0`	Expression for signum function (right-to-left rule) with
`1`		parentheses denoting grouping.
	`(5>4)∧5<10`	Logical and.
`1`		
	`0∨1`	Logical or.
`1`		
	`!3`	Factorial (operator is a composite symbol).
`6`		
	`2!4`	Generalized combination (dyadic), i.e., $\binom{4}{2}$.
`6`		
	`?5`	Random number between 1 and 5.
`1`		
	`⍟*1`	Natural log: ln *e*.
`1`		
	`10⍟2`	
`0.3010299957`		$\log_{10}2$.
	`○1`	
`3.141592654`		Pi times (monadic circle symbol).
	`1○(1÷6)`	
`0.5`		Sin 30 degrees (in radians).
	`)SAVE ASPACE`	Save workspace under the name ASPACE.
`15.58.21  12/20/69`		Time and date saved.

4.8   COMMENTS ON THE REMAINDER OF APL

APL achieves its power as a system for computing and for programming in five ways:

1. Through a rich assortment of primitive operations and mathematical functions.
2. By allowing the user to process arrays directly and by providing a variety of operations on arrays.
3. By permitting the user to define functions and to effectively write programs.
4. With appropriate input and output operations.
5. By including extensive program checkout facilities.

A study of these topics is a study of computing itself.

Because APL is useful to people with a variety of backgrounds and problems, the sequence in which the remainder of these topics is reviewed is of importance. The experienced reader should go directly to "Arrays and Operations on Arrays," covered in the next chapter. The reader being exposed to computing for the first time could go to Chapter 6 for an exposure to the major topics in computing and then return to arrays at a later date. Similarly, the user with a few simple calculations could also go directly to Chapter 6, although the use of arrays might simplify his programming considerably. Operations on arrays are not fully appreciated, frequently, until one is faced with the cumbersome task of programming the same functions using elementary operations. The array operations in APL are inclusive and serve as an excellent reference on the subject. Those faced with implementing similar algorithms in other languages might first look to APL.

5 | ARRAYS AND OPERATIONS ON ARRAYS

5.1 BASIC CONCEPTS

Most computations deal with single data values called scalars. This is so, perhaps, because most people are accustomed to thinking in terms of single values—regardless of whether they lend themselves to the physical situation at hand. Suppose, for example, that a market researcher stands on a street corner, for a period of time, and counts sporty automobiles of a given make. He might come up with the following list:

Category Number	Name	Total Number Observed
1	Riviera	7
2	Toronado	4
3	Thunderbird	6
4	Eldorado	5
5	Mark III	2

Clearly, each total of observations for a given category is a scalar value. Yet, the scalar values collectively form a *family* of related items. In this case, each value is a count giving a number of automobiles. The list of totals can also be interpreted as a linear sequence of values called a *vector*. Each value has an *index* given by the category number. The index can be used to select a value from the vector. For example, the index 4 would denote the value 5, which is said to be the fourth *component* of the vector. The concept is easily extended to other dimensions. If the above observations were repeated for each of five days, then the following collection of data might result:

		Day				
		1	2	3	4	5
	1	7	5	7	6	9
	2	4	3	2	5	3
Category	3	6	8	8	7	6
	4	5	2	3	4	5
	5	2	0	3	1	4

where the total observations for category 2 on day 3 is the value 2; here, the value 2 is selected by two indexes: the row index and the column index. A two-dimensional collection of values is termed a *matrix*. A vector or a matrix is a special case of a collection of related data called an *array*, which is extended to as many dimensions as are required by a given application. In the above example, a three-dimensional array of data values would be created if observations were taken on several street corners, that is,

Corner		Day				
1		1	2	3	4	5
	1	7	5	7	6	9
	2	4	3	2	5	3
Category	3	6	8	8	7	6
	4	5	2	3	4	5
	5	2	0	3	1	4

Corner		Day				
2		1	2	3	4	5
	1	10	5	8	3	9
	2	2	5	4	6	2
Category	3	8	5	9	4	5
	4	0	3	2	4	5
	5	1	4	2	1	3

The total of observations corresponding to the indexes (2,4,1), denoting corner 2, category 4, and day 1, is the value 0. An array with more than two dimensions is called, appropriately, a three-dimensional array, or a four-dimensional array, etc. If a component (often called an element can be denoted by an index, then it is not necessary to give a unique name to each individual value, and only the array, as a whole, must be named.

Thus, a variable name is given to an entire array of data items and an element within the array is selected by an appropriate number of indexes termed a subscript. If the three-dimensional array given above were assigned the name *AUTO*, for example, then the subscripted name *AUTO*[1;1;5] would denote the value 9. In computer terminology, each index is termed a subscript, so a vector array needs one subscript, a matrix needs two subscripts, a three-dimensional array needs three subscripts, etc. Subscripts are treated in more detail in succeeding sections.

It is not difficult to imagine situations where it is more convenient to regard an array as a whole rather than distinct elements. If one wanted to display every element of a vector, for example, it would be more convenient, and economical as well, to simply give the name of the vector and let the computer print the elements, regardless of how many there were. This is where APL achieves its power as a programming language and as a means for describing the functional characteristics of discrete systems. Primitive operations and mathematical functions are extended to accept arrays as operands, and additional functions are defined, primarily, for use on arrays. In treating entire arrays, two items are of significance: the *name* of the array and the *dimension* of the array. A vector has one dimension, which is the number of elements. Similarly, a matrix has two dimensions: the number of rows and the number of columns. It follows that a three-dimensional array has three dimensions, a four-dimensional array has four dimensions, etc. The dimensions of an array are conveniently referred to as its *size*. For some array operations, the size of the operands must agree. In others, it is necessary that the size be known and operators are available for obtaining this value.

5.2   VECTORS AND VECTOR OPERATIONS

In APL, a vector of numeric values is created by typing the numbers with at least one intervening space between components. The vector can be used in an expression, much like a scalar operand, and the result is stored in the active workspace by using the specification operation. When a vector is created in this way, the components must be constants and may not be scalar variables. Later, methods are presented for forming arrays from scalar variables and from arrays which already exist. For example:

```
V←3 .5 ⁻16 7.4 10
```

Thus, V is specified as a vector of five components. The size of V is determined and saved automatically by the APL system and the user need not be concerned with the bookkeeping aspects of array processing. As with a scalar, an array may be displayed by simply giving the array name:

```
      V
3 0.5 ¯16 7.4 10
```

Element-by-Element Operations

The primitive operations and mathematical functions defined for scalars are extended to arrays on an element-by-element basis for operands of the same size. For example:

```
      A←1 2 3 4 5
      B←6 7 8 9 10
      A+B
7 9 11 13 15
      C←A+1 2 3 4 5
      C
2 4 6 8 10
      1 2 3 4 5 -A
0 0 0 0 0
      A×A
1 4 9 16 25
      -A
¯1 ¯2 ¯3 ¯4 ¯5
      ÷A
1 0.5 0.3333333333 0.25 0.2
      !A
1 2 6 24 120
      A÷2 2 2 2
0.5 1 1.5 2 2.5
      A÷2 4 6 8 10
0.5 0.5 0.5 0.5 0.5
      A*3 3 3 3
1 8 27 64 125
      A<B
1 1 1 1 1
      A>B
0 0 0 0 0
```

```
      C←¯27 12 16.8 6E25 0
      D←0 12 ¯123.4 13 99.873
      C≥D
0 1   1  1  0
      E←1 0 0 1 0
      E∧C≥D
0 0   0  1  0
      E∨C≥D
1 1   1  1  0
      C=E
0 0   0  0  1
      C⌈D
0 12   16.8   6E25   99.873
      ⌊C
27 12   16.8   6E25   0
      F←1 ¯1 2 0
      *F
2.718281828   0.3678794412   7.389056099   1
      C+F
LENGTH ERROR
      C+F
      ∧
      1 2 3×30 20 10
30 40   30
      A←2 3 4
      A*3
8 27   64
```

The last two statements which are included in the previous example should be noted. In the statement, $A ← 2\ 3\ 4$, the variable A is respecified. Although it previously existed in the active workspace with a dimension of 5, it now has a dimension of 3 with components 2, 3, and 4. This leads to an important fact. Computer storage is maintained dynamically in APL. The size of an array never needs to be specified and the system uses whatever storage is necessary. In the statement, $A*3$, each component of the vector A is raised to the third power. The operation uses a vector and a scalar. This exhibits an important point. If a scalar is used in an element-by-element operation with an array, then it is used with each component of that array. Further examples will clarify the latter point:

```
          │A←13 ¯256 59.67 0
          │A>0
1     0   │1   0
          │2│1 2 3 4 5 6
1     0   │1  0  1  0
          │A←6  7  8
          │A+1
7     8   │9
          │B←1  2  3
          │C←B+2×A
          │C
13    16   19
          │A←2  4  6  8  10
          │A×A>5
0     0   │6   8   10
          │A←1 2 3 4 5 6 7 8 9 10 11 12
          │A×0=3│A
0     0   │3  0  0  6  0  0  9  0  0  12
          │ANGL←○1÷6 4 3 2
          │1○ANGL
0.5   0│.7071067812   0.8660254038   1
          │
```

Two final remarks on element-by-element operations are in order. First, element-by-element operations are extended to arrays of higher dimensions, even though methods for their generation have not been introduced as yet. Second, when an operation is performed on two arrays or an array and a scalar, it applies uniformly to all components of that structure.

Subscripting

Given an array, regardless of how it was formed, how is a specific element selected for display or for use in computation? The answer is with a subscript, denoted by square brackets. For example, A_i is represented in APL as $A[I]$ and is interpreted to be the Ith component of the vector A. The square brackets must follow the array name or array expression, and a subscript may be a constant, a variable, or an expression. A subscript may even be an array as noted later. For example:

```
          │I←2
          │V←2  4  6  8  10
          │V[1]
2         │
          │V[I]+V[I+2]
12        │
          │2 3 4 5+6 7 8 9
8    10   │12   14
          │(2 3 4 5+6 7 8 9)[3]
12        │
```

If more than one subscript is required, then they are separated by semi-colons. Given the matrix,

$$M = \begin{pmatrix} 1 & 2 & 3 & 4 \\ 5 & 6 & 7 & 8 \\ 9 & 10 & 11 & 12 \end{pmatrix}$$

stored in an active APL workspace, the subscripted variable $M[2;2]$ indicates the value 6 while the subscripted variable $M[3;4]$ denotes the value 12. A subscripted variable can also appear on the left-hand side of the specification arrow or in any context that a scalar variable can be used. For example:

```
      V←¯12 13.768 .4E¯13 6
      V[2]←113.768
      V
¯12  13.768  4E¯14  6
```

The APL system offers some protection against referencing nonexistent values. If an attempt is made to select an element not in the range of an array, the system responds with an appropriate error message; for example,

```
      V←2 4 6 8
      V[I+1]
VALUE ERROR
      V[I+1]
        ^
      I←2
      V[I+7]
INDEX ERROR
      V[I+7]
        ^
      V[I+1]
6
```

Generating a Vector

One of the difficulties in dealing with arrays is the typing of long sequences of numbers. When the numbers represent distinct data values, no alternative method for entering the information exists. But, when the numbers are the same or are consecutive integers, something can be done. The monadic form of the operator *iota*, that is, ιN, generates a vector of length N which contains the positive integers 1 through N. The iota function has several names of which *index generator* is perhaps the best known. Here, N must be a positive integer. For example:

```
        N←5
        ιN
1   2   3   4   5
        ι4
1   2   3   4
        ι2×N
1   2   3   4   5   6   7   8   9   10
        V←ι6
        V
1   2   3   4   5   6
        (ι6)*2
1   4   9   16   25   36
```

The above definition permits a vector with a length of zero to be denoted. The expression $\iota0$ creates a vector of zero length, termed an *empty vector*, and if a specification operation is involved, assigns it to the given variable. For example:

```
        ι0

        V←ι0
        V

```

Thus, a vector with a zero length prints as a blank line, which is reasonable for a variable that is regarded as empty. A scalar variable, on the other hand, may not be empty, and the language contains no facility for making that specification. Another method of generating an array is through the dyadic version of the operator ρ, called *rho*. The function is commonly known as the *reshape function*, although the precise meaning of that particular terminology will not become evident until matrices are discussed in the next section. When M is a scalar, the function $M\rho N$ generates a vector of length M using the operand N. If N is a scalar, then it is repeated M times in the generated vector. If N is a vector and its size is less than M, then it is repeated cyclically. If the size of N is greater than M, then the first M components are used. For example:

```
          5ρ2
2  2      2   2   2
          V←¯2 3 18.4 639. ¯9.200
          V
¯2  3     18.4  639  ¯9.2
          W←3ρV
          W
¯2  3     18.4
          10ρι3
1  2      3  1  2  3  1  2  3  1
          V←0ρ1
          V

```

When M is equal to zero in the reshape operation $M\rho N$, an empty vector is created. The result of the reshape operation is always an array.

Dimension of a Vector

The monadic interpretation of the operator ρ gives the size of a vector although the precise definition is also more general and applies to arrays of higher dimension. Applied to a vector V, ρV gives the number of elements in V. Applied to a scalar N, ρN generates a null value which prints as a blank line. For example:

```
          V←3 5 45E12 100 .67 ¯.00123 8
          ρV
7
          V×0=3|ιρV
0  0      4.5E13  0  0  ¯0.00123  0
          W←ι0
          ρW
0
          ρι0
0
          ρ0ρ100
0
          ρ3×4

          A←1ρ4
          A
4
          ρA
1
```

The monadic ρ operator always gives a vector as a result. The number of components in the result is equal to the number of dimensions* in the

*Later the dimensions of an array will be referred to as the *coordinates* of an array.

operand. Thus, a scalar has no dimension, a vector has one dimension, a matrix has two dimensions, etc.

Forming a Vector

It was stated earlier that methods are available for creating arrays (although the present discussion is limited to vectors) from scalar and array variables that already exist in the active workspace. The comma is used as the operator symbol in one of two ways: (1) As a monadic operator it denotes the *ravel operation* which is a means of creating a vector from either a scalar or an array of higher dimension. It is useful for operations which require that an operand be a vector. (2) As a dyadic operator, the symbol denotes *catenation* and chains scalars or vectors together in the usual fashion. After a catenation operation, the dimension of the resultant vector is the sum of the number of data items in the two operands. For example:

```
               V←5
               ρV
    ϸ
               V←,5
               V
    5
               ρV
    1
               V←10  20
               W←30  40  50
               X←V,W
               X
  10    20   30    40    50
               V,2E13
  10    20    2E13
               Y←13,W
               Y
  13    30   40    50
               A←3+B←2
               C←(A*2),(B*3),0
               C
  25    8   0
               ¯68.3,1.23 6
  ¯68.3 │ 1.23   6
               74.1 ¯109.3 16=74.1,¯109.3,16
  1    1  1
```

When catenating scalar constants, it is only necessary to separate them with one or more spaces. When catenating variables, the dyadic catenation operator must be used. The concept also applies to expressions although the right-to-left rule applies and the user should exercise caution. Consider two examples:

```
                    A←2
                    B←3
                    (A*2),2×B-1
    4    4
                    A*2,2×B-1
    4    16
```

In the first example, the value of the expressions $A*2$ and $2 \times B-1$ were computed and then catenated. In the latter case, $2 \times B-1$ is computed, catenated to the scalar 2, and A is raised to the power indicated by the catenated vector. Parentheses are useful for avoiding ambiguity even if it is only on the part of the user.

It was also mentioned that a variable must be specified before it could be used. The rule applies to all operators of the language including catenation. This is demonstrated in the following example:

```
                    )CLEAR
    CLEAR   WS
                    V←1  2  3
                    W,V
    VALUE   ERROR
                    W,V
                    ∧
                    W←ι0
                    W,V
    1    2   3
```

Catenation provides a convenient method of accumulating values, once the process has been started as in the previous script. A familiar example is the Fibonacci sequence where the ith term is the sum of the $(i-1)$st and $(i-2)$nd terms; for $i \geq 3$. A one-line program to add a term to the sequence is given in the next script:

```
                    FIB←0  1  2  3  5  8
                    FIB←FIB,FIB[(ρFIB)-1]+FIB[ρFIB]
                    FIB
    0    1   2   3   5   8   13
```

Catenation explains the form of output used in some previous examples. Recall that statements of the general form:

```
         A←2+B←1+C←2
         A,B,C
  5   3  2
```

were used. It is evident now that a vector of the form (5 3 2) is formed by catenation, and then and only then is the result printed.

Vector Reduction—Summation, Product, and Similar Functions

Assume that the market researcher, mentioned in the beginning of this section, desired to perform some elementary calculations on his data. For example, he might be interested in the total number of observations, the maximum value, and the minimum value for a given day. Ordinarily, he would have to prepare a repetitive program as follows:

Sum	*Maximum*	*Minimum*
1. Set $SUM \leftarrow 0$.	1. Set $MAX \leftarrow 0$.	1. Set $MIN \leftarrow 10E10$, or a very high value.
2. Set $I \leftarrow 1$.	2. Set $I \leftarrow 1$.	2. Set $I \leftarrow 1$.
3. Add the Ith component to SUM.	3. Compare the Ith component with MAX.	3. Compare the Ith component with MIN.
4. Set $I \leftarrow I+1$.	4. If MAX is greater than or equal to it, go to step 5; otherwise replace MAX with the Ith component.	4. If MIN is less than or equal to it, go to step 5; otherwise replace MIN with the Ith component.
5. If I is greater than the size of the vector, stop; otherwise, go to step 3.	5. Set $I \leftarrow I+1$.	5. Set $I \leftarrow I+1$.
	6. If I is greater than the size of the vector, stop; otherwise, go to step 3.	6. If I is greater than the size of the vector, stop; otherwise, go to step 3.

In APL, a composite function called *reduction* achieves the same result in one operation. The general form of a reduction operation is: $\oplus / V$, where $\oplus$ is a dyadic primitive operator or mathematical function, the character / is known as the solidus, and V is a vector expressed as a variable or the result of an expression. Reduction is defined as follows:

$$\oplus / V \equiv V[1] \oplus V[2] \oplus V[3] \ldots V[(\rho V)-1] \oplus V[\rho V]$$

The dyadic operations are performed from right to left in the usual fashion. Thus, for example:

```
         DAY1←7 4 6 5 2
         SUM←+/DAY1
         MAX←⌈/DAY1
         MIN←⌊/DAY1
         SUM,MAX,MIN
24    7   2
          !3
6
          ×/⍳3
6
          V←6 4 10 17 3
          AV←(+/V)÷ρV
          AV
8
          SD←(((+/V*2)÷ρV)-((+/V)÷ρV)*2)*.5
          SD
5.099019514
```

A defined function (see Section 5.3) may not be used as the operator in reduction; the reduction operation is extended, appropriately, to arrays of higher dimension. Clearly, the reduction operation applied to a vector reduces it to a scalar, hence the name. In general, reduction reduces the number of dimensions* in an operand by one. The capability of applying the same operation to all elements of an array is very useful. Thus far, it has been used for summation, product, maximum, and minimum. It can also be used in a logical sense to determine if *all* components possess a given property or if *any* component possesses another property. For example:

```
         X←¯1 2 5 ¯4 19
         N←⍳ρX
         ∧/(X*N)≥0
0
         ∨/(X*N)≤0
1
         ∧/1 2 3 4=⍳4
1
         ∨/(⍳ρA)≠A←1 2 3 4 5 6 7
0
```

*Later, the number of dimensions in an array will be referred to as its *rank*, so that reduction reduces the rank of an array by one.

Reduction of a vector of dimension zero gives the identity element, as listed in Table 4.1. Reduction of a scalar or a vector of one component gives that value. That is:

```
            +/ι0
 0
            */0ρ1
 1
            ×/¯5
  ¯5
            -/1ρ5
 5
```

Character Data

A great many interesting and useful applications of computers involve data that are not strictly numeric. Text exiting, information retrieval, message dissemination, formula manipulation and theorem proving, record keeping, and data processing are only a few examples. Therefore, any programming system without facilities for processing nonnumeric data is severely limited in scope. In fact, most scientific applications require, minimally, that comments and column headings be printed. APL permits character data to be entered, processed, and output—as required by a particular application. Character data are enclosed in quote symbols in APL to distinguish them from the name of something or a construct in the language. One character is interpreted as a scalar item so that sequences of characters form an array. For example:

```
            A←'ABCD25+'
            ρA
 7
            A[3]
 C
            A[ρA]
 +
            B←'12345'
            B[4]←'T'
            B
 123T5
```

A series of characters enclosed in quote symbols is termed a *literal*, which can contain any keyboard character *including composite symbols*

and the space character. Since elements of a literal array are restricted
to single characters, there is no need to distinguish between them and they
are printed without intervening spaces. The quote character, used as a
delimiter for literals, is a special case. If it is to be used in a literal,
then it must be represented by a double quote. For example:

```
       A←'BE CAREFUL OF THE SYMBOL ''φ'''
       A
BE CAREFUL OF THE SYMBOL 'φ'
       ρA
28
```

It should be noticed that literals are printed without the enclosing quote
symbols.

In general, arrays with characters as components can be processed as
numeric arrays except for the following cases:

1. An operation or function whose domain is strictly a numeric value is
   not permitted.
2. Numeric and character arrays may not be intermixed.

Thus, character arrays may be generated, catenated, indexed, compared
(for equality only), and used with the same utility functions as numeric
arrays:

```
       5ρ'X'
XXXXX
       A←'MISSION'
       B←'''IMPOSSIBLE'''
       ρB
12
       A,B
MISSION'IMPOSSIBLE'
       A,' ',B
MISSION 'IMPOSSIBLE'
       A←'123A456B789C101112D'
       6ρA
123A45
       'LOOP'='LOOP'
1 0  0 1
       'LOOP'≠'LOOP'
0 1  1 0
       C1←'ABCDEFGHIJKLM'
       C2←'ABCDEFGH1JKLM'
       ∧/C1=C2
0
```

Character data require some interpretation. A single character enclosed in quote symbols is a scalar; all other constructs are interpreted as vectors—including the null sequence:

```
             S←'A'
             ρS
     b
             V←0ρ'L'
             V
     b
             W←ρ' '
             W
     0
             ρW
     1
```

Mixed Output

Although arrays of mixed data* cannot be stored, arrays can be inter-mixed for output (and for output only) by separating the nonhomoge-neous data with a semicolon. Spaces are not inserted between the mixed data items in the print line.

```
            '1.23 SQUARED IS ';1.23*2
     1.23 SQUARED IS 1.5129
            NAME←'JANE'
            B←34
            W←24
            H←34
            NAME,'''S MEASUREMENTS ARE: ';B,W,H
     JANE'S MEASUREMENTS ARE: 34   24   34
```

Summary of Vector Operations

A brief summary of the vector operations presented in this section (i.e., Section 5.2) is included here for reference and for review.

1. *Specification.*   Numeric vectors are entered as:

$$V \leftarrow C_1\, C_2\, C_3 \cdots C_n$$

where C_i is a numeric scalar constant and C_i is separated from C_{i+1} by at least one space. A character vector is enclosed in quote sym-bols and called a literal; each character becomes a component of the resultant vector:

$$V \leftarrow 'A_1 A_2 A_3 ... A_n'$$

*That is, character and numeric data.

where A_I is any character in the keyboard (including composite symbols and spaces. Within a literal, a quote symbol is represented by two quote marks.

2. *Element-by-element operations.* Where $\oplus$ is an appropriate operator, an expression of the form:

$$V \oplus W$$

computes the $\oplus$ operation on the vectors in an element-by-element manner. If either operand is a scalar, then it is extended to all components of the other operand.

3. *Subscripting.* If I is a scalar constant or scalar variable, then:

$$V[I]$$

selects the Ith component of the vector V. $V[I]$ may be used in a scalar expression or may appear to the left of a specification arrow.

4. *Generation.* A vector may be generated in two ways. The index generator:

$$\iota N$$

generates a vector of length N which contains the positive integers 1 through N. The reshape function:

$$M \rho N$$

generates a vector of length M using the operand N. If M is greater than the size of N, then N is repeated cyclically. If the size of N is greater than M, then the first M components of N are used.

5. *Dimension.* The dimension of a vector V is given by:

$$\rho V$$

If V is an empty vector, than $(\rho V) = 0$. If the operand is a scalar, then the result is a null value which prints as a blank line.

6. *Formation.* A vector is formed from existing constituents in two ways. The monadic ravel operation:

$$,M$$

creates a vector from the operand M. If M is a scalar then a vector with one component is formed. If M is a higher-dimensioned array, then it is unraveled in index order (see the next section on matrices and arrays of higher dimension). The catenation operation:

$$M,N$$

chains the operands together in the usual fashion. The dimension of the resultant vector is the sum of the dimensions of the operands.

7. *Reduction.* The reduction operation of the form:

$$\oplus/V$$

applies the dyadic operator $\oplus$ to all elements of the vector V in the following manner:

$$V[1]\oplus V[2]\ldots V[(\rho V)-1]\oplus V[\rho V]$$

where the right-to-left rule holds in the above expression.

8. *Mixed output.* Numeric and character data may be intermixed for printing by separating the nonhomogeneous data with a semicolon.

5.3 MATRICES AND ARRAYS OF HIGHER DIMENSION

Nearly everyone is familiar with matrices and their indexing properties. In the matrix A, for example, the component $A[I;J]$ is the scalar value found in the Ith row and the Jth column. In arrays of higher dimension, however, indexing properties are not as well known—and frequently lead to some confusion.

Consider the problem of stringing out the components of a matrix in some order. Two methods can be identified by inspection: row major order and column major order. Applied to the matrix

$$A = \begin{pmatrix} 8 & 7 & 1 & 9 \\ ^{-}4 & 2 & 3 & 6 \\ 0 & ^{-}5 & 4 & 1 \end{pmatrix}$$

the two lists would appear as follows:

Row Major Order		Column Major Order	
Component	Indices	Component	Indices
8	$A[1;1]$	8	$A[1;1]$
7	$A[1;2]$	$^{-}4$	$A[2;1]$
1	$A[1;3]$	0	$A[3;1]$
9	$A[1;4]$	7	$A[1;2]$
$^{-}4$	$A[2;1]$	2	$A[2;2]$
2	$A[2;2]$	$^{-}5$	$A[3;2]$
3	$A[2;3]$	1	$A[1;3]$
6	$A[2;4]$	3	$A[2;3]$
0	$A[3;1]$	4	$A[3;3]$
$^{-}5$	$A[3;2]$	9	$A[1;4]$
4	$A[3;3]$	6	$A[2;4]$
1	$A[3;4]$	1	$A[3;4]$

The indices appear most naturally* in row major order, and that method is referred to in APL as *index order*. Whenever the components of an array are unraveled, they always appear in index order. Similarly, consider a three-dimensional array as follows:

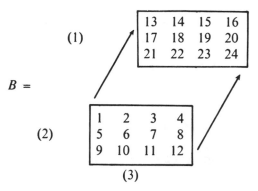

$B =$

(1)

13	14	15	16
17	18	19	20
21	22	23	24

(2)

1	2	3	4
5	6	7	8
9	10	11	12

(3)

where the numbers in parentheses indicate the first coordinate, the second coordinate, and the third coordinate, respectively. For example, $A[2;1;3]=15$. In index order, the array is listed as follows:

Component		Indices
1		$B[1;1;1]$
2		$B[1;1;2]$
3		$B[1;1;3]$
4		$B[1;1;4]$
5		$B[1;2;1]$
6		$B[1;2;2]$
7		$B[1;2;3]$
8		$B[1;2;4]$
9		$B[1;3;1]$
10		$B[1;3;2]$
11		$B[1;3;3]$
12		$B[1;3;4]$
13		$B[2;1;1]$
14		$B[2;1;2]$
15		$B[2;1;3]$
16		$B[2;1;4]$
17		$B[2;2;1]$
18		$B[2;2;2]$
19		$B[2;2;3]$
20		$B[2;2;4]$
21		$B[2;3;1]$
22		$B[2;3;2]$
23		$B[2;3;3]$
24		$B[2;3;4]$

*See Knuth (19) p. 296.

Is there a means of visualizing higher-dimensional arrays? Not in general but the following technique will usually suffice:

1. Visualize a *vector* as a horizontal row of components.
2. Visualize a *matrix* as a rectangular arrangement of components.
3. Visualize a *three-dimensional* array as a sheet of paper containing one or more matrices—each of which is termed a plane (as shown above).
4. Visualize a *four-dimensional* array as a book of sheets of paper, each containing a three-dimensional array.
5. Visualize a *five-dimensional* array as a library of books (or four-dimensional arrays)—rarely will the user need to go beyond five dimensions, although the idea can be easily extended.

Then, a component of an array is conceptualized as follows:

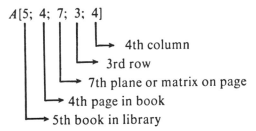

It should be noted that higher-dimensional arrays are synthesized on a right-to-left basis from vectors, matrices, three-dimensional arrays, etc.

Generating a Matrix or an Array of Higher Dimension

When discussing vectors, the reshape function of the form $M\rho N$ was used to generate a vector from a scalar or another vector. The left operand, that is, M, was a scalar and determined the dimension of the vector. A logical question might be, "What structure would be generated if the left operand were a vector?" The answer is that an array would be generated and the dimension of each coordinate is determined by the value of the respective component in the vector. For example, the expression:

$$3 \quad 4\rho 1$$

generates a matrix with 3 rows and 4 columns where each component is the value 1. Thus, the Ith component of the vector left operand indicates the extent of the Ith coordinate of the generated array. In the examples which follow, an array of dimension two or greater is printed for the first time. Higher-dimensional arrays are printed as matrices and are indented from the left margin.

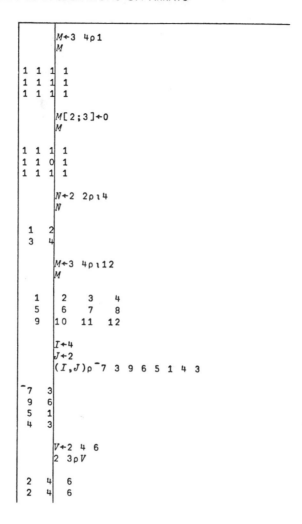

It should be noted that the array (matrix in the above examples) is formed from the right operand in *index order*. As with vectors, the right operand is used cyclically. If it contains more than the necessary number of components, then only those required are used. The concepts apply to character arrays and higher-dimensional arrays as shown in the following examples:

```
      2 3 4ρι24
 1  2  3  4
 5  6  7  8
 9 10 11 12

13 14 15 16
17 18 19 20
21 22 23 24

      W←3 2 2ρ'ABCDEFGHIJKLMNOPQRSTUVWXYZ'
      W
AB
CD

EF
GH

IJ
KL

      W[1;2;2]←W[2;1;2]←W[3;2;1]←' '
      W
AB
C

E
GH

IJ
 L

      1 5ρι5
1 2 3 4 5

      5 1ρι5
1
2
3
4
5

      3 1 1ρι3
1

2

3

      A←5 0ρ3
      A

      ρA
5 0
      A←(ι0)ρ3
      A

      ρA
0
```

The last two statements require further explanation. In the reshape operation, of the form $M\rho N$, the result is an empty array if any component of M is zero. If M is the empty array, then the result is a scalar. If N is a matrix or an array of higher dimension, then the elements of N are taken in index order. That is,

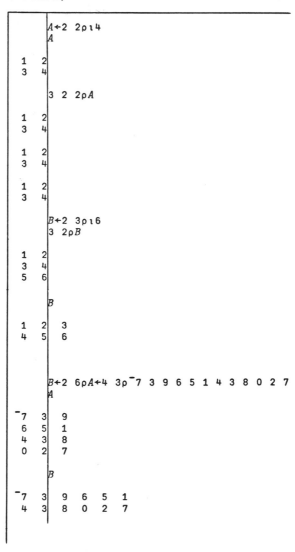

Shape of an Array

The monadic rho operator (ρ) applied to a vector gives the dimension (or size) of that vector. The result is always a vector so that, when dealing with a nonempty vector V, $(\rho\rho V)=1$. When applied to a matrix on a higher-dimensional array, the monadic rho operator (often called the *dimension operator* or the *size operator*) gives a vector whose components denote the number of components in each of the dimensions of the array. For example,

```
        M←3 4ρ5
        ρM
3   4
        N←1 1ρ7
        ρN
1   1
        N
    7
```

The *rank* of an array A is specified as:

$$\rho\rho A$$

and gives the number of indices (i.e., subscripts) necessary to select a component of A. For example:

```
        M←3 4ρ5
        ρρM
2
        N←1 1ρ7
        ρρN
2
        ρρ1 2 3 4ρ'CAT'
4
```

The following list gives dimension and rank vectors for frequently used arrays:

Operand (A)	ρA	$\rho\rho A$	$\rho\rho\rho A$
Scalar		0	1
Vector	I	1	1
Matrix	I J	2	1
Three-dimensional	I J K	3	1

Selection and Indexing

Although subscripting is essentially a dyadic operation, it appears different from other dyadic operations in that left and right brackets are used as operator symbols and that subscripts, which are actually operands, are separated by semicolons. The use of square brackets to enclose subscripts is reasonably familiar but the use of a semicolon to separate subscripts has probably puzzled the curious reader. The answer lies in the fact that a subscript which is ordinarily taken to be a scalar has been extended, in APL, to include arrays. Thus a subscript can be a vector or a matrix or a higher-dimensional array and the quantity selected has the same form—but obviously not the same value. Therefore, a semicolon is used to separate structured subscripts. This extended form of subscripting is generally known as *indexing* and the subscripts are called *indices*.

When the array being indexed is a vector, then the result R of the indexing operation $V[N]$ has the following properties:

1. R is formed by selecting from vector V those components whose indices are the operand N.
2. $(\rho R) = \rho N$ and $(\rho \rho R) = \rho \rho N$.

For example:

```
        V← ¯7 3 9 6 5 1 4 3
        V[1 3 4 7 8]
¯7   9   6   4   3
        I←ι3
        V[I]
¯7   3   9
        W←V[6ρ2 6]
        W
3    1   3   1
        WW←V[4]
        WW
6
        ρWW

        WWW←V[,4]
        WWW
6
        ρWWW
1
        V[ιρV]
¯7   3   9   6   5   1   4   3
```

In general, if the index for a coordinate is omitted, then the entire coordinate is assumed. In the previous example:

```
        V
¯7   3   9   6   5   1   4   8
        V[]
¯7   3   9   6   5   1   4   3
```

The index to a vector can also be a matrix or an array of higher dimension and properties (1) and (2) above hold. That is:

```
        V←¯7 3 9 6 5 1 4 3
        M←3 2ρ6 2 7 5 4 3
        V[M]

    1   3
    4   5
    6   9


        A←'AEFORTW'
        M←3 3ρ6 2 1 3 4 5 6 7 4
        M

    6   2   1
    3   4   5
    6   7   4

        A[M]

TEA
FOR
TWO
```

An indexed variable, of the variety presently being discussed, may appear to the left of the specification operator, and only the selected components are affected. That is:

```
        V←'TEAAFORTTWO'
        V[4 8]←' '
        V
TEA FOR TWO
        V[ι3]←'GIN'
        V,' SOUNDS BETTER'
GIN FOR TWO SOUNDS BETTER
```

When the array being indexed is a matrix, then the result R of the indexing operation $W[M;N]$ has the following properties:

1. R is formed by selecting from W those components whose row index is M and column index is N.
2. $(\rho R)=(\rho M),\rho N$ and $(\rho\rho R)=(\rho\rho M)+\rho\rho N$.

Careful analysis of the second property reveals that succeedingly complex results are developed by using higher-dimensional arrays as indices.

```
              M←3 4ρ⁻7 3 9 6 5 1 4 3 8 0 2 7
              M

 ⁻7  3  9  6
  5  1  4  3
  8  0  2  7

              M[1 2;1 2]

 ⁻7  3
  5  1

              M[1 3;2 4]

  3  6
  0  7

              M[2;1 3]
 5  4
              N←2 2ρ1 2 3 2
              A←M[N;2]
              ρA
 2  2
              ρρA
 2
              A

  3  1
  0  1


              M[2;N]

  5  1
  4  1

              B←M[,2;N]
              ρB
 1  2  2
              ρρB
 3
              B

  5  1
  4  1

              A←M[N;1 3]
              ρA
 2  2  2
              ρρA
 3
              A

 ⁻7  9
  5  4

  8  2
  5  4
```

If the row index is omitted, all rows are assumed, and if the column index is omitted, all columns are assumed. That is:

```
           M←3 4ρι12
           M[;2 4]

    2      4
    6      8
   10     12

           M[3;]
 9   10    11    12
```

The concepts are extended systematically to arrays of higher dimension, both as arrays being indexed and the indices themselves.

Ordinarily, the lower bound for a coordinate index is 1 and the upper bound is the dimension of that coordinate. For example, the first component of a vector A is $A[1]$ and the last component is $A[\rho A]$. This is generally known as *1-origin indexing*. *0-origin indexing* is permitted to satisfy certain classes of applications, and the origin applies to other functions in the language as well. The system command:

$$)ORIGIN \quad 0$$

is used to change the origin from 1 to 0 and

$$)ORIGIN \quad 1$$

is used for the reverse process. In 0-origin indexing, the first component of a vector A is $A[0]$ and the last is $A[^-1+\rho A]$. For example:

```
           V←7 8 9 4 3 1
           ιρV
 1   2     3   4   5   6
           V[ιρV]
 7   8     9   4   3   1
           V[1 3 5]
 7   9     3
           )ORIGIN 0
WAS 1
           ιρV
 0   1     2   3   4   5
           V[ιρV]
 7   8     9   4   3   1
           V[1 3 5]
 8   4     1
           ι1
 0
           )ORIGIN 1
WAS 0
           ι1
 1
```

The indexing origin also affects the coordinate axis, all operations involving indices, and the random number functions.

Fundamental Operations

Analogous to the operations and functions which are defined on scalars (and extended systematically to arrays), APL contains a wealth of functions designed to facilitate the use of arrays. They are treated in the next section, which covers functions on arrays. The remainder of this section is concerned with a brief exposition of scalar operations and functions and vector operations as they are extended to arrays of higher dimensions.

As with vectors, element-by-element operations apply to arrays in the usual manner. For example:

```
       M←3 4ρι12
       2×M+1

  4     6    8   10
 12    14   16   18
 20    22   24   26

      ⁻M

⁻1    ⁻2   ⁻3   ⁻4
⁻5    ⁻6   ⁻7   ⁻8
⁻9   ⁻10  ⁻11  ⁻12

      ⌊M÷3

0   0   1   1
1   2   2   2
3   3   3   4

      ⌈M÷3

1   1   1   2
2   2   3   3
3   4   4   4

      ÷M

1                 0.5            0.3333333333    0.25
0.2               0.1666666667   0.1428571429    0.125
0.1111111111      0.1            0.09090909091   0.08333333333
```

```
        3|M

1  2   0  1
2  0   1  2
0  1   2  0

        N←3 4ρ13-ι12
        M>N

0 0 0  0
0 0 1  1
1 1 1  1

        U←3 5ρ1 0 1
        V←3 5ρ1 1 0 1 1
        U

1 0 1  1 0
1 1 0  1 1
0 1 1  0 1

        V

1 1 0  1 1
1 1 0  1 1
1 1 0  1 1

        U∧V

1 0 0  1 0
1 1 0  1 1
0 1 0  0 1

        C←2 2 3ρι12
        C-3

¯2 ¯1   0
 1  2   3

 4  5   6
 7  8   9
```

Clearly, the extension of monadic scalar operations and functions to arrays does not require further definition. Dyadic operations and functions are extended on an element-by-element basis but only under the following conditions:

1. One of the operands is a scalar.
2. The arrays are *conformable*, that is, the same size.
3. One of the arrays is a single-element array of any rank.

Further, if two single-element arrays are used as operands, then the rank of the operand with the greatest rank is chosen for the result. For example:

```
      M←3 4ρι12
      M+N←1 1 1ρ10

 11   12   13   14
 15   16   17   18
 19   20   21   22

      N

 10
      ρN
1  1  1
      P←1 1ρ5
      Q←N+P
      Q

 15
      ρQ
1  1  1
      ρρQ
3
```

The *ravel* operation when applied to a matrix or an array of higher dimension generates a vector whose components are the components of the array taken in *index order*. For example:

```
      M←3 4ρι12
      M

 1    2    3    4
 5    6    7    8
 9   10   11   12

      ,M
1  2  3  4  5  6  7  8  9  10  11  12
```

The result R of the ravel operation on M is always a vector, so the following relationships hold:

$$(\rho R) = \times/\rho M$$
$$(\rho\rho R) = 1$$

The *catenation* of two arrays requires a ravel of the two operands and a catenation of the two resultant vectors. The result of catenation is always a vector, although the result can be reshaped as required. For example:

```
       M←3 4ρ'A'
       N←2 4ρ'B'
       5 4ρ(,M),,N
AAAA
AAAA
AAAA
BBBB
BBBB
```

The result R of the operation satisfies the following properties:

$$(\rho R) = (\rho,M)+\rho,N$$
$$(\rho\rho R) = 1$$

As logical extensions of scalar operations and functions, fundamental operations on arrays provide a basis for a class of functions defined primarily for array processing. They are divided into two groups: composite functions and mixed functions. *Composite* functions, which include reduction, inner product, and outer product, are extensions to arrays of the dyadic scalar operations and functions. *Mixed* functions include the remainder which are generally classed as not being primitive functions or composite functions.

Summary of Fundamental Array Operations

A brief summary of fundamental array operations presented in this section is included here for reference and for review:

1. *Generation.* An array A is generated as:

$$M\rho N$$

where M is a scalar or vector giving the coordinates of A, and N is an array whose components are used cyclically.

2. *Shape.* The monadic operator ρ gives the size of an array:

$$\rho A$$

The result is always a vector and each of its components gives the dimension of a coordinate of the operand. The rank of A is specified as:

$$\rho\rho A$$

and gives the number of subscripts (or indices) necessary to select a component of A.

3. *Indexing.* The concept of a subscript (or index) is extended to include arrays as indices so that a single index can select one or more

components of an array. Ordinarily, 1-origin indexing is used; however, with the)*ORIGIN* command, the index origin may be changed to 0 and back to 1.

4. *Element-by-element operations.* Scalar operations and mathematical functions apply to matrices or a component-by-component basis. Thus, in an expression of the form:

$$M \oplus N$$

the operator is applied to both operands which must be conformable. If either is a scalar, it is extended to all components of the other operand.

5. *Ravel.* The ravel function

$$,A$$

yields a vector of the components of A taken in index order.

6. *Catenation.* Two arrays can be catenated by raveling the operands and then executing a vector catenation:

$$(,A),,B$$

5.4 FUNCTIONS ON ARRAYS

Several functions on arrays, such as reduction, perform an operation along one of the coordinates of an array. Therefore, it is important to identify which number goes with which coordinate. In the matrix generated by the expression,

$$M \leftarrow 3 \quad 4\rho\iota 12$$

there are three rows and four columns. The coordinates are numbered by their index in the vector generated by the monadic rho operator. Thus, ρM is equal to 3 4; the dimension of the first coordinate is 3 and the dimension of the second coordinate is 4. Similarly, for the three-dimensional array 2 3 4$\rho\iota$24, the following dimensions apply:

Coordinate	Dimension
1	2
2	3
3	4

If 0-origin indexing is used, then there is a 0 coordinate. The versatility inherent in origin indexing requires, minimally, that the first and last coordinate be identified. Therefore, if no coordinate is specified for a function on an array, then the *last* coordinate is assumed. Special provisions apply to the first coordinate. For example, reduction along the first co-ordinate is indicated by the composite symbol $\neq$, which is a solidus over-struck by a minus symbol.

Reduction

Reduction is applied along the Ith coordinate of an array with an expression of the form

$$\oplus/[I]A$$

where $\oplus$ is a dyadic operator and A is an array. For example:

```
                M←2 3ρι6
                +/[1]M
5    7          9
                +/[2]M
6    15
                (+/[2]M)=+/M
1    1
                N←2 2 3ρι12
                N

     1    2    3
     4    5    6

     7    8    9
    10   11   12

                ×/[1]N

     7   16   27
    40   55   72
```

Reduction effectively reduces the rank of an array by one. Special cases are treated in the preceding section under vector reduction.

Inner Product

The familiar matrix product of the form:

$$\begin{pmatrix} a_{11}a_{12}a_{13} \\ a_{21}a_{22}a_{23} \end{pmatrix} \begin{pmatrix} b_{11}b_{12} \\ b_{21}b_{22} \\ b_{31}b_{32} \end{pmatrix} = \begin{pmatrix} a_{11}b_{11}+a_{12}b_{21}+a_{13}b_{31} & a_{11}b_{12}+a_{12}b_{22}+a_{13}b_{32} \\ a_{21}b_{11}+a_{22}b_{21}+a_{23}b_{31} & a_{21}b_{12}+a_{22}b_{22}+a_{23}b_{32} \end{pmatrix}$$

is expressed in APL as:

$$C[I;J] = +/A[I;] \times B[;J]$$

The preceding operation is termed the inner product and is written more succinctly in APL as:

$$A +. \times B$$

and is characteristic of the class of functions:

$$Af.gB$$

where f and g are primitive scalar operations and mathematical functions. For example:

```
            A←2  3ρι6
            B←3  2ρ7-ι6
            C←A+.×B
            C
    20     14
    56     41

            B←3  3ρι9
            A+.×B
    30     36    42
    66     81    96

            U←2  2ρ1  0  0  1
            V←2  2ρ1  1  1  0
            U
  1 0
  0 1

            V
  1 1
  1 0

            Uv.∧V
  1 1
  1 0
```

The dimension of the last coordinate of the first operand must agree with the dimension of the first coordinate of the second operand to satisfy a conformality requirement. As shown in the next examples, the inner product applies to a combination of vector and matrix operands:

```
        A←3 3ρι9
        X←2 4 6
        B←A+.×X
        B
28  64   100
        X+.×A
60  72   84
        X+.×3 5 7
68
        U←2 2ρ1 0 0 1
        V←1 0
        U∧.∨V
0   1
```

Given the result R of the inner product $Af.gB$, then the following definitions apply:

Type of Operands	Definition
Vector	$R = f/AgB$
Vector and matrix	$R[I] = f/AgB[;I]$
Matrix and vector	$R[I] = f/A[I;]gB$
Matrix and matrix	$R[I;J] = f/A[I;]gB[;J]$

where I and J are scalars. In all cases, the following identities apply:*

$$(\rho R) = (^-1 \downarrow \rho A), 1 \downarrow \rho B$$
$$(\rho\rho R) = ((\rho\rho A) + \rho\rho B) - 2$$

Outer Product

The familiar multiplication table is an example of multiplying *each* component of one vector by *all* components of another. That is:

×	1	2	3	4
1	1	2	3	4
2	2	4	6	8
3	3	6	9	12
4	4	8	12	16

In APL, the outer product of vectors A and B is written $A \circ . \times B$ where the component in the Ith row and the Jth column is defined as:

$$R[I;J] = A[I] \times B[J]$$

*The *take* function of the form $1 \downarrow B$ is decribed subsequently.

As with inner product, the definition applies to the scalar dyadic operations and functions. For example:

```
      (ι4)∘.×ι4

1 |  2    3    4
2 |  4    6    8
3 |  6    9   12
4 |  8   12   16

      (2 2ρι4)∘.+10 20

11 | 21
12 | 22

13 | 23
14 | 24
```

In general, outer product is regarded as each component of the first operand applied to every component of the second operand. The result R of the outer product $A \circ .fB$ is defined as

Type of Operands	Definition
Vector	$R[I;J] = A[I] fB[J]$
Vector and matrix	$R[I;J;K] = A[I] fB[J;K]$
Matrix and vector	$R[I;J;K] = A[I;J] fB[K]$
Matrix and matrix	$R[I;J;K;L] = A[I;J] fB[K;L]$

where

$$(\rho R) = (\rho A), \rho B$$
$$(\rho \rho R) = (\rho \rho A) + \rho \rho B$$

Transposition

The notion of interchanging the rows and columns in a matrix is a fundamental concept in mathematics and is useful in many data analysis programs. For example, a program designed to group data by row for analysis, that is,

		Subject		
		A	B	C
	1	×	×	×
Variable	2	×	×	×
	3	×	×	×
	4	×	×	×

would be useful for grouping the data by subject. All that is needed is a
means of transposing the data matrix.

The *row-column* transposition of a matrix in APL is written $\phi\!\!\!\backslash M$ and
produces a matrix whose rows are the columns of M and whose columns
are the rows of M. For example:

```
      M←3 4ρι12
      M

1   2    3    4
5   6    7    8
9  10   11   12

      ⍉M

1   5    9
2   6   10
3   7   11
4   8   12
```

The monadic operator symbol is the circle symbol overstruck with the
reverse solidus. More generally, the monadic transpose operation is the
interchange of the last two coordinates of the operand.

```
       N←2 3 4ρι24
       N

 1   2    3    4
 5   6    7    8
 9  10   11   12

13  14   15   16
17  18   19   20
21  22   23   24

       NTRANS←⍉N
       NTRANS

 1   5    9
 2   6   10
 3   7   11
 4   8   12

13  17   21
14  18   22
15  19   23
16  20   24

       ρN
2  3   4
       ρNTRANS
2  4   3
```

The problem of augmenting a matrix A with a matrix B, depicted as:

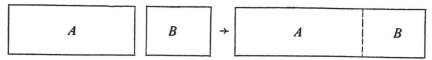

is easily solved with the ravel, catenation, and transpose functions.

```
A←3 4ρι12
B←3 2ρ0
C←⍉(((ρA)+ρB)[2],(ρA)[1])ρ(,⍉A),,⍉B
A

1    2    3    4
5    6    7    8
9   10   11   12

B

0 0
0 0
0 0

C

1    2    3    4    0    0
5    6    7    8    0    0
9   10   11   12    0    0
```

The dyadic form of transposition uses a left operand which specifies the coordinates that should be interchanged. For example:

```
M←3 4ρι12
2 1⍉M

1    5    9
2    6   10
3    7   11
4    8   12

(⍉M)=2 1⍉M

1 1 1
1 1 1
1 1 1
1 1 1
```

Given the dyadic transportation operation $N\mathbin{⍉}M$, then ρN must equal $\rho\rho M$ and the $N[I]$th coordinate of the result is the Ith coordinate of M. Therefore, the components of N must specify all the coordinates of the array result. If $(\rho M)=3$, then 1 2 3 or 1 1 2 or 1 2 1 or 3 1 2 would be a suitable value for N whereas 1 1 3 would be illegal. That is:

```
          M←2 3 4ρι24
          N←3 1 2
          M

    1     2    3    4
    5     6    7    8
    9    10   11   12

   13    14   15   16
   17    18   19   20
   21    22   23   24

          ρM
2   3     4
          Q←NⱲM
          Q

    1     13
    2     14
    3     15
    4     16

    5     17
    6     18
    7     19
    8     20

    9     21
   10     22
   11     23
   12     24

          ρQ
3   4     2
```

The result R of dyadic transposition on M is defined as follows:

Operation	$ρρM$	$ρρR$	Result	Notes
1 1ⱲM	2	1	$R[I] = M[I;I]$	Main diagonal of M
1 2ⱲM	2	2	$R[I;J] = M[I;J]$	No transposition specified
2 1ⱲM	2	2	$R[I;J] = M[J;I]$	Same as $ⱲM$
1 1 1ⱲM	3	1	$R[I] = M[I;I;I]$	Main diagonal of M
1 1 2ⱲM	3	2	$R[I;J] = M[I;I;J]$	
1 2 1ⱲM	3	2	$R[I;J] = M[I;J;I]$	
1 2 2ⱲM	3	2	$R[I;J] = M[I;J;J]$	
1 2 3ⱲM	3	3	$R[I;J;K] = M[I;J;K]$	No transposition specified
1 3 2ⱲM	3	3	$R[I;J;K] = M[I;K;J]$	Same as $ⱲM$
2 1 1ⱲM	3	2	$R[I;J] = M[J;I;I]$	
2 1 2ⱲM	3	2	$R[I;J] = M[J;I;J]$	
2 1 3ⱲM	3	3	$R[I;J;K] = M[J;I;K]$	
2 2 1ⱲM	3	2	$R[I;J] = M[J;J;I]$	
2 3 1ⱲM	3	3	$R[I;J;K] = M[J;K;I]$	
3 1 2ⱲM	3	3	$R[I;J;K] = M[K;I;J]$	
3 2 1ⱲM	3	3	$R[I;J;K] = M[K;J;I]$	

The following values for N where $\rho \rho M = 3$ are illegal: 1 1 3, 1 3 1,
1 3 3, 2 2 2, 2 2 3, 2 3 2, 2 3 3, 3 1 1, 3 1 3, 3 2 2, 3 2 3, 3 3 1,
3 3 2, and 3 3 3.

Reversal and Rotation

In examples requiring a descending sequence of integers, the following
expressions was written:

```
            N←7
            (N+1)-ι7
   7    6   5   4   3   2   1
```

which is simply the reversal of ιN. The idea of reversing the components
of an array is a cumbersome task in programming, and a function to do
the job prevents many problems therein. The circle symbol overstruck
by the vertical stroke is the operator for the monadic reversal operation
which appears as follows: ϕA. If A is a vector, then the components are
reversed. If A is an array, then ϕA indicates a reversal along the last
coordinate. If reversal is desired around the Ith coordinate, then the coordinate index must be specified as follows: $\phi[I]A$. $\phi[1]A$ may be indicated by: $\ominus A$, where the operator is the circle symbol overstruck with a
minus sign.

```
            A←ι6
            φA
   6    5   4   3   2   1
            B←2 3ρι6
            B

   1    2   3
   4    5   6

            φ[1]B

   4    5   6
   1    2   3

            φ[2]B

   3    2   1
   6    5   4

            (φ[2]B)=φB

   1  1  1
   1  1  1
```

```
        C← 2 3 4ρι24
        C

 1      2   3    4
 5      6   7    8
 9     10  11   12

13     14  15   16
17     18  19   20
21     22  23   24

        φ[1]C

13     14  15   16
17     18  19   20
21     22  23   24

 1      2   3    4
 5      6   7    8
 9     10  11   12

        A←3 3ρ'TEAFORTWO'
        A

TEA
FOR
TWO

        φ[1]A

TWO
FOR
TEA
```

Reversal does not change the structure of the operand so the result assumes its dimension and rank.

The dyadic form of the φ operator is used to rotate an array cyclically. The operation is of the form:

Vector Rotation	Array Rotation
$K \phi A$	$K \phi [I] A$

If A is a vector, then K must be a scalar and A is rotated to the left $(\rho A) \mid K$ components. Thus, if K is positive, rotation is to the left, whereas if K is negative, rotation is to the right. For example:

```
          A←ι6
          2φA
3  4      5  6  1  2
          ⁻3φA
4  5      6  1  2  3
          (4φA)=⁻2φA
1  1      1  1  1  1
```

If A is an array of higher dimension, then the coordinate along which the rotation is to take place must be specified as a coordinate index. If it is omitted, the last is assumed. The first coordinate may be specified as $K\ominus A$ where $\ominus$ is a circle overstruck with the minus sign. The dimension of K must agree with the respective dimension of A; if K is a scalar, then it is extended to all indices of A. The sign and magnitude of each component of K determines the rotation that is applied to the respective dimension of A and a positive K indicates rotation toward the index origin. For example:

```
          A←3 4ρι12
          A

  1       2    3    4
  5       6    7    8
  9      10   11   12

          2ϕ[2]A

  3       4    1    2
  7       8    5    6
 11      12    9   10

          (¯1ϕA)=¯1ϕ[2]A

1 1 1    1
1 1 1    1
1 1 1    1

          1ϕ[1]A

  5       6    7    8
  9      10   11   12
  1       2    3    4

          1 0 2ϕA

  2       3    4    1
  5       6    7    8
 11      12    9   10

          3 1 2 0ϕ[1]A

  1       6   11    4
  5      10    3    8
  9       2    7   12
```

```
              B←2 3 4ρι24
              B

     1        2    3    4
     5        6    7    8
     9       10   11   12

    13       14   15   16
    17       18   19   20
    21       22   23   24

              1φ[2]B

     5        6    7    8
     9       10   11   12
     1        2    3    4

    17       18   19   20
    21       22   23   24
    13       14   15   16

              3φ[1]B

    13       14   15   16
    17       18   19   20
    21       22   23   24

     1        2    3    4
     5        6    7    8
     9       10   11   12

              (3φ[1]B)=1φ[1]B

  1 1 1  1
  1 1 1  1
  1 1 1  1

  1 1 1  1
  1 1 1  1
  1 1 1  1

              2φ[3]B

     3        4    1    2
     7        8    5    6
    11       12    9   10

    15       16   13   14
    19       20   17   18
    23       24   21   22
```

As with reversal, the dimension and rank of the result are taken from the
dimension and rank of the right operand since the structure is not changed
by rotation.

Compression and Expansion

The *compression* operation provides a means of suppressing some components of an array while retaining others. The general form of compression is:

$$U/A$$

where U is a logical vector that is conformable with A, the array being compressed. In vector compression, components corresponding to a 1 are retained while those corresponding to a 0 are suppressed. If either operand is a scalar or a one-component array, it is extended to apply to all components of the other operand. The result of vector compression is always a vector. For example:

```
          | U←1  0  1  0
          | V←'ABCD'
          | U/V
    A C   |
          | U/ϕι4
   4    2 |
          | U/5
   5    5 |
          | 1/ι4
   1    2 | 3   4
```

In matrix compression, it is necessary to specify along which coordinate the compression should operate. Similar to reduction, $U/[1]M$ and $U{\neq}M$ denote the first coordinate and $U/[2]M$ and U/M specify the last coordinate. More specifically, $U{\neq}M$ denotes compression *along* the first coordinate and suppresses rows while U/M operates *along* the second coordinate and suppresses columns. For example:

```
      M←3 4ρι12
      M

1     2     3     4
5     6     7     8
9    10    11    12

      1  0  1/[1]M

1     2     3     4
9    10    11    12

      1  1  0  1/M

1     2     4
5     6     8
9    10    12

      N←3 4ρ'TAEAFBORTCWO'
      N

TAFA
FBOR
TCWO

      P←1  0  1  1/N
      P

TEA
FOR
TWO

      0  1  1/[1]P

FOR
TWO
```

In compression of rank-3 arrays, compression operates along a co-ordinate and entire matrices are suppressed. For example:

```
              Q←2 3 3ρι18
              Q

      1       2    3
      4       5    6
      7       8    9

     10      11   12
     13      14   15
     16      17   18

              1 0/[1]Q

      1    2  3
      4    5  6
      7    8  9

              0 1 1/[2]Q

      4       5    6
      7       8    9

     13      14   15
     16      17   18

              1 0 1/Q

      1       3
      4       6
      7       9

     10      12
     13      15
     16      18
```

In general, the rank of the result of compression is always equal to the rank of the right operand, including scalars and one-component arrays after they have been extended.

Expansion is the converse of compression and is written as follows:

$$U \backslash A$$

where U is a logical vector. $U \backslash A$ expands A to the form given by U, so that $(\rho A) = +/U$, by inserting padding for components that correspond to zero components of U. Numeric arrays are padded with zeros and character arrays are padded with space characters. With arrays of rank 2 or greater, $U \nleftarrow A$ denotes the first coordinate and $U \backslash A$ specifies the last. Since the operation is closely related to compression, it is further described by example:

```
          V←'TEAFORTWO'
          (12ρ1 1 1 0)\V
TEA  FOR  TWO
          U←9ρ1 0
          Y←U/ι9
          Z←(~U)/ι9
          Y
1    3    5    7    9
          Z
2    4    6    8
          (U\Y)+(~U)\Z
1    2    3    4    5    6    7    8    9
          M←2 4ρι8
          1 0 1\[1]M

     1    2    3    4
     0    0    0    0
     5    6    7    8


          1 0 1 1 1\M

     1    0    2    3    4
     5    0    6    7    8

          Q←2 2 2ρι8
          1 1 0\[2]Q

     1    2
     3    4
     0    0

     5    6
     7    8
     0    0

          1 0 1\[1]Q

     1    2
     3    4

     0    0
     0    0

     5    6
     7    8
```

The conformability requirement for $U \backslash [I] A$ is that $(+/U) = (\rho A)[I]$.

Take and Drop—The Selection of Leading and Trailing Components

To a limited extent, the capability of selecting the leading or trailing components of a vector is provided with prefix and suffix vectors and the compression operation. A *prefix vector* of order *n* is a logical vector containing *n* leading ones; the remaining components are zero. Similarly, a *suffix vector* of order *n* contains *n* trailing ones. Thus, compound expressions to take or drop components of a vector are given as follows:

```
            X←¯7 3 9 6 5 1 4 3
            U←(3ρ1),((ρX)-3)ρ0
            U
1   1       1  0   0   0   0   0
            U/X
¯7   3      9
            (~U)/X
6   5       1  4   3

            V←(((ρX)-3)ρ0),3ρ1
            V
0   0       0  0   0   1   1   1
            V/X
1   4       3
            (~V)/X
¯7   3      9  6   5
```

The *take* and *drop* functions in APL eliminate the need for compound expressions of this sort and apply to rank-*n* arrays as well. The general form of the *take operation* is:

$$T \uparrow A$$

where *T* must be an integer or vector of integers. *T* must contain one component for each coordinate of *A*. If *A* is a vector, then *T* may be a scalar or a one-component array. The rank of the result is always the rank of the left operand. If *A* is a vector and *T* is positive, then $T \uparrow A$ selects the first *T* components of *A*. If *T* is negative, then the last *T* components are selected. If $T=0$, then the result is the null vector. If $T > \rho A$, then the right operand is padded with zeros or blanks, as required. For example:

```
            V←¯7 3 9 6 5 1 4 3
            3↑V
¯7   3      9
            ¯5↑V
6   5       1  4   3
            ρρ0↑V
1

            W←'IRREGARDLESS'
            ¯6↑(8↑W)
REGARD
```

If A is an array, then ρT must equal $\rho\rho A$ and $T[I]$ determines the components selected along the Ith coordinate of A. The components of T may be positive or negative and indicate first or last components, respectively. For example:

```
                M←3 4ρι12
                M

         1      2    3    4
         5      6    7    8
         9     10   11   12

                N←1 3
                N↑M

         1    2  3

                ‾2 2↑M

         5      6
         9     10

                ρ3 0↑M
    3    0
                A←2 3 4ρι24
                A

         1      2    3    4
         5      6    7    8
         9     10   11   12

        13     14   15   16
        17     18   19   20
        21     22   23   24

                ‾1 3 4↑A

        13     14   15   16
        17     18   19   20
        21     22   23   24

                2 2 ‾2↑A

         3      4
         7      8

        15     16
        19     20
```

The *drop operation* is defined analogously but drops the indicated components instead of taking them. The form of the drop is:

$$T \downarrow A$$

If the right operand is a vector, then $(\rho A)\downarrow A$ gives an empty vector. If $T>\rho A$, then the operation yields an empty array, which assumes the rank of T.

```
             V←¯7 3 9 6 5 1 4 3
             3↓V
   6    5    1   4   3
             ¯5↓V
  ¯7    3    9
             ρρ(ρV)↓V
   1
             C←'/*COMMENT*/'
             ¯2↓(2↓C)
COMMENT
             M←3 4ρι12
             M

    1        2    3    4
    5        6    7    8
    9       10   11   12

             N←1 3
             N↓M

    8
   12

             ¯2 2↓M

    3    4

             ρ3 0↓M
   0    4
             A←2 3 4ρι24
             A

    1        2    3    4
    5        6    7    8
    9       10   11   12

   13       14   15   16
   17       18   19   20
   21       22   23   24

             ¯1 0 0↓A

    1        2    3    4
    5        6    7    8
    9       10   11   12

             0 ¯1 2↓A

    3        4
    7        8

   15       16
   19       20
```

Set Operations—Index of and Membership

One of the functions that depends upon the index origin is that which gives the index of the earliest occurrence of a scalar value C in a vector V. If 1-origin indexing is used, then the indices of components in V run from 1 through ρV. If 0-origin indexing is used, then the indices of the components in V run from 0 through $(\rho V)-1$. The *index of* operation is written:

$$V\iota C$$

and gives the index of the earlier occurrence of scalar C in vector V. If the right operand is a vector, then the result is a vector of the same size—the components of the result are the indices of the right operand in V. The left operand must be a vector. This concept is extended to rank-n arrays so that for the result R of the operation $V\iota A$:

$$(\rho R)=\rho A$$
$$(\rho\rho R)=\rho\rho A$$

If U component of A is not found in V, then it is given the index $1+\lceil/\iota\rho V$. For example:

```
        V←¯7 3 9 6 5 1 4 3
        Vι3
2
        Vιι5
6    9  2    7    5
        A←'ABCDEFGHIJKLMNOPQRSTUVWXYZ'
        Aι'TEA FOR TWO'
20   5  1   27    6   15   18   27   20   23   15
        W←V,10 11
        Wι3 4ρι12

        6  11    2    7
        5   4   11   11
        3   9   10   11

        (ρW)+1
11
        W
¯7   3  9    6    5    1    4    3   10   11
        M←2 3ρι6
        WιM

        6  11    2
        7   5    4

        )ORIGIN 0
WAS 1
        Vι3
1
        Vιι5
8    5  8    1    6
        )ORIGIN 1
WAS 0
```

The *membership function* yields a logical value (i.e., 0 or 1) if a given component (or scalar quantity) is an element of a specified array. The function, written $A \in B$, gives a result that is the same size as A. If a component of A is contained in B, then the respective component of the result is 1; otherwise, it is given the value 0. B can be a scalar, vector, matrix, or rank-n array.

```
        C←'ABCDEFGHIJKLMNOPQRSTUVWXYZ'
        D←'TEA FOR TWO'
        D∈C
1    1  1   0   1   1   1   0   1   1   1
        E←(D∈C)/D
        E
TEAFORTWO
        F∈C
1    1  1   1   1   1   1   1   1
        (3 4ρι12)∈ι6
  1 1 1 1
  1 1 0 0
  0 0 0 0
        ((5|ι25)∈0)/ι25
5   10  15    20    25
        (2 4 6 8 10 12 14 16)∈3 4ρι12
1    1  1   1   1   1   0   0
```

Grade Up and Down—Sequencing of Components

The need to sort a trivial list of values occurs frequently in computer applications—yet it is one of the more cumbersome and time-consuming operations. The *grade up* function uses the monadic operator ⍋ (formed by overstriking a delta Δ with a vertical stroke) and yields a vector of indices that would order the vector right operand in ascending sequence. The general form of grade up is:

$$R = \,\!⍋ V$$

where the result R is the same size as V. For example:

```
        V←¯7 3 9 6 5 1 4 3
        ⍋V
1   6   2   8   7   5   4   3
        V[⍋V]
¯7  1   3   3   4   5   6   9
```

In the above example, the index of the smallest component ⁻7 is 1, the
index of the next highest component 1 is 6, etc. The ordering of duplicate
components is determined by their position in V.

The *grade down* function:

$$R = \psi V$$

is analogous to the grade up function except the ordering is given in descending sequence, and the operator is formed from a del (∇) and a vertical stroke. For example:

```
        |V←⁻7 3 9 6 5 1 4 3
        |⍒V
3   4   |5   7   2   8   6   1
        |V[⍒V]
9   6   |5   4   3   3   1   ⁻7
        |M←3 4⍴V,8 0 2 7
        |M

  ⁻7  3|  9   6
   5  1|  4   3
   8  0|  2   7

        |3 4⍴(,M)[⍋,M]

  ⁻7  0|  1   2
   3  3|  4   5
   6  7|  8   9
```

The operand for grade up and grade down is limited to vectors, and the
size of the result is the size of the operand. The indices in the vector are
affected by the index origin.

Deal — Generation of Numbers at Random without Replacement

The roll function, discussed previously, generates numbers pseudo-
randomly from a given set with replacement. Therefore, the probability
of drawing a unique component from the given set by this process exists
only within probabilistic limits. The *deal function, A?B,* where A and B
are integer scalars or one-component arrays, generates a vector of A components from the vector ιB without replacement. Thus, each component
generated is unique. The result is dependent upon the index origin.

```
        |3?5
5   1   |2
        |7?7
4   5   |6   2   1   3   7
```

Decode and Encode—Base Value and Representation

The ordinary polynomial of the form:

$$a_n x^n + a_{n-1} x^{n-1} \ldots a_2 x^2 + a_1 x + a_0$$

arises in a variety of ways in computing, the most frequent being with regard to the positional number system—or a fixed-base value representation. Given a vector whose components represent coefficients of *descending* powers of a *base* value, then the base ten value of the polynomial is usually computed using nested multiplication or a component-by-component vector multiplication and a sum reduction. In the latter case, it is first necessary to develop a weighting vector of successive powers of the base value. For example, the coefficient vector $A \leftarrow 1\ 2\ 3\ 4$ to the base ten is computed as follows:

```
        A←ι4
        X←1000  100  10  1
        +/A×X
1234
```

Similarly, $B \leftarrow 1\ 0\ 1$ to the base two and $C \leftarrow 1\ 0\ 0$ to the base eight are computed as:

```
        B←1  0  1
        Y←4  2  1
        +/B×Y
5
        C←1  0  0
        Z←64  8  1
        +/C×Z
64
```

Actually, the operation is more general and applies to: the hours, minutes, and seconds in a day; the gallons, quarts, pints, and ounces in a barrel; the yards, feet, and inches in a mile, etc. That is, the radix vector need not be successive powers of a given base value. For example, the seconds in 3 hours, 4 minutes, and 17 seconds is computed as follows:

```
        A←3  4  17
        B←3600  60  1
        S←+/A×B
        S
11057
```

Yet in this example, the most natural way of representing the days, hours, and minutes·is:

> 24 hours per day,
> 60 minutes per hour, and
> 60 seconds per minute.

which is termed a *radix vector*. The *base value function* allows the radix vector to be expressed in natural order and delegates the intermediate calculations to the computer. Base value is often called the *decode* function and is expressed as:

$$B \perp A$$

where B represents the radix and A is the vector of coefficients. If B is a scalar, then it is extended to all components of A. If B is a vector, then it must be the same size as A. Thus:

```
              A←ι4
              10⊥A
     1234
              2⊥1 0 1
     5
              24 60 60⊥3 4 17
     11057
```

The function utilizes a weighting vector, internally, which is developed as follows:

$$W[\rho W] = 1$$
$$W[I-1] = B[I] \times W[I]$$

Here, B is the radix vector. The result R of the base value function is defined as:

$$R = +/A \times W$$

or as:

$$R = A +. \times W$$

The *representation function*, also called *encode*, provides the inverse of decode. The function is expressed as:

$$B \top S$$

where B is the radix vector and S is a scalar value. The dimension of the result is the size of B. For example:

```
         | 10 10 10 10T1234
 1   2   | 3  4
         | 2 2 2T5
 1   0   | 1
         | 2 2T5
 0   1   |
```

R [1] is not used in either function and the components of the radix or co-efficient vectors are not restricted to integral or positive values. For example:

```
         | 109 3 .5⊥1 2 3
 5.5     |
         | ⁻3 ⁻3 ⁻3⊥1 2 3
 6       |
         | ⁻3 ⁻3 ⁻3T6
 1   1   | 0
         | 0 ⁻3 ⁻3T6
 1   1   | 0
```

Summary of Functions on Arrays

A brief summary of the functions designed for use on arrays is included here for reference and review:

1. *Reduction.* Reduction is applied along the Ith coordinate of A with the operation:

$$\oplus/[I]A$$

If $[I]$ is elided, the last coordinate is used. Alternately, the first coordinate may be specified with:

$$\oplus\!\!\not{}A$$

2. *Inner product.* The inner product of arrays A and B is specified as:

$$Af.gB$$

where f and g are scalar operations or mathematical functions. The ordinary matrix product is specified as:

$$A+.\times B$$

3. *Outer product.* The outer product of two arrays is specified as:

$$A\ .fB$$

where the given scalar operation or function f is applied to *each* component of one array by *all* components of the other; f may not be a defined function.

4. *Transposition.* The row-column transpose of a matrix is specified as the monadic operation:

$$\lozenge M$$

and is extended to rank-n arrays by exchanging the last two co-ordinates. The dyadic form of transposition permits the user to specify the coordinates that are interchanged and has the form:

$$N \lozenge M$$

where $\rho N = (\rho\rho M)$.

5. *Reversal.* The reversal of components along the Ith coordinate of A is specified by:

$$\phi[I]A$$

If $[I]$ is elided, the last coordinate is used. Alternately, the first coordinate is specified by:

$$\ominus A$$

6. *Rotation.* The rotation of components along the Ith coordinate of A is specified by:

$$K\phi[I]A$$

If K is a scalar, it is extended to all indices of A. If K is a vector, its size must agree with the respective dimension of A. If $[I]$ is elided, the last coordinate is assumed. The first coordinate is specified by:

$$K\ominus A$$

If K is positive, rotation is towards the lowest index for the specified coordinate. If K is negative, it is towards the high-numbered index for that coordinate.

7. *Compression.* Compression along the Ith coordinate is specified by:

$$U/[I]A$$

where U is a logical vector where $\rho U = (\rho A)[I]$. If $[I]$ is elided, the last coordinate is assumed. The first coordinate is specified as:

$$U \nmid A$$

8. *Expansion.* Expansion along the Ith coordinate of A is specified by:

$$U\backslash[I]A$$

where U is a logical vector and $(+/U) = (\rho A)[I]$. If $[I]$ is elided, the last coordinate is assumed and the first coordinate is specified by:

$$U \bar{\downarrow} A$$

9. *Take.* The take function:

$$T \uparrow A$$

selects the first $T[I]$ components (if $T[I]$ is positive) along the Ith coordinate of A. If $T[I]$ is negative, the last components are selected. If A is a vector, the T must be a scalar or one-component array.

10. *Drop.* The drop function:

$$T \downarrow A$$

deletes the first $T[I]$ (or last) component of A along the Ith co-ordinate depending upon whether $T[I]$ is positive (or negative). If A is a vector, then T must be a scalar or a one-component array.

11. *Index of.* The earliest occurrence of A (or components of A) in vector V is specified by:

$$V \iota A$$

The result is the same size as A.

12. *Membership.* The membership function yields the value 1 if A (or component of A) is an element of vector B; that is,

$$A \epsilon B$$

Otherwise, the function yields the value 0. The result is the same size as A.

13. *Grade up.* The grade up function

$$\not\Downarrow V$$

yields the permutation of indices (of V) that would order V, so that the components of $V[\not\Downarrow V]$ are in ascending sequence.

14. *Grade down.* The grade down function

$$\not\Downarrow V$$

yields the permutation of indices (of V) that would order V so that the components of $V[\not\Downarrow V]$ are in descending sequence.

15. *Deal.* The function,

$$A?B$$

generates a vector of size ρA from ιB pseudo-randomly without replacement. The result is dependent upon the index origin.

16. *Decode.* Decode yields the base ten value of coefficients A to the radix R:

$$R \perp A$$

If R is a scalar it is extended to all components of A; the dimension of the result is the dimension of A.

17. *Encode.* Encode yields the vector of coefficients A of the radix R that is equivalent to the scalar S:

$$R \top S$$

The dimension of the result is the dimension of R.

5.5 ANNOTATED SCRIPT OF ARRAY OPERATIONS

```
            V←¯7 3 9 6 5              Creating a numeric vector.
            ρV                        Dimension of V.
5
            W←5ρ2 3 1                 Generating a vector with the reshape function.
            W
2  3        1  2  3                   Numeric vector printed with intervening spaces.
            V,W                       Catenation of two vectors.
¯7  3       9  6  5  2  3  1  2  3
            V×W                       Element-by-element operation on vectors of the
¯14  9      9  12  15                    same size.
            V*2                       Right operand extended to all components of V.
49  9       81  36  25
            (V×V)=V*2                 Compound expression giving a logical result.
1  1        1  1  1
            C←'TEA FOR TWO'           Vector of characters.
            ρC                        Size of C  each character is a component.
11
            C[4]←C[8]←'|'             Indexing and specification.
            C
TEA|FOR|TWO                          Character vector printed without spaces.
            'TEN FACTORIAL IS ';!10   Mixed output requires semicolon.
TEN FACTORIAL IS 3628800
            (V÷W)[3]                  Indexing of an expression.
9
            I←2
            V[(2×W[I])-3]             Subscripted subscript.
9
            ι6                        Index vector of integers 1 through 6.
1  2        3  4  5  6
            ι0                        Null vector.
                                      Prints as blank line.
            ρι0                       Size of null vector.
0
            ρρι0                      Rank of null vector.
1                                     1  it is a one-dimensional array.
            ρ(ι997),8,(ι2)            Size of a partial result.
1000
```

```
          X←V,1  4  3            Catenation of vectors.
          X[2  4  6  8]          Vector as an index.
3    6    1   3
          +/ι4                   Sum reduction.
10
          ⌈/V                    Largest value in V —maximum reduction.
9
          ⌊/V                    Smallest value in V—minimum reduction.
⁻7
          Vι⌈/V                  Index of the largest value in V.
3
          +/ι0                   Identity element for sum reduction.
0
          ×/ι0                   Identity element for product reduction.
1
          ∧/C='TEA  FOR  TWO'    And reduction    test for equality.
0                                No! they are not the same.
          U←2  2ρ1  0  0         Generation of a 2×2 logical matrix.
          U                      Display of matrix.

1    0                           Output is indented.
0    1


          M←2  2ρι4              Generation of a matrix using reshape and an index vector.
          M

     1    2
     3    4


          M×U                    Element-by-element operation on two arrays.

     1    0
     0    4


          M*2                    Scalar operand extends to all components of M.

        1              4
        9             16


          !M                     Monadic operation on array —applies to all components.

      1              2
      6             24
```

```
        A←2 3 4ρι24                    Generation of a rank-3 array.
        A

   1    2    3    4                    Displayed as two planes since the first coordinate has
   5    6    7    8                       two dimensions.
   9   10   11   12

  13   14   15   16
  17   18   19   20
  21   22   23   24

        ρA                             Size of A.
2    3  4
        ρρA                            Rank of A.
3                                      3—we knew it all the time.


        J←5
        ρJ                             Size of a scalar.
ꞵ                                      Prints as a blank line.
        ρρJ
0                                      Rank of a scalar is zero.
        A[2;1;4]←0                     Subscripts separated by semicolons—specification of a
        A                                component of an array.

   1    2    3    4
   5    6    7    8
   9   10   11   12

  13   14   15    0
  17   18   19   20               Note the zero component.
  21   22   23   24

        4 6ρA                          Restructuring   A taken in index order.

   1    2    3    4    5    6
   7    8    9   10   11   12
  13   14   15    0   17   18
  19   20   21   22   23   24

        B←2 3ρι6
        B

   1    2    3
   4    5    6

        ,B                             B is raveled in index order.
1    2  3    4    5    6
        ρ5                             Size of a scalar value.
ꞵ
        ρ,5                            Ravel always produces a vector result.
1
```

```
      M←3 4ρι12
      M

1     2   3   4
5     6   7   8
9    10  11  12

      M[1 3;2 4]

 2    4
10   12

      M[2;]
5 6   7   8
      M[;4]←19 20 21
      M

1     2   3  19
5     6   7  20
9    10  11  21

      V←ι5
      V[2]
2
      ι2
1 2
      V[ιρV]
1 2   3   4   5
      )ORIGIN 0
WAS 1
      V[2]
3
      ι2
0 1
      V[ιρV]
1 2   3   4   5
      M←3 2ρι6
      M

 0    1
 2    3
 4    5

      +/M
1 5   9
      +/+/M
15
      ×/[1]M
0 6   20
      )ORIGIN 1
WAS 0
```

`M[1 3;2 4]`	Vector subscripts select rows and columns.
`M[2;]`	Cross section of an array—all components corresponding to elided index are selected.
`M[;4]←19 20 21`	Respecification of an entire column.
`V←ι5`	Index vector in 1-origin indexing.
`V[2]`	Second component in 1-origin indexing.
`ι2`	Index vector in 1-origin indexing.
`V[ιρV]`	Index vector and vector indices agree.
`)ORIGIN 0`	Change indexing origin to zero.
`V[2]`	Index of 2 selects third component. Components of the vector remain the same.
`ι2`	Index vector in 0-origin indexing.
`V[ιρV]`	Index vector and vector indices still agree.
`M←3 2ρι6`	Generation of a matrix in 0-origin indexing.
`+/M`	Reduction along the last coordinate.
`×/[1]M`	Reduction along the first coordinate.

```
       A←2 3 4ρι24
       A

  1    2    3    4
  5    6    7    8
  9   10   11   12

 13   14   15   16
 17   18   19   20
 21   22   23   24

       +/[2]A                    Reduction of a rank-3 array along the second coordinate.

 15   18   21   24
 51   54   57   60

       A←2 3ρι6                  Generation of matrices A and B such that the last coordinate
       A                            of A agrees with the first coordinate of B.

  1    2    3
  4    5    6

       B←3 4ρφι12
       B

 12   11   10    9
  8    7    6    5
  4    3    2    1

       A+.×B                     Ordinary matrix product (generalized inner product).

 40   34   28   22
112   97   82   67

       AL.ΓB                     Inner product using L and Γ.

  4    3    3    3
  6    6    6    5

       A+.×3ρ2                   Inner product of matrix and vector.
 12   30
       (3ρ2)+.×ι3                Inner product of two vectors.
 12
```

```
      V∘.+V←ι3          Outer product of two vectors.

2  3  4
3  4  5
4  5  6

      M←2 3ρι6
      M

1  2  3
4  5  6

      ⍉M                Monadic transpose   interchanges last two coordinates.

1  4
2  5
3  6

      A←2 2 3ρι12
      A

1   2   3
4   5   6

7   8   9
10  11  12

      3 1 2⍉A           Dyadic transpose  left operand denotes coordinates to be
                            interchanged.
1  7
2  8
3  9

4  10
5  11
6  12

      1 1⍉M             Main diagonal of M.
1  5
      ⌽ι6               Reversal of index vector.
6  5  4  3  2  1
      ⌽'OWT ROF AET'    Reversal of character vector.
TEA FOR TWO
      ⌽[2]M             Reversal along the second coordinate.

3  2  1
6  5  4

      ⌽[1]M             Reversal along the first coordinate.

4  5  6
1  2  3

      ⌽M                Reversal along the last coordinate.

3  2  1
6  5  4
```

```
        4⌽' TWO TEA FOR'        Vector rotation to the left.
   TEA FOR TWO
        ⁻3⌽⍳7                   Vector rotation to the right.
5  6   7  1  2  3  4

        1 2⌽[2]M               Rotation along second coordinate applying different rota-
                                   tion to each row.
   2  3| 1                         (rotation of rows)
   6  4| 5

        0 1 2⌽[1]M             Rotation along first coordinate (rotation of columns).
   1  5| 3
   4  2| 6

        1⌽[1]M                 Left operand extended to all coordinates.
   4  5| 6
   1  2| 3

        1⌽[2]M
   2  3| 1
   5  6| 4

        1⌽[2]A

   4 | 5   6
   1 | 2   3

  10 |11  12
   7 | 8   9

        U←1 0 0 1
        V←'ABCD'
        U/V                     Compression.
AD
        U/⌽⍳4
4  1
        1/⍳4                    Left operand extended.
1  2  3  4
        U/4                     Right operand extended.
4  4
```

```
N←3 4ρι12
N2←U/[2]N
N2
```
Compression along second coordinate.

```
1   4
5   8
9   12
```
Entire columns suppressed.

```
N1←1 0 1/[1]N
N1
```
Compression along first coordinate.

```
1   2    3    4
9   10   11   12
```
Entire rows suppressed.

```
U\[2]N2
```
Expansion along second coordinate.
(converse of compression)

```
1   0   0   4
5   0   0   8
9   0   0   12
```
Padded with zeros

```
1 0 1\[1]N1
```

```
1   2    3    4
0   0    0    0
9   10   11   12
```

```
A←U/V
U\A
```

A   D

```
B←U/ι4
C←(~U)/ι4
(U\B)+(~U)\C
```
Character arrays padded with spaces.

```
1   2   3   4
```
Reforming a numeric vector.

```
V←ι7
3↑V
```

```
1   2   3
```
Take leading components of a vector.

```
¯2↑V
```

```
6   7
```
Take trailing components of a vector.

```
3↓V
```

```
4   5   6   7
```
Drop leading components of a vector.

```
¯2↓V
```

```
1   2   3   4   5
```
Drop trailing components of a vector.

```
N
```
Recall N.

```
1   2    3    4
5   6    7    8
9   10   11   12
```

```
2 3↑N
```
Take 2 rows and 3 columns.

```
1   2   3
5   6   7
```

```
¯1 ¯2↓N
```
Drop 1 row (trailing) and 2 columns.

```
3   4
7   8
```

```
        A←'ABCD'
        B←'C'
        A⍳B                       Index of B in A.
3
        A⍳'BDK'                   Extended to vector right operands.
2  4    5
        V←10 13 6 4 1 5 3
        V⍳5                       Components not in V are given index of (ρV)+1.
5  8    7  4  6
        W←⍳6
        W⍳3 4ρ⍳12                 Applies to array right operands, as well.

    1 2 3  4                      Components not in W are given index of (ρW)+1.
    5 6 7  7
    7 7 7  7

        E←(0=2|⍳100)/⍳100         Vector of even numbers ≤ 100.
        (⍳6)∊E                    Membership function.
0  1    0  1  0  1                Result—logical vector.
        (3 4ρ⍳12)∊E               Left operand matrix.

   0 1 0 1
   0 1 0 1                        Result—logical matrix.
   0 1 0 1

        V←¯7 3 9 6 5 1 4 3        Respecification of V.
        ⍋V                        Grade up—sequence of indices that would order V in
1  6    2  8  7  5  4  3              ascending sequence.
        V[⍋V]
¯7 1    3  3  4  5  6  9
        ⍒V                        Grade down—sequence of indices that would order V in
3  4    5  7  2  8  6  1              descending sequence.
        7?10                      Generation of random numbers without replacement.
9  3    5  4  8  6  2
        10⊥1 2 3 4                Base value of vector.
1234
        2⊥1 0 1
5
        2 2 2⊤5                   Representation of decimal value.
1  0    1
```

6 | TOPICS IN PROGRAMMING

6.1 THE REALM OF AUTOMATIC COMPUTATION

The facilities presented thus far in APL make it effective as a general-purpose desk calculator a very powerful one, indeed, but nevertheless, a desk calculator. What, then, is the difference between a collection of basic operations and conventions, such as the ones that have been presented, and a more general automatic programming system? The answer is almost obvious. First, it is necessary to subordinate some of the detail usually involved with programming to the programming system itself. APL achieves this result through *arrays* and a wide range of *array operations*, which were presented in the preceding chapter. Next, the system must contain facilities for operating in the automatic mode; that is, it must contain features so that sequences of statements can be stored internally and be fetched automatically instead of making it necessary for the user to enter each statement just before it is executed. *Defined functions* serve this need. Many algorithms are more than mere sequences of statements. Repetition, iteration, or looping is required. Through a branching operation and statement labels, a variety of *sequence and control* features are available for execution within defined functions. Input/output is always significant and is often emphasized because of the human factors problems involved with programming and using a computer. APL allows character and numeric data to be entered in a variety of forms and to be displayed, as required. Automatic computation is not without its disadvantages, and the elimination of syntactic* and logical errors from a program, called *debugging*, is at best a chore. APL includes a *trace function* and a *stop control function* to aid in the debugging process.

Four new topics have been mentioned: functions, sequence and control, input/output, and program checkout. For the most part, these topics constitute the difference between automatic computing and the desk calculator mode of operation. Obviously, the topics are nontrivial and each is worthy of considerable attention. On the other side of the coin, however, there is much that is usually said about these topics that does not need to be said—that is, either the information can be inferred from fundamental concepts or it results from having to describe a well-known or intuitive process in terms of elementary operations. The vehicle used here for describing these topics in computing is the facilities available in the APL language. The reader benefits in three ways: (1) He is exposed to the topics, as intended; (2) he is exposed to the more powerful features of APL; and (3) the use of APL to introduce the topics is straightforward and economical of time and energy.

6.2   DEFINED FUNCTIONS

The right triangle problem of Section 4.4 exhibited what was loosely defined as a program. For review, the program uses the base and height of a right triangle and computes its diagonal, perimeter, and area. Suppose that one needed to run this program for various values of the base and height. Not only would it be uneconomical and tedious to enter the statement repeatedly, but the mechanics of the process would probably generate many errors and the user would finally end up finding a shorter method or give up and do the calculations by hand. In short, it would be desirable to store the statements and then execute them for different values of the base B and height H. APL satisfies this need with a facility for defining and invoking functions.

A precise definition of a function is of particular interest, even though most readers have a working knowledge of the concept. Mathematically, a *function* is a mapping between two sets A and B and is expressed in a variety of ways:

$$a \epsilon A \overset{f}{\rightarrow} b \epsilon B$$
$$f{:}A \rightarrow B$$
$$f(a) \rightarrow b$$
$$fa \rightarrow b$$

---

*The dual role of most operators and the right-to-left rule sometimes result in an executable statement (i.e., one that does not cause an error message) that does not serve the intended purpose. Often, this type of error is more difficult to isolate than a logical error. For lack of a more appropriate classification, the name *syntactic error* is used.

The set A is called the *domain* of the function and B is called its *range*. Elements in the domain or range of a function need not be limited to single values to satisfy the above definition. For example, scalar addition is a function of two values and gives a single value as a result. Thus, there are monadic and dyadic functions– which is no surprise. The precise method of designating a function also deserves some discussion. Given a function (f) and operands A and B, it can be applied to the operands in the following ways:

Monadic Form	*Dyadic Form*
f(B)	f(A,B)
fB	fA B
	AfB

The latter form for both cases closely resembles ordinary mathematics and was selected for use in APL. The question of more than two arguments (or operands) naturally arises and is resolved by making one or both or the arguments vectors, matrices, or rank-*n* arrays as the case may be.

The Definition Mode

Ordinarily, the APL system is in the execution mode so that it can respond to requests for computation by the user. The *definition mode* is used for defining functions and is entered by typing the character ∇, pronounced "del," followed by a function header statement, which contains the name and declaration of syntax of that function. The system leaves the definition mode when the next del is received, that is, if it is not contained in a literal or a comment line.

After the function header is entered, APL responds with a number enclosed in brackets as follows:

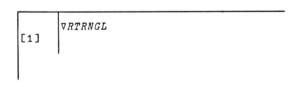

Statements within functions are sequenced by a decimal number, and the number of the next statement to be entered is given by the computer. The user enters the statements, comprising the function, successively until the function is completed. The statements are not checked as they are received by the computer and are stored in the active workspace under the function name. A final del then completes the function. That is,

```
        ∇RTRNGL
[1]     D←((H*2)+B*2)*.5
[2]     P←H+B+D
[3]     A←.5×B×H
[4]     ∇
```

The function is ready for use as follows:

```
        H←3
        B←4
        RTRNGL
        D,P,A
5    12  6
        H←5
        B←12
        RTRNGL
        D,P,A
13   30  30
```

It should be noted here that the above function is invoked by entering its name and that it requires no arguments. However, *RTRNGL* does not return an explicit result* so that its appearance in a mathematical expression results in an appropriate error message. For example:

```
        2×RTRNGL
VALUE   ERROR
        2×RTRNGL
         ∧
```

Functions can be modified in a variety of ways. The most elementary form of modification is given here; more complicated procedures are given in a following paragraph. Since *D, P,* and *A* were printed after each execution of *RTRNGL* in the preceding examples, it seems reasonable to reopen the function definition and simply add the necessary statement. A function is reopened by entering a del followed by the function name; the system responds by the number of the next statement to be entered. That is:

```
        ∇RTRNGL
[4]     D,P,A
[5]     ∇
```

*Such as a square root routine might return, for example.

Although the characteristics of the function remain the same (no arguments, implicit result), it now contains embedded output statements. For example:

```
          H←3
          B←4
          RTRNGL
5    12   6
          H←5
          B←12
          RTRNGL
13   30   30
```

After a few changes, it is usually desirable to obtain a listing of the function to insure that future modifications are made from a known foundation. This is achieved by using the quad* symbol ☐ as follows:

```
          ∇RTRNGL[☐]∇
     ∇    RTRNGL
[1]       D←((H*2)+B*2)*0.5
[2]       P←H+B+D
[3]       A←0.5×B×H
[4]       D,P,A
     ∇
```

In addition, statements can be inserted, replaced, or deleted—in conjunction with a display of the function. These facilities are covered under *function modification.*

Syntax of Function Definition

The foregoing function definitions were composed of several components. The statement following the initial *del* is the *function header.* The numbers in brackets are called the *statement numbers* and the associated statements are the *body* of the function. The function header essentially controls the form of the function. Six possibilities exist which are grouped into two classes depending on whether or not the function returns an explicit result. The forms are summarized in Table 6.1. An *explicit result* function produces a result and may appear as a constituent of a compound expression, much like the primitive operations and mathematical functions.

Of the six cases given in Table 6.1, four can be used with the right

*Sometimes called the *window* symbol.

TABLE 6.1   DEFINED FUNCTIONS

| | Form of Function Header | | |
Arguments	Explicit Result	No Explicit Result	Type
0	∇ R←FCN	∇ FCN	Niladic
1	∇ R←FCN Y	∇ FCN Y	Monadic
2	∇ R←X FCN Y	∇ X FCN Y	Dyadic

FCN = Function name.
X,Y = Dummy arguments.
R = Dummy result.

triangle problem—that is, since two arguments, base and height, are required. They are listed as follows:

1. Implicit argument—implicit result (this is the *RTRNGL* example given).
3. Implicit argument—explicit result (three values are computed so they must be returned as a vector of three components).
3. Explicit argument—implicit result.
4. Explicit argument—explicit result.

A function can have only one result, but it may be a scalar, vector, matrix, or rank-*n* array. The *implicit argument-explicit result* form requires no formal arguments but produces a result that may be used in a compound expression. That is:

```
      ∇R←RTR1
[1]   D←((H*2)+B*2)*.5
[2]   P←H+B+D
[3]   A←.5×B×H
[4]   R←D,P,A
[5]   ∇

      H←3
      B←4
      T←RTR1
      T
5  12  6
      RTR1+2
7  14  8
```

An explicit result function without arguments is analogous to a constant in that it can be used anywhere that an operand can be used, except to the left of a specification operation. The *explicit argument-implicit result* form allows more flexibility in assigning arguments but again restricts the function from being used as a constituent of a compound expression. For example:

```
       ∇X  RTR2  Y
[1]    D←((X*2)+Y*2)*.5
[2]    P←X+Y+D
[3]    A←.5×X×Y
[4]    D,P,A
[5]    ∇

       3  RTR2  4
5    12  6
       5  RTR2  12
13   30   30
       (25*.5)  RTR2  3×4
13   30   30
       T←3  RTR2  4
5    12  6
VALUE  ERROR
       T←3  RTR2  4
           ∧
```

The preceding example is the first in which formal arguments have been used. Formal arguments, such as X and Y above, are used during function definition as *dummy variables*. When the function is used, they must be replaced with expressions that have a value. Every occurrence of a dummy variable within a function is effectively replaced by the value that the argument assumes at the point of activation. The use of a dummy variable within a function definition does not affect its value outside the function definition. That is:

```
       ∇R←X  PLUS  Y
[1]    R←X+Y
[2]    ∇
       X←10
       Y←20
       1  PLUS  2
3
       (17  PLUS  ¯4)-1
12
       X,Y
10   20
```

The *explicit argument-explicit result* form requires one or more arguments and returns a result that can be used in a mathematical expression. For example:

```
        |∇R←X RTR3 Y
[1]     |D←((X*2)+Y*2)*.5
[2]     |P←X+Y+D
[3]     |A←.5×X×Y
[4]     |R←D,P,A
[5]     |∇
        |T←3 RTR3 4
        |T
5   12  |6
        |(3 RTR3 4)*2
25  14  |4   36
```

Careful attention should be given to the arguments and result of a defined function. As with primitive operations and mathematical functions, they may be any constituent that is acceptable to the body of the function. Consider again the *PLUS* function given above.

```
        |∇R←X PLUS Y
[1]     |R←X+Y
[2]     |∇
```

Clearly, the values which replace dummy variables *X* and *Y* may be anything acceptable to the operator +.

```
        |2 PLUS ι5
3   4   |5   6   7
        |(ι5) PLUS φι5
6   6   |6   6   6
        |(3 3ρι9) PLUS ⍉3 3ρι9
    2   |6   10
    6   |10  14
    10  |14  18
```

In other functions, the argument must be an operand of a specific type. Consider a *SORT* function defined and used as follows:

```
        |∇DONE←SORT LIST
[1]     |DONE←LIST[⍋LIST]
[2]     |∇
        |SORT ¯7 3 9 6 5 1 4 3
¯7  1   |3   3   4   5   6   9
        |φ SORT ¯7 3 9 6
9   6   |3   ¯7
```

However, since the grade up function requires a vector as an operand, the function produces a length error if applied to a scalar value. That is (using the above function definition):

```
      SORT 5
LENGTH ERROR
SORT[1] DONE←LIST[⍋LIST]
                 ∧
```

This could have been avoided by judicious use of the ravel operation as follows:

```
      ∇D←SORT L
[1]   D←(,L)[⍋,L]
[2]   ∇
      SORT ‾7 3 9 6
‾7  3  6  9
      SORT 5
5
```

Local and Global Variables

In APL, all variables are *global* unless specified otherwise. Essentially, this means that a variable used inside and outside of a function refers to the same data item. For example:

```
      ∇SETH Y
[1]   H←Y
[2]   ∇
      H←2
      SETH 5
      H
5
      ∇Z←GETH
[1]   Z←H
[2]   ∇
      GETH
5
      H←2
      GETH
2
```

Another example is the $RTR3$ function defined previously. That is:

```
      |∇R←X RTR3  Y
[1]   |D←((X*2)+Y*2)*.5
[2]   |P←X+Y+D
[3]   |A←.5×X×Y
[4]   |R←D,P,A
[5]   |∇
```

In the function, the variables D, P, and A are used as temporary variables —but might possibly conflict with important variables outside of the function definition. For example:

```
      |P←1.0545E¯27
      |A←6.02250E23
      |D←0.367894411
      |T←3 RTR3  4
      |P
12
      |A
6
      |D
5
```

Thus, the values D, P, and A that were stored previously have been respecified from within the invoked function.

In a case such as this, the variables D, P, and A could have been declared as local variables. A *local variable* is one that retains its value only within the execution of the function in which it is declared. A variable which is local to a function is *dominant* over global variables with the same name when that function is active. Local variables for a function are placed as a list after the function prototype in the function header statement. Each local variable listed in the function header must be preceded by a semicolon. For example:*

---

*The system command)CLEAR activates a clean workspace for the user. A clean workspace contains no defined functions, variables, or other system conditions.

```
              )CLEAR
CLEAR    WS
              ∇R←X RTR3 Y;P;D
[1]      D←((X*2)+Y*2)*.5
[2]      P←X×Y+D
[3]      A←.5×X×Y
[4]      R←D,P,A
[5]      ∇
              P←1.0545E⁻27
              A←6.02250E23
              T←3 RTR3 4
              P
1.0545E⁻27
              A
6
              D
VALUE    ERROR
              D
              ∧
```

Local variables are particularly useful when developing a function that is to be used by a number of people to avoid conflict with variables that might otherwise be in use as global variables.

Function Modification

In the course of developing a function, especially at the terminal, many problems arise which require that the function be modified in some way. In most cases, the modification involves a display of the function (or part of it) followed by an addition, deletion, insertion, or replacement of one or more statements.

As mentioned previously, the body of a function is not checked by the computer as it is entered—however, the function header is. This fact is used with examples of function editing. The following function is defined for use in examples:

```
              ∇DUMMYFCN
[1]      LINE1
[2]      LINE2
[3]      LINE3
[4]      LINE4
[5]      LINE5
[6]      LINE6
[7]      ∇
```

The various methods of modifying a function are presented in the following form:

Type of modification or operation,
Comments (if any),
General form, and
An example.

FCN is used as a dummy function name and *N* is a statement number.

1. *List a closed function.*
   General form:

$$\nabla FCN[\square] \nabla$$

   Example:

```
        |∇DUMMYFCN[□]∇
     ∇  |DUMMYFCN
 [1]    |LINE1
 [2]    |LINE2
 [3]    |LINE3
 [4]    |LINE4
 [5]    |LINE5
 [6]    |LINE6
     ∇  |
```

2. *List a closed function and leave it open to perform additional modifications.*
   General form:

$$\nabla FCN[\square]$$

   Example:

```
        |∇DUMMYFCN[□]
     ∇  |DUMMYFCN
 [1]    |LINE1
 [2]    |LINE2
 [3]    |LINE3
 [4]    |LINE4
 [5]    |LINE5
 [6]    |LINE6
     ∇  |
 [7]    |
```

3. *List an open function.*
   General form:

   $$[\Box]$$

   Example:

   ```
   ∇LISTFCN
   [1]   LINE1
   [2]   LINE2
   [3]   [□]
         ∇ LISTFCN
   [1]   LINE1
   [2]   LINE2
         ∇
   [3]
   ```

4. *List an open function and leave definition mode.*
   General form:

   $$[\Box]\,\nabla$$

   Example:

   ```
   ∇LISTFCN
   [1]   LINE1
   [2]   LINE2
   [3]   [□]∇
         ∇ LISTFCN
   [1]   LINE1
   [2]   LINE2
         ∇
   ```

5. *Display a statement of a closed function.*
   General form:

   $$\nabla\,FCN[N\,\Box]\,\nabla$$

   Example:

   ```
         ∇DUMMYFCN[4□]∇
   [4]   LINE4
   ```

6. *Display a statement of a closed function and leave it open for further modification.*
General form:

$$\triangledown\ FCN[N\square]$$

Example:

```
                 ▽DUMMYFCN[ 3□]]
         [3]     LINE3
         [3]
```

7. *Display a statement of an open function and leave definition mode.*
General form:

$$[N\square]\ \triangledown$$

Example:

```
                 ▽LISTFCN
         [1]     LINE1
         [2]     LINE2
         [3]     LINE3
         [4]     [2□]▽
         [2]     LINE2
```

8. *Display a statement of an open function and change it.*
General form:

$$[N\square]$$

Example:

```
                 ▽LISTFCN
         [1]     LINE1
         [2]     LINE2
         [3]     LINE3
         [4]     [2□]
         [2]     LINE2
         [2]     LINE TWO
         [3]     [□]▽
             ▽   LISTFCN
         [1]     LINE1
         [2]     LINE TWO
         [3]     LINE3
             ▽
```

9. *List a closed function beginning with line N leaving it open or closed.*
General forms:

$$\nabla \ FCN[\square N]$$
$$\nabla \ FCN[\square N] \ \nabla$$

Examples:

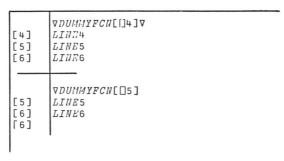

```
            ∇DUMMYFCN[[]4]∇
    [4]     LINE4
    [5]     LINE5
    [6]     LINE6


            ∇DUMMYFCN[□5]
    [5]     LINE5
    [6]     LINE6
    [6]
```

10. *Display a function header.*
General forms:

$$\nabla \ FCN[0 \ \square] \ \nabla$$
$$[0\square]$$

Examples:

```
            ∇DUMMYFCN[0□]∇
    [0]     DUMMYFCN


            ∇LISTFCN
    [1]     LINE1
    [2]     [0□]
    [0]     LISTFCN
    [0]
```

Thus, a function header has statement number zero. It can be modified, as any other statement, using that statement number.

11. *Override a statement number.*
General form:

$$[N]...$$

Example:

```
            ∇DUMMYFCN
    [7]     [3] LINE THREE
    [4]     [7] LINE7
    [8]
```

12. *Insert a statement.*
    General form:

    $$[N.M]...$$

    Example:

```
      │∇DUMMYFCN
[8]   │[4.2] INSERT LINE
[4.3] │[□]
    ∇ │DUMMYFCN
[1]   │LINE1
[2]   │LINE2
[3]   │LINE THREE
[4]   │LINE4
[4.2] │INSERT LINE
[5]   │LINE5
[6]   │LINE6
[7]   │LINE7
    ∇ │
[8]   │∇
      │∇DUMMYFCN[□]∇
    ∇ │DUMMYFCN
[1]   │LINE1
[2]   │LINE2
[3]   │LINE THREE
[4]   │LINE4
[5]   │INSERT LINE
[6]   │LINE5
[7]   │LINE6
[8]   │LINE7
    ∇ │
```

In the preceding example, the statements are renumbered when the function is closed.

13. *Delete a statement.*
    Comment: This operation is essentially implementation-dependent.
    General forms:

    [N] *line feed*   (IBM 1050 terminal)
    [N] *attention*   (IBM 2741 terminal)

Example:

```
           ∇DUMMYFCN
[9]        [5]
               ∇

[6]        [□]
       ∇   DUMMYFCN
[1]        LINE1
[2]        LINE2
[3]        LINE THREE
[4]        LINE4
[6]        LINE5
[7]        LINE6
[8]        LINE7
       ∇
[9]        ∇
           ∇DUMMYFCN[□]∇
       ∇   DUMMYFCN
[1]        LINE1
[2]        LINE2
[3]        LINE THREE
[4]        LINE4
[5]        LINE5
[6]        LINE6
[7]        LINE7
       ∇
```

14. *Enter the definition mode for an existing function.*
    General form:

$$\nabla FCN$$

Example:

```
           ∇DUMMYFCN
[8]
```

15. *Open a function, change a statement, and leave the definition mode.*
    General form:

$$\nabla FCN[N]... \ \nabla$$

Example:

```
              ∇DUMMYFCN[1] LINE ONE∇
              ∇DUMMYFCN[□]∇
         ∇    DUMMYFCN
   [1]        LINE ONE
   [2]        LINE2
   [3]        LINE THREE
   [4]        LINE4
   [5]        LINE5
   [6]        LINE6
   [7]        LINE7
         ∇
```

16. *Open a function, change a statement,* and *remain in the definition mode.*
   General form:

$$\nabla FCN[N]...$$

   Example:

```
              ∇DUMMYFCN[1] LINE WON
   [2]        [□]
         ∇    DUMMYFCN
   [1]        LINE WON
   [2]        LINE2
   [3]        LINE THREE
   [4]        LINE4
   [5]        LINE5
   [6]        LINE6
   [7]        LINE7
         ∇
   [8]
```

The closing del need not be placed in a separate statement. A del found anywhere in a statement, except a comment line or within quotes, will close that definition.

A *comment line* may be inserted with the composite character ⍝, formed by overstriking a ∘ with a ∩, which must be the first character of a line. ⍝ is called the *lamp* symbol, for example:

```
              ∇R←X PLUS Y
   [1]        ⍝ THIS IS A VERY SIMPLE FCN
   [2]        R←X+Y
   [3]        ⍝ THIS DEL DOES NOT END FCN ∇
   [4]        ⍝ BUT THE NEXT ONE DOES ...
   [5]        ∇

              1 PLUS 2
   3
```

6.3 SEQUENCE AND CONTROL

As mentioned previously, statements within a function are executed sequentially. It is well known, on the other hand, that many algorithmic processes require that parts of a function be repeated. The branch operation in APL provides a facility whereby the normal sequence of operation is interrupted and execution of the function is resumed with another statement.

Exit from a Function

Thus far, a function has been entered at its first statement, that is, statement number one, and it was executed until no statements remained. In other words, control flowed out of the function. The branch operation, to be covered next, passes program control to a given statement, by means of its statement number. It can also be used to exit from a function by branching to a statement numbered zero or to a nonexistent statement number. The three ways of exiting from a function are summarized as follows:

1. By flowing out of the function.
2. By branching to a statement numbered zero.
3. By branching to a nonexistent statement number.

Branching

The general form of the *branch operation* is:

$$\rightarrow S$$

where S is any program constituent that can be reduced to a numeric value. The branch is a monadic operation and causes execution of the function to be directed to the statement numbered by the value of the expression to the right of the branch operator. In a statement with a branch operation, no symbols can appear to the left of the branch operator.* If the operand of the branch operator is omitted, the current function is terminated as well as the entire sequence of functions (if any) which invoked the current function.

Branching can be used in a variety of ways. If $N=3$ and $V=3\ 4\ 5\ 7$, for example, then all of the following branch statements transfer function control to the statement numbered 3:

$$\rightarrow 3$$
$$\rightarrow N$$
$$\rightarrow V$$

*Except a statement label followed by a colon (covered in the next section).

In the latter case, the system always uses the first element of a vector to determine the number of the statement to which to branch. This convention is described more formally later. The operand to the branch operator can also be an expression. If $N = 3$, then the following statement:

$$\rightarrow(N*2)+1$$

branches to statement numbered 10. In the next example, the computer branches to the statement numbered 10 if $A > B$ and to statement numbered 20 if $A \leq B$:

$$\rightarrow((A>B)\times 10)+(A\leq B)\times 20$$

The following script, which contains a function to compute gross pay, uses a branch operation similar to the one just mentioned:

```
        ∇PAY←HOURS GROSSPAY RATE
[1]     →((HOURS≤40)×2)+(HOURS>40)×4
[2]     PAY←RND HOURS×RATE
[3]     →0
[4]     PAY←RND RATE×40+1.5×HOURS-40
[5]     ∇
        35 GROSSPAY 1.00
35
        40 GROSSPAY 2.50
100
        50 GROSSPAY 1.63
89.65
        32 GROSSPAY 2.19
70.08
```

The function uses the RND function to round the gross pay to two decimal places.

```
        ∇R←RND T
[1]     R←(⌊0.5+100×T)÷100∇
```

The next function,* which builds a table of integers along with their squares and cubes, exhibits a situation where a branch is taken or an exit is made from the function.

*This version will be improved upon in subsequent examples.

```
      ∇TABLE N;I
[1]   →(N>0)×2
[2]   I←0
[3]   I←I+1
[4]   I,(I*2),(I*3)
[5]   →(I≤N)×3
[6]   ∇

      TABLE 5
1   1   1
2   4   8
3   9   27
4   16  64
5   25  125
6   36  216
```

After this brief introduction, the branching operation can be treated in more detail. In the statement

$$\to S$$

the numeric value of S determines the statement number of the statement to be executed next. S may also indicate that the function is to be terminated, in which case a statement from a calling function is executed next. The following conditions apply:

1. If the value of $1\uparrow S$ is a statement number in the function being executed, then the next statement executed is the one numbered as $1\uparrow S$.
2. If the value $1\uparrow S$ is not a statement number in the function being executed, then the execution of the function terminates.
3. If S is an empty vector, then no branch takes place and the next statement in sequence is executed.

The last case has not been seen before and can take a variety of forms. In general, an empty (i.e., null) vector can be computed in the following ways: $0/S$, $0\rho S$, and $S\times\iota 0$. Given an expression XrY which can produce the value 0 or 1, then the following statements:

$$\to(XrY)/S$$
$$\to(XrY)\rho S$$
$$\to S\times\iota XrY$$

branch to statement numbered S or execute the next statement depending upon whether XrY produces the value 1 or 0, respectively.* Note here

*Ordinarily, r will be one of the operators: $<\ \leq\ =\ \geq\ >\ \neq\ \vee\ \wedge\ \not\vee\ \not\wedge\ \epsilon$.

that S can be zero resulting in a branch-out of the function if the relationship XrY is true. For example:

```
        ∇BFCN
[1]     'ENTRY'
[2]     →(X>Y)/S
[3]     'CONTINUE'
[4]     →0
[5]     'BRANCH TAKEN'
[6]     ∇
        X←10
        Y←5
        S←5
        BFCN
ENTRY
BRANCH TAKEN
        X←0
        BFCN
ENTRY
CONTINUE
        X←10
        S←0
        BFCN
ENTRY
```

A branch to one of two statements $S1$ or $S2$ can be specified in the following ways:

$$→(S1, S2)[1+XrY]$$
$$→((XrY), \sim XrY)/S1,S2$$

Clearly, the last form can be extended, as required. A branch to one of several statements can be specified as:

$$→ N\phi L$$

or

$$→L[N]$$

where N is a counter, L is a vector of statement numbers, ϕ is the rotation operator, and the branch operation selects $1 \uparrow L$ as the statement number of the next statement to be executed.

As examples of the preceding variations, consider three simple problems:

   1. Generation of N terms in the Fibonacci sequence.*

*Introduced in Section 5.2.

2. Evaluating the step function:

$$y=0, \qquad \text{if } x \le 0$$
$$y=13.2, \quad \text{if } 0 < x < 131.4$$
$$y=50, \qquad \text{if } x \ge 131.4$$

3. Providing a multibranch function *TROUBLEREPORT* whose operand is an integer indicating an error message to be selected.

All three functions are provided in the next script.

```
       ∇L←FIB N;I
[1]    →(N≥2)/4
[2]    'VALUE ERROR'
[3]    →0
[4]    L←1 2
[5]    I←2
[6]    →(I≥N)/0
[7]    L←L,L[(ρL)-1]+L[ρL]
[8]    I←I+1
[9]    →6
[10]   ∇

       FIB 5
1   2  3   5   8
       FIB 10
1   2  3   5   8   13   21   34   55   89


       ∇Y←STPFCN X
[1]    →((X≤0),((X>0)∧X≤131.4),X>131.4)/2 3 5
[2]    →Y←0
[3]    Y←13.2
[4]    →0
[5]    Y←50
[6]    ∇

       STPFCN ‾1
0
       STPFCN 100
13.2
       STPFCN 1E3
50
```

```
        ∇E←TROUBLEREPORT I;L
[1]     →((I>5)∨I≤0)/14
[2]     L←2×1+ι6
[3]     →(I-1)⌽L
[4]     E←'NUMBER NOT IN SYSTEM'
[5]     →0
[6]     E←'INCORRECT SIGN-ON'
[7]     →0
[8]     E←'ALREADY SIGNED ON'
[9]     →0
[10]    E←'NUMBER IN USE'
[11]    →0
[12]    E←'NUMBER LOCKED OUT'
[13]    →0
[14]    'IMPROPER TROUBLE REPORT'
[15]    →
[16]    ∇


        TROUBLEREPORT 2
INCORRECT SIGN-ON
        TROUBLEREPORT 5
NUMBER LOCKED OUT
        TROUBLEREPORT 10
IMPROPER TROUBLE REPORT
```

Statement Labels

One of the disadvantages of branching, as it has been presented thus far, is that function modification can rearrange the statement numbers, requiring a probable modification of some branching statements as well. APL obviates this difficulty by permitting statements to be given a name, called a statement label. A *statement label* is an ordinary scalar variable which has the value of the statement number with which it is associated. A statement label is local to the function in which it is used and assumes its value when the function definition is closed and resequencing has been performed.

A statement is given a label by preceding the body of the statement by a name and separating the two with a semicolon as follows:

$$LOOP\colon\ A \leftarrow B + C$$
$$\vdots$$
$$\rightarrow LOOP$$

The following script, which uses statement labels, modifies the previous *TABLE* program so that the output is produced in columns that are vertically aligned:

```
        ∇TABLE N;I
[1]     →(N≤0)/ERROR
[2]     OUTP←ι0
[3]     I←0
[4]     NEXTI: →(N<I←I+1)/PRINT
[5]     OUTP←OUTP,I,(I*2),(I*3)
[6]     →NEXTI
[7]     PRINT: (N,3)ρOUTP
[8]     →0
[9]     ERROR: 'INVALID OPERAND TO ''TABLE'' FCN'
[10]    ∇

        )DIGITS 3
WAS 10
        TABLE 6


        1          1          1
        2          4          8
        3          9         27
        4         16         64
        5         25        125
        6         36        216


        TABLE 0
INVALID OPERAND TO 'TABLE' FCN
```

Upon reviewing the output, it seems reasonable to edit the above function so that an appropriate title is given:

```
          ∇TABLE[1.1]
[1.1]     ' '
[1.2]     '      N           N*2           N*3'
[1.3]     ∇
          ∇TABLE[□]∇
    ∇     TABLE N;I
[1]       →(N≤0)/ERROR
[2]       ' '
[3]       '      N           N*2           N*3'
[4]       OUTP←ι0
[5]       I←0
[6]       NEXTI:→(N<I←I+1)/PRINT
[7]       OUTP←OUTP,I,(I*2),(I*3)
[8]       →NEXTI
[9]       PRINT:(N,3)ρOUTP
[10]      →0
[11]      ERROR:'INVALID OPERAND TO ''TABLE'' FCN'
    ∇


          TABLE 5

      N          N*2          N*3

      1            1            1
      2            4            8
      3            9           27
      4           16           64
      5           25          125
```

Looping

When an algorithm requires that a sequence of steps be repeated, the corresponding program can be constructed in one of two ways: (1) The program steps can be duplicated the necessary number of times; and (2) the program can be written to execute the same steps iteratively. For long or complex programs, or when the exact number of iterations is not known beforehand, the iterative method is usually preferred.

A series of statements to be executed many times is called a *loop*, and the statements in the loop are called the *range of the loop* or the *body of the loop*. One pass through the loop is termed an *iteration*. A loop must be executed a certain number of times, and some mechanism must determine whether the required number has been reached. One of the mechanisms for doing this is a *control variable* which is set to a given value initially (usually zero) and is increased by another value (usually one) for each iteration that is to be made. The process also requires a *limit value*, which determines the upper limit on the number of iterations. Loops may also be programmed in another manner. The control variable may be set initially to the limit value and it is decreased for each iteration until zero is reached. If the control variable is used as an index or data value in the loop, then this use frequently determines the direction in which the control variable should be sequenced. In still other cases, a control variable is not required and the program iterates until a specified condition is met— such as a residual value being less than a certain

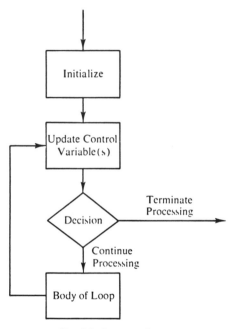

Fig. 6.1 Program loop.

tolerance value. Figure 6.1 depicts the required steps in a loop; they are summarized as follows:

1. *Initialization.* Variables are given initial values; special conditions are checked; and control variables are given appropriate values. Program control is never returned here.
2. *Update.* The control variable is updated to correspond to the next iteration.
3. *Decision.* A test is made whether the necessary number of iterations has been made. If so, then an exit is made from the loop; otherwise, control passes to the body of the loop.
4. *Body of the loop.* The required calculations are made for each iteration. Control passes to the update step.

The preceding steps have described the *method of leading decisions*. Clearly, it is feasible to place the decision step after the body of the loop—except in one case. That is when a check should be made to determine if the loop should be executed zero times. Because of the array operations in APL, the need for loops is diminished significantly. The next script computes the square root R of a value X and uses the following relationship:

$$R \leftarrow R + .5 \times (X \div R) - R$$

The program uses an initial guess $(R=1)$ and iterates until the residual $|(R*2) - X$ is less than a given tolerance E.

```
        ∇R←SQRT X;E
  [1]   →(X>0)/INIT
  [2]   'VALUE ERROR'
  [3]   →0
  [4]   INIT: E←.001
  [5]   R←1
  [6]   TEST: →((|(R*2)-X)<E)/0
  [7]   R←R+.5×(X÷R)-R
  [8]   →TEST
  [9]   ∇

        SQRT 1
  1
        SQRT 25
  5
        SQRT 6.25
  2.5
        SQRT ¯1
  VALUE ERROR
```

The next example uses a control variable and smooths a given function by a simple averaging method. Consider a vector X with indices running from 1 to ρX. A given component $X[I]$, for $I>1$ and $I<\rho X$, is smoothed by the expression:

$$S[I] = (X[I-1] + X[I] + X[I+1]) \div 3$$

The function returns a vector which has two less components than the original vector.

```
      ∇S←SMOOTH X;I;L
[1]   →((ρX)>3)/INIT
[2]   'DATA ERROR'
[3]   →0
[4]   INIT: I←1
[5]   L←(ρX)-1
[6]   S←ι0
[7]   LOOP: I←I+1
[8]   →(I>L)/0
[9]   S←S,(X[I-1]+X[I]+X[I+1])÷3
[10]  →LOOP
[11]  ∇

      SMOOTH 1 3 5 7 9
3  5  7
      SMOOTH 2 10 6 8 16 12 2 4 6 8 7
6  8  10  12  10  6  4  6  7
```

Collectively, defined functions and sequence and control facilities enable APL to be used as a programming language in addition to its direct mode of execution. One topic, usually associated with programming, has yet to be introduced: input and output. Although APL contains no facilities for file processing, it does contain operators for both character and numeric I/O. Moreover, input and output operators can be embedded in mathematical expressions and may be used as ordinary constants or variables are used.

6.4   INPUT AND OUTPUT

It is most desirable in a programming language to provide input facilities that are under control of a program that is being executed. That is, the program should be able to indicate to the user that it is time for him to enter some data. Output is not as significant, but a more general facility should be provided than simply permitting the user to enter a statement where the last operation is not a specification. The material is presented as four topics: numeric input, evaluated input, character input, and output.

Numeric Input

The quad symbol □ is used to indicate numeric input to a program. In this context, it can appear anywhere that a constant or variable can be used, except directly to the left of a specification operator. The computer halts execution of the statement containing the quad symbol and makes an input request to the terminal as shown below. After the desired value is entered, execution continues as though that value were actually a part of the statement. For example:

```
            X←2×□
    □:
            2
            X
    4
            Y←□÷□
    □:
            3
    □:
            6
            Y
    2
```

The computer prints the symbols □: to indicate that it is time to enter a value, spaces the carriage one line, and unlocks the keyboard. The user follows by typing the value and presses RETURN. The computer then continues with the execution of that statement. Consider another example:

```
            ∇ROOT;X
    [1]     LOOP:  X←□*.5
    [2]     X
    [3]     →LOOP
    [4]     ∇

            ROOT
    □:
            25
    5
    □:
            36
    6
    □:
            →
```

The example, as shown, contains what is termed an *input loop*. It is possible to escape from the □ request by typing → as was done in the example. If necessary, the input quad can be identified by preceding the statement containing the input quad with a statement that outputs an appropriate literal. The following examples give some other uses of the numeric input operation:

```
        ∇GAME
[1]     'ENTER 0, 1, 2, OR 3'
[2]     START: →□φ(A,B,C,BINGO)
[3]     A: 'SORRY, TRY AGAIN'
[4]     →START
[5]     B: 'WRONG AGAIN'
[6]     →START
[7]     C: 'GETTING WARMER'
[8]     →START
[9]     BINGO: 'BINGO'
[10]    ∇

        GAME
ENTER   0, 1, 2, OR 3
□:
        0
SORRY, TRY AGAIN
□:
        1
WRONG AGAIN
□:
        3
BINGO


        ∇STATEMENT
[1]     →□
[2]     'STATEMENT NO. TWO'
[3]     ∇
        STATEMENT
□:
        2
STATEMENT NO. TWO
        STATEMENT
□:
        0
```

Evaluated Input

The quad symbol, as used for input, is actually more general than implied previously. The input request is satisfied by any valid APL expression, which is evaluated at the time of entry, and substituted for the quad. For example:

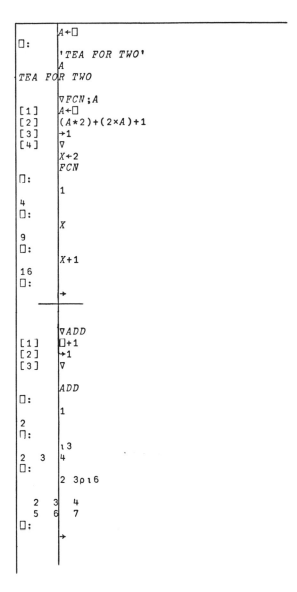

```
                A←□
        □:
                'TEA FOR TWO'
                A
    TEA FOR TWO

                ∇FCN;A
        [1]     A←□
        [2]     (A*2)+(2×A)+1
        [3]     →1
        [4]     ∇
                X←2
                FCN
        □:
                1
        4
        □:
                X
        9
        □:
                X+1
        16
        □:
                →
```

```
                ∇ADD
        [1]     □+1
        [2]     →1
        [3]     ∇

                ADD
        □:
                1
        2
        ⍞:
                ι3
        2   3   4
        □:
                2 3ρι6

            2   3   4
            5   6   7
        □:
                →
```

Character Input

The requirement that literals must be enclosed in quote symbols partially negates the generality of use principle of APL. The convention is particularly cumbersome for text editing applications where the eventual user may not be familiar with the APL language.

The quote-quad symbol ⍞ (formed by overstriking a quad symbol with a quote symbol) is used to enter character data. The operator functions in a manner similar to the quad operator with the following exceptions:

1. No input symbol is printed to alert the user.
2. The carriage is not indented.

The user types his character data *without* enclosing them in quote symbols. For example:

```
       T←▯
TEA FOR TWO
       T
TEA FOR TWO
       ρT
11
       V←▯
MISSION 'IMPOSSIBLE'
       V
MISSION 'IMPOSSIBLE'
       ρV
20
       C←▯
A
       ρC

       ρρC
0
```

An input loop can also occur with character input. An escape is provided with the following sequence: O, BACKSPACE, U, BACKSPACE, T. So that the symbols print as: *Ø*. For example:

```
       ∇ABC;B
[1]    B←▯
[2]    ρB
[3]    →1
[4]    ∇

       ABC
THESE EXAMPLES USE THE ▯ SYMBOL
31
-*-
3
BE CAREFUL OF φ
15
''
2
THE NEXT LINE WILL BE O-U-T
27
Ø
```

Output

A quad or quote-quad symbol appearing immediately to the left of a specification symbol indicates that the value of the expression to its right is to be printed. The output operation is frequently used in a long expression to print intermediate results or in a multiple specification statement. For example:

```
        □←X←Y←3*2
9
        B←' BYE'
        □←A←'GOOD',B
GOOD BYE
        □←A←'GOOD',B
GOOD BYE
        □←X←5
5
        B←□←2 6ρ□←A←4 3ρ ̄7 3 9 6 5 1 4 3 8 0 2 7

 ̄7  3  9
 6  5  1
 4  3  8
 0  2  7

 ̄7  3  9  6  5  1
 4  3  8  0  2  7
```

6.5 PROGRAM CHECKOUT

It is needless to say that all programs do not work correctly. The symptoms are usually obvious:* The program stops or incorrect results are computed. With a halted function, the user can diagnose the difficulty, modify his function, and continue. The reasons for incorrect results can be detected by a perusal of the statements, by tracing his function, or by inserting stops at various statements so that he can investigate the function at that point during the course of execution.

Halted Functions

A function is halted for one of two reasons: (1) The execution of a statement cannot be completed; and (2) the function runs for an inordinate length of time and the user presses the ATTN key to halt execution. Case (2) is actually part of case (1).

---

*In some problems in numerical analysis, it is difficult to determine whether or not the results are correct but that is a problem for numerical analysts and frequently involves algorithmic methods, accuracy, and test cases.

If the execution of a statement cannot be completed, the following steps ensue:

1. An error message (see Appendix B) is printed identifying the error that was encountered.
2. The name of the function and the statement number of the statement being processed are printed.
3. The erroneous statement is printed.
4. A caret is printed to indicate how far execution has progressed in that statement.

Thus, the execution of the active function is *suspended* and all functions which called for the execution of that function (either directly or indirectly) are left *pending*. A function in the latter state is said to be *pendent*. If a function is halted by the ATTN key, then only step 2 takes place. A suspended function remains suspended until one of three operations is given: (1) A branch, →*S*, is entered to resume execution at the statement whose number is *S*; (2) a branch to zero, →0, is given to terminate that function; and (3) a branch without a right operand, →, is entered to clear the suspended and pendent functions.

When a function is suspended, the system is in the execution mode and the user can perform calculations, define functions, and even modify the suspended function. He may not, however, modify a function that is pendent. Consider the following erroneous function:

```
        ∇EFCN
[1]     A←1
[2]     B←2
[3]     U←1∧∧1
[4]     A,B,U
[5]     ∇

        EFCN
SYNTAX ERROR
EFCN[3] U←1∧∧1
             ^
        5*2
25
        ∇R←X PLUS Y
[1]     R←X+Y
[2]     ∇
        1 PLUS 2
3
        ∇EFCN[3]U←1∧1∇
        →3
1    2  1
```

While *EFCN* was suspended, the user was able to define and execute another function. Then, *EFCN* was modified and execution was resumed.

The APL system contains a *state indicator* which gives a list of pendent and suspended functions. The state indicator is displayed with the system command)*SI*, which may be used at any time the system is in the direct mode. The)*SI* display requires some explanation. Consider the following display:

$$)SI$$
$$A[5] \quad *$$
$$B[6]$$
$$C[7]$$

Entries marked with an asterisk indicate suspended functions; other entries denote pendent functions. *A*[5] denotes that function *A* was suspended just before statement 5 was completed. *B*[6] means that function *A* was invoked in statement 6 of function *B*. *C*[7] indicates that function *B* was invoked from statement 7 of function *C*. The state indicator can be cleared by entering a → without an operand for each * in the list.

Tracing a Function

If a program gives incorrect results and the reason is not obvious from reviewing the statements, then the user has good reason to trace the execution of that function.

The trace of a function *FCN* is specified as follows:*

$$T\Delta FCN \leftarrow V$$

where *V* is a vector whose components correspond to statement numbers in *FCN*. Any statement in *FCN* whose statement number is in *V* is traced. The trace function works as follows: (1) The value of every statement, whether or not the last operation is a specification, is printed; and (2) the value of the expression to the right of a branch statement is printed. All output is identified by function and statement number. For example:

---

*It should be obvious now why names cannot begin with *T*Δ.

```
        ∇R←SQRT X;E
[1]     →(X>0)/INIT
[2]     'VALUE ERROR'
[3]     →0
[4]     INIT: E←.001
[5]     R←1
[6]     TEST: →((|(R*2)-X)<F/0
[7]     R←R+.5×(X÷R)-R
[8]     →TEST
[9]     ∇
        SQRT 1
DOMAIN ERROR
SQRT[6] TEST:→((|(R*2)-X)<F/0
                                ∧
        )ST
SQRT[6] *
        ∇SQRT[6] TEST: →((|(R*2)-X)<E)/0∇
        →6
1
        SQRT 1
1

        )DIGITS 3
WAS 10
        SQRT 25
5
        T∆SQRT←6 7
        SQRT 1
SQRT[6] 0
1
        SQRT 9
SQRT[6]
SQRT[7] 5
SQRT[6]
SQRT[7] 3.4
SQRT[6]
SQRT[7] 3.02
SQRT[6]
SQRT[7] 3
SQRT[6] 0
3
        SQRT 16
SQRT[6]
SQRT[7] 8.5
SQRT[6]
SQRT[7] 5.19
SQRT[6]
SQRT[7] 4.14
SQRT[6]
SQRT[7] 4
SQRT[6]
SQRT[7] 4
SQRT[6] 0
4
        T∆SQRT←10
        SQRT 4
2
        )DIGITS 10
WAS 3
```

The expression $T\Delta FCN \leftarrow 0$ or $T\Delta FCN \leftarrow \iota0$ discontinues the trace.

Stop Control

When program errors cannot be detected with the trace function, then it is necessary to halt execution at specific statements so that the user can "poke" around to ascertain the status of variables and indicators. The stop control feature operates very similarly to the trace function and serves that purpose. A statement of the form:

$$S\Delta FCN \leftarrow V$$

is used to establish stop control. Here, *FCN* is the function under study and *V* is a vector of statement numbers. Execution of the function is halted *just before* each statement whose statement number is in *V*. For example:

```
         A←B←C←D←0
         ∇SFCN
   [1]   A←1
   [2]   B←2
   [3]   C←3
   [4]   D←4
   [5]   'FINI'
   [6]   ∇
         S∆SFCN←2 4
         SFCN

   SFCN[2]
         B
   0
         →2

   SFCN[4]
         D
   0
         →4
   FINI
         A,B,C,D
   1   2 3   4
         S∆SFCN←0
         SFCN
   FINI
```

The function name and statement number is printed each time the function is halted. Stop control is discontinued by $S\Delta FCN \leftarrow 0$ or $S\Delta FCN \leftarrow \iota0$.

Program checkout in an APL environment is affected significantly by the interactive mode of operation. When the user does not have terminal facilities, checkout is enhanced by inserting output statements at appropriate places in the program. When the program is completely verified, then the output statements can be removed.

6.6   ANNOTATED SCRIPT OF TOPICS IN PROGRAMMING

Defined Functions

```
        ∇P←X TIMES Y
[1]     P←X×Y
[2]     ∇
        2 TIMES 2
4
        Z←(25*.5) TIMES 2+2
        Z
20
        X←10
        ∇R←ABS X
[1]     R←X⌈-X
[2]     ∇
        ABS ¯5
5
        X
10
        ∇ATTR V
[1]     SUM←+/V
[2]     MAX←⌈/V
[3]     MIN←⌊/V
[4]     RNGE←MAX-MIN+1
[5]     AV←(+/V)÷ρV
[6]     ∇
        ATTR ι6
        SUM,MAX,MIN,RNGE,AV
21   6  1   4   3.5
        ∇ATTR
[6]     [0]R←ATTR V
[1]     [6]R←SUM,MAX,MIN,RNGE,AV
[7]     [□]
      ∇ R←ATTR V
[1]     SUM←+/V
[2]     MAX←⌈/V
[3]     MIN←⌊/V
[4]     RNGE←MAX-MIN+1
[5]     AV←(+/V)÷ρV
[6]     R←SUM,MAX,MIN,RNGE,AV
      ∇
[7]     ∇
        ATTR ι6
21   6  1   4   3.5
        ∇ATTR[0]R←ATTR V;SUM;MAX;MIN;RNGE;AV∇
        SUM←100
        ATTR ι2
3   2   1   0   1.5
        SUM
100
```

Function header (dyadic function   explicit result).
End of function definition.
Execution of function.
Defined function embedded in expression.

Value of X specified.
Monadic function header.
R and X are dummy variables.

X retains value of 10.

Function header (implicit result).
V is dummy variable.
SUM, MAX, MIN, $RNGE$, and AV are global variables.

No explicit result.

Reopen function definition.
Change function header.
Add statement.
Display function.

Close of display.
Close function definition.
Explicit result

Make SUM, MAX, MIN, $RNGE$, and AV local variables and assign value to SUM.

SUM retains global value

```
       ∇L←FIB N;I
[1]    →(N≥2)/FIBSTART
[2]    'VALUE ERROR'
[3]    →0
[4]    FIBSTART:L←1 2
[5]    I←2
[6]    FIBTEST:→(I≥N)/0
[7]    L←L,L[(ρL)-1]+L[ρL]
[8]    I←I+1
[9]    →FIBTEST∇

       FIB 7
1   2  3   5   8   13   21
       T∆FIB←4 5 7 8
       FIB 7
FIB[4]  1   2
FIB[5]  2
FIB[7]  1   2   3
FIB[8]  3
FIB[7]  1   2   3   5
FIB[8]  4
FIB[7]  1   2   3   5   8
FIB[8]  5
FIB[7]  1   2   3   5   8   13
FIB[8]  6
FIB[7]  1   2   3   5   8   13   21
FIB[8]  7
1   2  3   5   8   13   21
       T∆FIB←0

       ∇X TABLE Y
[1]    X∘.*ιY
[2]    ∇
       2 3 5TABLE 4
```

Define function with statement labels and branching.

Close definition.

Set trace on statements 4,5,7, and 8.

Discontinue trace.

Function definition (two arguments implicit result).

	3	5
2	3	5
4	9	25
8	27	125
16	81	625

```
       )DIGITS 3
WAS 10
       2 3 5 TABLE 4
```

Display only 3 digits of a numeric value.

2	3	5
4	9	25
8	27	125
16	81	625

```
       )DIGITS 10
WAS 3
```

Reestablish normal printing.

Input and Output

```
        'FIVE FACTORIAL IS ';!5              Mixed output.
FIVE FACTORIAL IS 120
        ∇FACTORIAL
[1]     K←□                                  Request for evaluated input   uses quad symbol.
[2]     K;' FACTORIAL IS ';!K
[3]     →1
[4]     ∇
        FACTORIAL                            Invoke function.
□:                                           Request for input.
        4                                    Carriage moved up one line and indented.
4 FACTORIAL IS 24
□:
        X←3                                  Input may be expression.
3 FACTORIAL IS 6
□:
        X+5                                  Evaluated input.
8 FACTORIAL IS 40320
□:
        →                                    Escape from input loop.

        ∇CHARACTERS
[1]     'LENGTH IS ';ρ▯                      Character input   uses quote-quad symbol.
[2]     →1
[3]     ∇
        CHARACTERS                           Invoke function.
ABC                                          Keyboard unlocked but not indented   no quote
LENGTH IS 3                                      marks required.
A       B
LENGTH IS 7
BE CAREFUL OF THE SYMBOL φ
LENGTH IS 26
NEXT IS 'O-U-T'
LENGTH IS 15
                                             Escape from character input loop by entering: O,
                                             BACKSPACE, U, BACKSPACE, T.
```

7 | COMPUTER SYSTEMS AND DEVICES

7.1 BASIC SYSTEMS CONCEPTS

Certainly, there is more to computing than using a well-designed language via a remote terminal device. First, the equipment must be selected, configured, and then either purchased or leased. Many factors must be taken into consideration: characteristics of the equipment, areas of application, requirements, conversion, compatibility, growth potential—to name only a few. Next, the equipment must be operated; when, how, and by whom is frequently of major significance. Lastly, programs must be either developed or obtained in some way. Often, in fact, the cost of programs exceeds the cost of the equipment itself. No major solution to these problems is given—perhaps no easy solution exists. Yet, the reader, whether he be an APL user, a FORTRAN programmer, or a manager or administrator, must be familiar with the major problem areas of installation management. Not all users have access to an APL system or even a computer with remote computing facilities, but most scientists, engineers, analysts, or managers depend on computers in their work and have to deal with subsidiary problems, such as these, that exist in the world of automatic computation.

Factors in Systems Design and Evaluation

Although the processor is the most expensive unit in a computer system, its functioning, and its selection as well, is usually obscured by the total system configuration and the other units in the system; that is, the storage unit and the various input/output units. If the purpose of the system is to service a real-time need, then the speed of the processor is usually determined by the timing requirements of a physical process. If the computer system is to be used for general-purpose computing, then the amount of storage, the speed and type of I/O units, and the overall system organization also affect the effectiveness of the system.

The selection of a processing unit for a given application is usually based on five factors: the basic speed of the machine measured in machine cycles per *something*, the time required for the execution of critical instructions, the appropriateness of the instruction repertoire* to the projected work load, the functional organization of the processing unit, and other technoeconomic factors not necessarily related directly to the functioning of the devices under consideration. These factors are summarized in Table 7.1 along with those for selection of storage units and input/out-

TABLE 7.1   SYSTEM DESIGN FACTORS

Processing Unit	*Storage Unit*	*I/O Units*
1. Basic speed (cycles per)	1. Basic speed (accesses per)	1. Data rates
2. Time required for execution of critical instructions	2. Size	2. Access time
3. Instruction repertoire	3. Organization (inter-leaving)	3. Storage capacity
4. Width of data path	4. Width of data path	4. Data organization (serial, direct)
5. Processor organization (parallelism, registers)		5. Data channel capacity
6. Technoeconomic factors		

put units. Appropriate evaluation and analysis techniques are given in Table 7.2. The organization of the processing unit is particularly significant and relates to factors other than the raw speed of the circuitry. Two areas are usually candidates for study: the dependence upon references to storage and the implementation of parallel processes. The dependence upon storage is usually minimized by providing *multiple arithmetic registers* and by fetching instructions ahead of sequence and holding them in an *instruction* stack.† Parallel processes are implemented through mul-

---

*That is, the extent to which frequently used operations must be synthesized from more elementary operations.

†In fact, in the IBM System/360 model 195 and in the CDC 7600, it is frequently possible to retain an entire loop in the instruction stack.

TABLE 7.2 COMPUTER EVALUATION AND ANALYSIS TECHNIQUES

Technique Used	Area of Widespread Use
1. Cycle time	Measures the speed of storage or a processing unit. Used mainly as a general indication of system capability.
2. Add time	Used mainly to compare high-performance scientific systems. This measure is usually combined with other evaluation techniques.
3. Instruction times	Compares the relative times for a given set of basic instructions. Frequently used to obtain an overall feeling for the speed of a processor.
4. Instruction mix	Gives the time required to execute a *set* of instructions, which are representative of a given class of programs. Usually combined with techniques (1), (2), and (3) for evaluating high-performance scientific systems.
5. Kernel problems	Representative programs are coded using the instruction repertoire of the computer being evaluated. Gives a measure of internal computing speed.
6. Benchmark job streams	A means of measuring the throughput of a system. A collection of jobs is run and the total elapsed time is measured. This technique is affected by I/O performance and the software available with the computer system.
7. Simulation	A complete computer system is simulated by another computer system. Particularly useful during the design phase of computer development.

tiple execution units for arithmetic operations and by partially executing instructions along the branch and no-branch paths while waiting for the completion of a conditional instruction.

The storage unit is important for two reasons: (1) It determines the number* of programs that can reside in high-speed storage and the effective size of each; and (2) it regulates the speed of the processing unit since the instructions and operands (i.e., data) are stored there and must be retrieved before execution can take place. Therefore, the actual size of main storage and the manner in which it is organized is usually of concern. With regard to the latter case, speed is hampered by the fact that most storage mechanisms are *destructive* in the sense that once a unit of

*Chapter 8 contains a description of multiprogramming and time sharing wherein two or more programs share high-speed storage.

data is fetched, another unit cannot be fetched until the first unit is effectively restored.*   Therefore, it is desirable to have the storage unit organized into two or more banks so that information can be fetched from one bank while the other is in a restore cycle. The width of the data path from the storage unit to the processing unit is also relevant. If, for example, the operand for a particular instruction requires eight bytes and the width of the data path is only four bytes, then two storage fetches are required before execution of that instruction can be initiated.

In spite of the complexity and importance of the processing and storage units, the biggest hindrance to good system design and performance is input and output (I/O). The difficulty is not surprising due to the fact that I/O devices are electromechanical while the processing unit and storage are electronic. However, significant advances have been made. In early computers (see Figure 7.1), all data entering or leaving the system had to pass through the processing unit on their way to or from storage, requiring that the system run effectively at I/O speeds. The *data channel* (also Figure 7.1), which is generally regarded as a small hardware-wired proc-

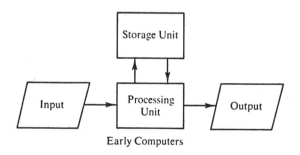

Early Computers

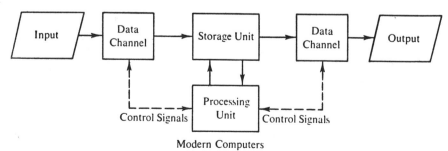

Modern Computers

Fig. 7.1 Input/output and system organization.

*Which, as a matter of fact, is performed automatically by the circuitry.

essing unit used only for the transfer of data, has enabled I/O devices to communicate directly with storage, allowing processing and input/output to overlap to some degree—that is, if provided for in the computer programs. Fortunately, efficient methods of doing input/output are available with most operating systems and programming languages.

Evaluation of a prospective computer system in light of the complexity of modern computers is indeed an involved process. Factors affecting a decision or sequence of decisions are as often economic and political as they are technical. Nevertheless various methods have been used to assess the potential effectiveness of a computer system and are summarized in Table 7.2. Some techniques measure raw computing speed and are useful for applications requiring high internal speeds, such as particle physics, or for those where the internal performance must be known explicitly to satisfy the needs of a physical process. Other evaluation techniques measure sequences of instructions and even total system throughput—a term which implies the maximum amount of work that a complete system can do in a given period of time. Simulation is another useful device for evaluating or analyzing performance and relies on another computer to obtain the best results from the simulation effort.

The performance of a system is influenced to such an extent by system organization and input/output facilities that both are presented as separate sections in this chapter. Section 7.2 presents the most popular ways that systems are organized to increase performance, and Section 7.3 compares I/O devices and mass storage facilities that are currently available commercially.

Yet, other factors, which can only be mentioned in passing, influence system evaluation. The problem of *conversion*, that is, converting an installation's programs to run on the new machine, is of major consequence for installations with a large investment in programming. Standard programming languages such as FORTRAN and COBOL are definite assets in this respect. The possibility of *growth* should also be of concern. The capability of adding storage boxes or I/O units without changing the processing unit can solve many problems caused by the natural increase in data and in new applications.

Computer System Operation

The effectiveness of a computer system is greatly affected by the methods used for operation. Three methods have come into widespread use: the open shop, the closed shop, and time sharing. The *open shop* is characterized by the fact that users make arrangements for a block of computer time and have complete use of the system during that period. The open-shop system is particularly attractive to small scientific installations, data processing, or applications requiring a given level of security. The *closed shop* requires that the user submit his job to the computer center so that it can be run on the computer by operations personnel so as to satisfy installation guidelines. *Time sharing*, which exists in several forms, permits the user to access the computer system from a remote location using data communication facilities. Whereas in the open shop the user has access to the machine proper, the user rarely even sees the equipment in the closed-shop and time-sharing environments. An operating system (see Chapter 8) is normally used in a closed shop to obtain machine operating efficiency.

Programs

Without programs, a computer system is very little more than a showpiece—although a very dramatic and useful one indeed. Programs can be categorized in a variety of ways, depending upon the objectives of the person doing the classification. The needs of the user can best be met with the following categories: software, application packages, and problem programs. There is considerable overlap between the categories; however, the objective here is to give the reader a clear picture of the various kinds of programs.

Software generally includes the programs necessary to use the computer. Included in this category are *system control programs* (also known as operating systems, control programs, executive programs, and system monitors), *compilers* and *assemblers* (that are used to translate source programs into machine language programs), and *utility programs* (such as programs to dump core storage, initialize direct-access storage, etc.) necessary for maintaining a computer installation. Software is usually available from the computer manufacturer without charge or for a slight fee depending upon whether he has unbundled* or not. Software is also available from a software development company on a lease or proprietary basis or can be developed in-house.

Application packages are usually developed by computer manufacturers or software development companies to solve a well-defined class of problems. Included in this category are general-purpose programs related to the following topics: sort/merge, matrix algebra, linear programming, differential equations, report generation—to give only a few examples. Competition is keen in this category and the prospective user does well by surveying what is available.

Although many computer scientists would classify compilers, assemblers, utility programs, and application packages as problem programs, the category is reserved here for those programs developed by an installa-

---

Unbundling refers to the practice of pricing hardware and software separately.

tion for use there—or in a similar environment elsewhere—and which are not generally for sale. Payroll, inventory, scheduling, and most scientific programs fall into this class. Although most problem programs are developed in-house by professional programmers, analysts, scientists, engineers, and even contract programmers, they are occasionally developed by a software firm on a contract basis.

The category into which a particular program is placed is not of great importance. The important point is that the various kinds of programs do exist and that the interested reader should be made aware of that fact.

The Equipment—Purchase, Rent, Lease, or Buy Time

The installation in need of computing equipment has two alternatives: install the equipment in-house or buy time, as needed, from another installation. Frequently, an installation will do both as the work load increases and then sell time once the new equipment is installed.

In-house equipment can be purchased, rented, or leased from a computer-leasing company. A sophisticated (i.e., with respect to the use of computers) user with a substantial programming staff and a work load in excess of two eight-hour shifts per day is well off by purchasing equipment, if the financial arrangements can be made. Otherwise, rental from a computer manufacturer or lease from a leasing company is necessary. Computer manufacturers, as a rule, give shift premiums after the first shift, making rental attractive. As with many other commodities, the renter can usually expect modern equipment and conversion aids, whenever required. If an installation can be satisfied with equipment on a long-term basis, then perhaps the leasing company is a good alternative. The installation can reduce equipment costs considerably with a long-term agreement. With purchased or leased equipment, the installation must plan on maintenance services which are generally available from the manufacturer of the equipment.

Computer time is also available from service companies and from installations with excess time. From both sources, either a block of time is purchased or charges are made on an individual job basis. Individual charges are usually made on the basis of processor time, external storage, and operator time used. When a block of time is purchased, the group purchasing the time is frequently required to furnish their own operator and storage volumes.*

The remainder of the chapter is concerned with two topics: computer systems architecture and mass storage and input/output devices. These topics along with those that have been covered thus far should enable

---

*A storage volume is usually a removable unit of storage with a separate identity such as a reel of magnetic tape or a disc pack.

decision makers to effectively evaluate and install a prospective computer system.

7.2 COMPUTER SYSTEMS ARCHITECTURE

Systems programmers have developed ingenious methods to alleviate the I/O problem and to obtain more computing performance out of the processing unit. Several of these methods have influenced configuration and operability of the computer system and are presented here. In general, the system configurations involve adding at least another processing unit to the system complex; however, I/O problems are so acute that even the cost of adding another processor is usually justified.

Peripheral Computers

The use of a peripheral computer essentially replaces a potentially low-speed I/O medium with one of a higher speed. With early systems, and this is partially true today, most input to the system was on punched cards and a substantial amount of the output was to be printed. A nominal rate for card input is between 600 and 1000 80-column cards per

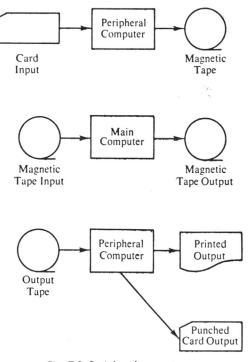

Fig. 7.2 Peripheral computers.

minute, and for printed output, it is 1000 to 1500 120-character lines per minute. These figures amount to an input rate of approximately 1200 characters per second and an output rate of approximately twice that amount or 2400 characters per second. The fact that an average figure for magnetic tape input/output is in the neighborhood of 100,000 characters per second led to the use of a peripheral computer to transfer input cards to tape and output information from magnetic tape to the printer or card punch, as shown in Figure 7.2. Thus, both input to and output from the main computer is via magnetic tape. This arrangement more than pays for the use of the peripheral computer, which can additionally be used to perform data editing and error checking.

Satellite Computers

The next step, logically, beyond the peripheral computer is a collection of satellite processors, as shown in Figure 7.3, that are attached to the main computer. Each satellite processor is capable of being programmed and can perform data editing and handle the I/O for a given device type. Therefore, a high-speed main computer can use a small computer to control a given I/O unit so that data are available and can be disposed of at

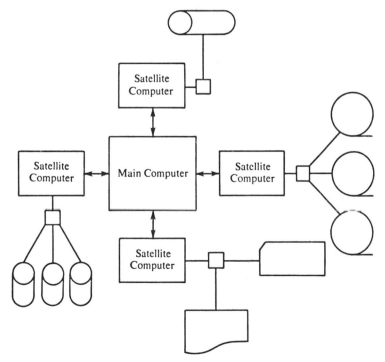

Fig. 7.3 Satellite computers.

electronic speeds. In most cases, the satellite computers contain features for interrupting the execution of the main computer and for sharing portions of main storage.

Attached Support Processors

An attached support processor (ASP) combined the facilities of several satellite computers into one high-speed general-purpose computer. An attached support computer is usually connected to the main computer in one of two ways: (1) with common access to main storage including intersystem communication features; and (2) with a channel-to-channel adapter permitting a data transfer at electronic speeds. An ASP facility generally relegates a significant amount of work to the support processor since it is a computer system in its own right; in some cases, a support processor has been known to have enough processor time available to process small jobs of its own. Generally, however, an attached support processor handles all low-speed input and output, editing, and error checking for a main high-speed processor and relives that processor of almost all responsibility for I/O processing. (See Figure 7.4.)

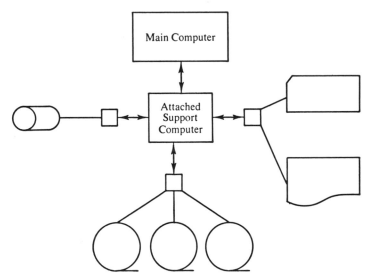

Fig. 7.4 Attached support processor.

Multiprocessing

A computer system which contains more than one processing unit is generally termed a *multiprocessing system.* Multiprocessing is used for either or both of two reasons: (1) reliability, and (2) increased throughput. In many systems where response is critical, an extra processing unit is made available, under program control, to take over in the event of malfunction in the primary processor.   In this case, the processing units must have access to the same storage units and must be able to exchange control signals resulting from a malfunction alert.   Some operating systems also include multiprocessing facilities as a means of increasing work through-put.   If the processing units share main storage, then the system control program is also shared and each processor, when looking for work, selects the next task that is ready for execution.   If the processing units share direct-access storage devices, then each processor has storage units of its own and selects its next unit of work from an input work queue   stored on the shared direct-access storage device.   Both configurations are de-picted in Figure 7.5.

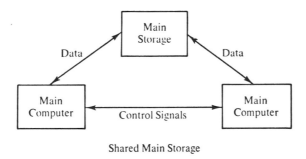

Shared Main Storage

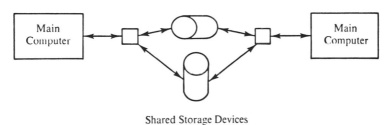

Shared Storage Devices

Fig. 7.5 Multiprocessing.

Although the information given here does not tell how to design a system or even use one, the various system configurations are representative of operational systems in the field today.   Clearly, any system design or evaluation would be performed by systems analysts and would involve a much deeper analysis of possible alternatives.   Systems architecture is a complex business indeed, and there is much to be gained by more fully appreciating the progress that has been made thus far.

7.3 MASS STORAGE AND INPUT/OUTPUT DEVICES

Mass storage and input/output devices are usually classified by the media on which the data are recorded. Unit record devices ordinarily pertain to punched cards where each document is a separate transaction such as a set of data, or a source statement from a program. Also included in this category are line printers where each line of printing is a discrete set of characters. Tape devices pertain to magnetic and punched tape where information is recorded serially as a continuous stream. Rotating devices include magnetic discs and magnetic drums where the media are rotated at high speed and recording and reading are performed with electronic read-write heads. The section on terminal devices presents keyboard and cathode ray tube display devices, and miscellaneous devices include work stations, optical character readers, magnetic card and strip devices, graph plotters, audio response units, and microfilm output facilities.

Unit Record Devices

Unit record devices include punched card readers, card punches, and line printers. Punched cards occur most frequently in two varieties:

1. 80-column cards occasionally referred to as Hollerith cards (see Figure 1.1); and
2. 96-column cards available with the IBM System/3 (shown as Figure 7.6).

Punched card readers are electromechanical devices which use optical photocells or sensing brushes to detect the presence or absence of a punch in a particular position on the card. Card punches operate similarly but use mechanical devices to punch holes under control of a computer program or an input/output control device. The speed of card readers ranges from approximately 300 cards per minute to about 1200 cards per minute. Card punches are generally slower and range from approximately 60 cards per minute to about 500 cards per minute.

Line printers print a line of information (usually 120 or 132 characters) at one time by one of two methods:

1. impact printing, and
2. chemical or photographic techniques.

The impact technique is used most frequently because it generally gives better-quality printing at a loss of line speed. Impact printing uses a type bar, a print wheel, or a print drum and involves impacting the paper

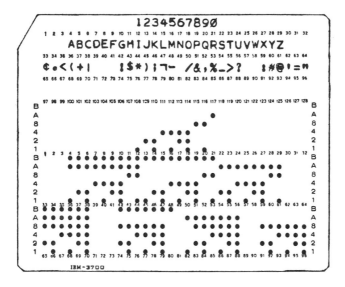

Fig. 7.6   96-column card (actual size).   (Courtesy of IBM Corporation.)

(and ribbon) with the printing mechanism or vice versa. Chemical or photographic techniques are generally used in printers with ultra-high line speed but often result in a lower printing quality. The speed of line printers generally ranges from approximately 200 lines per minute to about 1500 lines per minute.

Tape Devices

Tape devices use either magnetic tape or punched tape* and provide convenience, low cost, and relatively high speed. The major disadvantage is, of course, that data are stored serially and that access to a particular piece of data often involves searching down the tape until the required information is found. Punched tape (see Figure 1.2) comes in a variety of widths depending upon the number of tracks recorded. Punch tape readers usually operate at from approximately 250 characters per second to about 1000 characters per second. Tape punches are quite slow with

---

*Punched tape is usually constructed of paper although a mylar base is used for applications which require a durable medium.

speeds ranging from 50 characters per second to approximately 300 characters per second.

Although magnetic tape is also a serial device, it has some distinct advantages: (1) speed, (2) convenience, (3) capacity, and (4) low cost. Most magnetic tape is either $\frac{1}{2}$ inch or 1 inch wide and is constructed from a plastic-like base coated with iron oxide. The iron oxide is magnetized to indicate the presence of information. Obviously, magnetic tapes differ in length—especially after use. A new reel is approximately 2400 feet in length, costs approximately $20, and can hold significantly more information than $20 worth of punched cards. A 2400-foot reel can hold between one and twenty million characters depending upon the packing density. Table 7.3 gives the data rate for magnetic tape at various forward speeds and at different packing densities. Magnetic tapes are reusable, easy to carry and store, and come in seven-track and nine-track varieties. The choice of seven or nine-track is usually dependent upon the internal coding scheme of the main computer.

TABLE 7.3   DATA RATE FOR MAGNETIC TAPE

Tape Speed in Inches per Second	Density in Bytes per Inch			
	200	556	800	1600
36	7,200	20,016	28,800[a]	57,600[a]
75	15,000	41,700	60,000	120,000[a]
112.5	22,500	62,550	90,000	180,000

[a] Not generally available.

Rotating Devices

Rotating devices usually refer to magnetic disc and magnetic drum storage. A magnetic disc unit is a stack of rotating discs in which data are recorded. The number of discs, their capacity, and their removability differ between the various manufacturers. Figure 7.7 gives several views of a disc storage unit. Data are addressed by read-write head, track, and a sector address. The read-write head can be fixed or moving. A fixed head (view C) eliminates arm movement (since a particular read-write head is selected electronically), and the only delay in access involves rotation time. Moving heads move in and out together (view A) or independently (view B). With a moving head, data access requires that the head be moved to the required track prior to waiting for rotational delay. Magnetic discs are regarded as direct-access devices since information may be located directly instead of serially locating a particular address on the device. Removable disc packs are popular since they serve

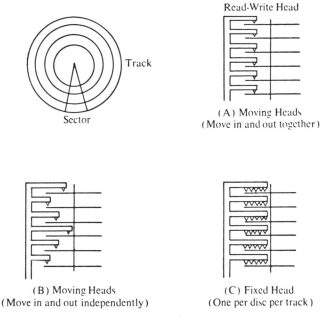

(A) Moving Heads
(Move in and out together)

Track

Sector

(B) Moving Heads
(Move in and out independently)

(C) Fixed Head
(One per disc per track)

Fig. 7.7 Magnetic disc storage.

as both a mass storage and an input/output medium. Disc units without removable discs are generally used solely for mass storage.

Magnetic drum, as a device type, usually has a storage capacity greater than that of magnetic disc and achieves a higher data rate. Magnetic drums are used mainly for mass storage and achieve high data rates because the drum, on which data are recorded, rotates at high speeds and the read-write heads are fixed—one per track (see Figure 7.8). The drum is usually a precision-built cylinder coated with iron oxide, which is magnetized to record data. Magnetic drums are frequently used by an operating system to store programs, such as I/O routines, compilers, etc., which are needed on a demand basis but are too lengthy to reside in main storage permanently.

Although the rotating devices discussed here provide direct-access facilities, they can also be used to store and retrieve data sequentially. Therefore, a sophisticated operating system can provide for considerable generality of use by permitting device types to be interchanged.

Terminal Devices

Terminal devices used with time-sharing systems, data inquiry facilities, and in general remote computing systems, are primarily of two types: key-

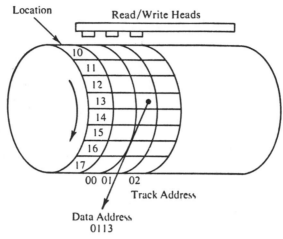

Fig. 7.8 Magnetic drum storage.

board devices and cathode ray tube (CRT) devices. Keyboard devices, such as the one used with APL, are easy to program and are used extensively for remote input and output. CRT devices generally come in two varieties: character generators and point-to-point displays. Display devices based on the character generator principle usually contain a data buffer so that information is retained on the screen as long as desired. This type of display device, when used for general-purpose computing, also contains a keyboard so that data can be entered, visually inspected, and sent to the computer.

Point-to-point display devices allow a considerable amount of flexibility in the type of information that can be displayed but generally require that the image be refreshed periodically by either the computer or a control device attached to the display unit. Input via a device of this type is usually accomplished with a light pen—a pencil-like device capable of interrupting the display control instructions.

Miscellaneous Input and Output Devices

Several other I/O devices are commercially available to meet the needs of specialized applications. A remote job entry (RJE) *work station* is usually composed of a card reader, card punch, line printer, and optionally a magnetic tape unit, and effectively allows a user to send a job into a closed-shop system from a remote location. Verbal output from a computer can be achieved with an *audio response unit*, which can select a message from an audio drum, and transmit it over a telephone line—all under program control. *Optical readers* can read magnetic characters printed in designated portions of a document (such as a bank check) or can perform a more general analysis using matrix matching, stroke analysis, or curve tracing. *Graph plotters* use pen and ink for drawing smooth curves or point-to-point figures under program control or from magnetic tape using an off-line device. Ultra-high mass storage is achieved with *magnetic cards* and *magnetic strips.* Both devices use iron oxide-coated media, which operate at low speeds, but are generally removable and capable of storing literally millions of characters on each card or strip. The newest computer output medium is called COM, which is an acronym for *Computer Output Microfilm.* For certain classes of application, microfilm output can incorporate both printed and graphic data and make the information available in one of the well-known forms of microfilm technology, that is, 16 mm film in rolls, 35 mm film, microfiche, or aperture cards (punched cards with microfilm windows).

8 | PROGRAMMING SYSTEMS AND LANGUAGES

8.1 THE CONCEPT OF AN OPERATING SYSTEM

In general, computer systems are used in three ways. The most convenient, obviously, is with a terminal device and a remote programming system, such as APL. However, two other methods are in widespread use. The first method is called *basic programming* and involves running each job separately as shown in Figure 8.1 and described in the following steps:

1. The user prepares his program in a programming language* and has the information punched into cards or recorded on magnetic or punched tape.
2. A compiler program, which can translate a program written in a programming language to one in machine language, is loaded into the computer.
3. The compiler program reads the program, prepared by the user, as data and produces a machine language program.
4. The user's machine language program is loaded into the computer; the program reads the user's data and produces results as output.

The operations are usually distinct and require an appropriate amount of manual intervention between one step and the next. The steps are essentially repeated for each user. The second method (Figure 8.2) uses a computer program, called an *operating system*, to reduce setup time be-

*Introduced in Chapter 2.

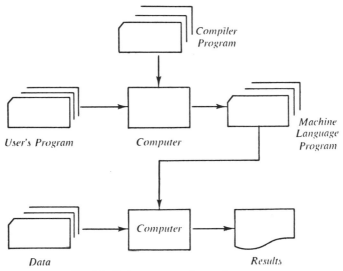

Fig. 8.1 Basic programming environment.

tween jobs and to minimize operator intervention. The steps, present in basic programming, also exist in an operating environment monitored by an operating system. The major difference is that sequencing between jobs is automatic and that jobs are submitted to the operating system as a batch. The last topic is treated in more detail in the following paragraphs.

Batch Processing

The term *batch processing* originated with early operating systems and refers to the practice of collecting a batch of jobs and submitting them to the computer on an input tape. Similarly, output for the entire batch of jobs was collected on an output tape. A peripheral computer, as discussed in Chapter 7, was used for the card-to-tape operation and for the processing of the output tape.

The input tape was accessed by the operating system and the problem programs alike, and when one job terminated, the operating system readied the next job for execution. The early batch environment can be characterized in several ways. First, when a job was given control of the processing unit, it had complete control until its work was finished. Next, I/O units were addressed physically so that when a user wanted to change an I/O device or device type, he had to recompile (or assemble) his program. Lastly, programs to perform input and output were either coded in assembler language or provided with a programming language, such as FORTRAN.

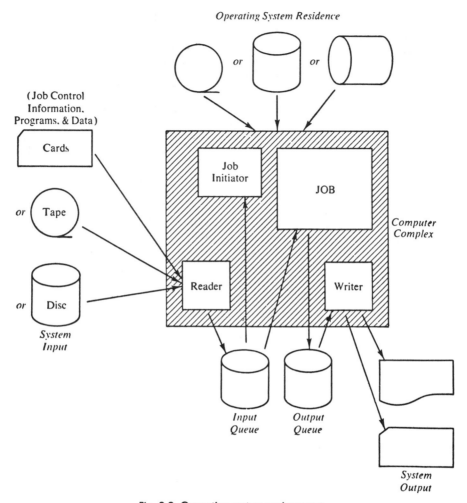

Fig. 8.2 Operating system environment.

The invention of the data channel (see Chapter 7) changed the situation considerably. Most importantly, it awakened an interest in operating systems and encouraged research and development personnel to explore ways of using the I/O-compute overlap available with those devices. This research was the forerunner of the modern operating systems, and as a result of it, three basic components of an operating system were recognized:

1. *Input-output systems*, which provide a software interface between programs and external I/O devices.

2. *Processing programs*, such as compilers, assemblers, and problem programs which process data and produce results.
3. *Supervisory systems*, which provide a logical interface between the hardware system and the remainder of the software system.

The new interest in operating systems had three happy consequences:

1. I/O procedures were generalized so that they now exist on a system-wide basis.
2. The programmer is now able to code his program without having to commit himself to a particular I/O unit. In other words, he is able to specify a device symbolically at compile time and postpone making an actual device assignment until run time.
3. It was recognized that the natural waits (i.e., for I/O, etc.) embedded in most programs could be used effectively to run other jobs in the machine.

Consequences (1) and (2) lead to what is now known as data management. The last consequence led to multiprogramming and time-sharing systems.

Section 8.2 discusses the architecture of various types of operating systems. In most modern systems, however, a minimal facility is provided, regardless of the number of user jobs that can reside in the system at one time:

1. The ability to process jobs sequentially and pass automatically to the next job when the first is completed.
2. The facility for controlling system input and output concurrently with the processing of the primary job. This involves the reading of jobs into the system and stacking them up on direct-access storage for subsequent processing, and the printing and punching of system output which is similarly stacked up in direct-access storage.

The latter facility is generally known as SPOOLing.*

Job Control

In preparing a program for execution on a computer, the programmer usually goes through the following steps:

1. *Design.* The problem is formally stated, the constraints are listed, and the overall logic is determined.
2. *I/O requirements.* The file organization, access methods, and external devices are specified. This is commonly known as data management.

---

*Which stands for Simultaneous Peripheral Output On Line.

3. *Programming.* A programming language is selected, program structure is established, and the program is developed.

The programs are then ready for computer processing, which requires use of the operating system. The following information must be available before computer processing can begin:

1. Job control information.
2. Input/output requirements.
3. Source program(s).
4. Data.

Job control information is usually presented on control cards which are interpreted by the operating system and provide the following information; job identification, priorities, and passwords; a specification of input/output requirements; and requests to have specific processing programs executed. Two types of data exist: problem data and source programs. Source programs are data to the language processors; for example, a FORTRAN or COBOL compiler. Problem data usually follow a request to have a problem program executed and exist in a form determined by the particular application. Depending upon the stage of program development, the job control information provided to the operating system may also contain debugging commands and request the services of "service programs" provided by the operating system. Figure 8.3 contains a sample deck setup.* The various types of control cards are of particular

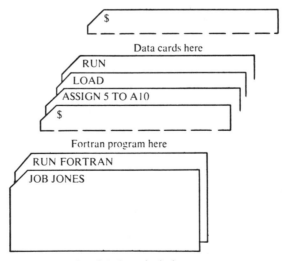

Fig. 8.3 Sample deck setup.

*The control cards presented here do not correspond to any existing operating system but are representative of facilities that normally exist.

interest. The JOB card establishes the programs and data as a unit of work to the operating system. The RUN card specifies that a particular processing program is to be executed. The $ card denotes end-of-data and is used to indicate the last card of a particular type. The ASSIGN card assigns a physical I/O device to a symbolic name specified in the program. The LOAD card initiates loading of the machine language programs into main storage and readies them for execution. The second RUN card causes the user's programs to be executed. Lastly, the user's program reads data from the job stream until the final $ card is read.

Normally, many users will be contending for the use of the computer system; it is the function of the operating system to utilize the job control information to recognize priorities and maintain job schedules in accordance with installation guidelines.

Control Programs

The input/output and supervisory systems, mentioned previously, were the forerunners of what are now regarded as control programs. They are responsible for the overall functioning of the computer system and have well-defined objectives, that is,

1. To maximize the use of the system's resources.
2. To provide for the continuous operation of the system.
3. To establish and maintain job priorities.
4. To insure the integrity of individual jobs.

The control programs which satisfy these needs are classed into three categories—system management, job management, and data management. First, the functions performed by the system in response to a job are introduced.

The system first reads the entire job (i.e., job control information, programs, and data) into main storage and places it on external storage as an input job stream; it then initiates the job as a unit of work to the operating system. This involves creating an initial program structure and forming a *job control block*, which will contain execution-control data and identify the job to the operating system. This function is accomplished by the *system management* control program which also performs the following job-oriented functions for each job on a system-wide basis:

1. Schedules the job for execution on either a priority or a sequential basis.
2. Performs actual input/output for all jobs.
3. Processes normal and abnormal job terminations.
4. Allocates main storage.
5. Controls the printing and punching of output files by peripheral devices.

Other functions are oriented toward a particular job. *Job management* routines interpret job control information, execute service requests, and monitor the execution of processing programs. *Data management* routines initiate input and output for the processing programs, maintain catalogs and libraries, and manage storage buffers.*

The three types of control programs have structural properties which, perhaps, are as significant as their functions. *System management* routines provide a logical interface between the hardware and the remainder of the software system. *Job management* routines provide a logical interface between processing problems and control programs. *Data management* routines provide a software interface between processing programs and external storage.

Most operating systems are interrupt-driven in the sense that the computing system processes a given unit of work until one of two events occurs: (1) It requires a system management function; or (2) a system management function is required for some other reason on a demand basis. In either case, the unit of work is interrupted and control is passed to a system management routine to interrogate the interrupt. These interrupts are termed hardware interrupts in that they are initiated from an I/O device, the processing unit, a machine instruction, or an external electronic device such as a timer or the computer console. System management's basic function is to respond to these interrupts by classifying them as to type and by initiating appropriate routines to process each. In so doing, system management maintains control over system facilities. The system facilities include the processing unit(s), main storage, and input/output devices. System management routines have several important characteristics which enable them to effectively perform the functions listed above:

1. They reside permanently in main storage.
2. They are not directly addressable by processing programs.
3. They execute in the supervisor state.†
4. Only one active copy of each exists in the system.

Job management's prime function is to monitor the execution of a job. Although job management routines, like data management routines, are considered control programs, they do not necessarily reside permanently in main storage. When system management gives control to a job, it normally returns where execution was last terminated. If a program in-

---

*A storage buffer is an area of main storage set aside for use by data management to increase the efficiency of I/O operations.

†The supervisor state is an internal machine state in which machine instructions critical to the operation of the system can be executed. Ordinarily, only control programs are allowed to execute in this state.

terrupt is pending, however, control is passed to a subsystem of job management called the *job monitor*. This is what is generally meant by a *software interrupt*. The job monitor interrogates the program interrupt condition and passes control to one of its own diagnostic routines or a routine provided by the user. A major portion of job management is concerned with job control information. Usually, job management contains a job control subsystem which reads the input job stream, interprets control cards, and calls appropriate routines to process them. Generally, a processing routine exists for each type of control card, although in some cases, data management routines are used to perform a major portion of the requested operation. The last major function of job management is to handle job terminations which may occur on a normal or abnormal basis.

Data management routines provide input/output support for processing programs and job management routines. They are grouped into four classes:

1. *Access routines* manage the transfer of data between an I/O device and main storage.
2. *Catalog service routines* manage the system catalog so that data files may be referenced by name.
3. *Device management routines* control the allocation of physical I/O devices to a job.
4. *External storage management routines* determine the manner in which space on direct-access volumes is allocated to the users of the system.

Although data management is concerned with input and output, it does none itself; but rather, it passes program control to a system management routine to have the operation performed.

The next section, on the architecture of operating systems, is concerned with the various types of systems. Basically, they all contain system, job, and data management routines but differ, for the most part, in how the overall system is organized.

8.2 OPERATING SYSTEMS ARCHITECTURE

Operating systems architecture refers to the overall design of hardware and software components and their operational effectiveness as a whole. To be effective, however, an operating system must not only be cognizant of the collection of hardware and software modules, but must also be designed in light of the programs and data which the system processes, and the people it serves. An *operating system* is an integrated set of control programs and processing programs designed to maximize the overall operating effectiveness of a computer system. Early operating systems increased system performance by simplifying the operations side of the system. Current operating systems additionally attempt to maximize the use of hardware resources while maintaining a high level of work throughput or providing a certain level of terminal response. A multitude of programmer services are usually provided as well.

Categories of Operating Systems

A *multiprogramming system* is an operating system designed to maintain a high level of work throughput while maximizing the use of hardware resources. As each job enters the system, an internal priority, which is a function of external priority and arrival sequence, is developed. This internal priority is used for processor scheduling. During multiprogramming operation, the program with the highest internal priority runs until a natural wait is encountered. While this wait is being serviced, processor control is turned over to the program with the next-highest priority until the first program's wait is satisfied, at which time processor control is returned to the high-priority program, regardless if the second program can still make use of the system. The first job has, in a sense, demanded control of the system. The concept is usually extended to several levels and is termed the *level of multiprogramming*.

One of the problems frequently faced by installation management involves running two different operating systems, each of which requires a dedicated but identical machine. A *hypervisor* is a control program that, along with a special hardware feature, permits two operating systems to share a common computing system. A relatively small hypervisor control program (see Figure 8.4) is required which interfaces the two systems. Although only one processor is involved, a hardware prefix register divides storage into two logically separate memories, each of which is utilized by an operating system. Input/output channels and devices are dedicated to one or the other operating system and use the hardware prefix register to know to which half of storage to go. All interrupts are indirectly routed to a *common interrupt routine* which decides which operating system should receive the most recent interrupt. Processor control is then passed to the hypervisor control program for dispatching. The hypervisor control program loads the prefix register and usually dispatches processor control to the operating system which received the last interrupt. Alternate dispatching rules are to give one operating system priority over another or to give one operating system control of the processor after a fixed number of interrupts have been received by the other side. Hypervisors are particularly useful when it is necessary to run an emulator and an operating system at the same time.

Although *time sharing* is used in a variety of contexts, it most fre-

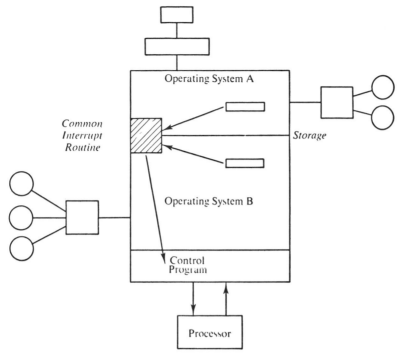

Fig. 8.4 Hypervisor multiprogramming.

quently refers to the allocation of hardware resources to several users in a time-dependent fashion. More specifically, a *time-sharing system* concurrently supports multiple remote users engaging in a series of interactions with the system to develop or debug a program, run a program, or obtain information from the system. The basic philosophy behind time sharing is to give the remote user the operational advantages of having a machine to himself by using his *think*, *reaction*, or I/O time to run other programs. Operation of a time-sharing system is summarized as follows:*

   Time-shared operation of a computer system permits the allocation of both space and time on a temporary and dynamically changing basis. Several user programs can reside in computer storage at one time while many others reside temporarily on auxiliary storage such as disc or drum. Computer control is turned over to a resident program for a scheduled time interval or until the program reaches a delay point (such as an I/O operation), depending upon the priority structure and control algorithm. At this time, processor control is turned over to another program. A nonactive program may continue to reside in computer storage or may be moved to auxiliary storage, to make room for

*See reference 18, p. 190.

other programs, and subsequently be reloaded when its next turn for machine use occurs.

A *virtual system* is one that provides a logical resource which does not necessarily have a physical counterpart. *Virtual storage* systems[5,6,11] (see Figure 8.5) are widely known and provide the user with a large single-level store achieved through a combination of hardware and software components. A virtual storage system is characterized by the fact that real

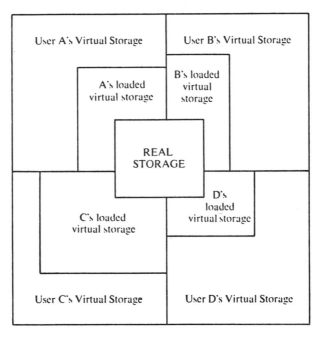

Fig. 8.5 Virtual storage.

storage contains only that part of a user's program which *need* be there for execution to proceed. The basic philosophy of virtual storage lends itself to paging (Figure 8.6) and is usually associated with *dynamic address translation*, as introduced later in the section.

A *virtual machine* (30) is an extension to the virtual storage concept which gives the user a *logical* replica of an actual hardware system. Whereas in a virtual storage system a user could run programs, in a virtual machine a user or installation can run complete operating systems. In addition to using the virtual storage concept, a virtual machine system contains a control program which allocates resources to the respective virtual machines and processes privileged instructions which are issued by a particular operating system.

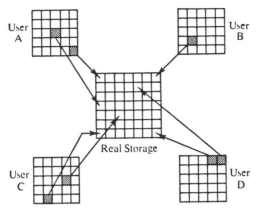

Fig. 8.6 Loaded virtual storage.

Although virtual systems are usually associated with time sharing, the concept is more general and applies equally well to multiprogramming systems. Virtual systems tend to be most effective in operating environments where dynamic storage allocation, dynamic program relocation, simple program structure, and scheduling algorithms are of concern.

In modern operating systems, the allocation of hardware resources among users is a major task. Two resources directly affect performance and utilization: storage management and scheduling. Both topics were introduced earlier. The most widely used implementation techniques are discussed here.

Storage Management

In an operating system, available storage is usually divided into two areas: a fixed area for the supervisor program and a dynamic area for the user programs. If no multiprogramming or time sharing is done, then a user program executes serially in the dynamic area. When he has completed his use of the CPU, then the dynamic area is allocated to the next user.

When more than one user shares the dynamic area, such as in multiprogramming or time sharing, then storage management becomes a problem for which various techniques have been developed. They are arbitrarily classed as multiprogramming techniques or time-sharing techniques, although the point of departure is not well defined. *Multiprogramming techniques* include fixed-partition, region-allocation, and roll in/roll out. *Time-sharing techniques* include core-resident, swapping, and paging.

In a *fixed-partition* system, the dynamic storage area is divided into fixed subareas called partitions. As a job enters the system, it specifies how much storage it needs. On the basis of the space requirements specified, it is assigned to a fixed partition and must operate within that area using planned program structure whenever necessary. In a *region-allocation* system, a variable number of jobs may use the system. Just before a job is initiated, a request is made to dynamically allocate enough storage to that job. Once a job is initiated, however, it is constrained to operate within that region. In a logical sense, fences are created within the dynamic area. *Roll in/roll out* is a variation of region allocation which effectively enables one job to borrow from another job if space requirements cannot be fulfilled from the dynamic area. The borrowed region is rolled back in and returned to the original owner whenever he demands the CPU or when the space is no longer needed by the borrower.

The most fundamental technique for storage management in time sharing is *core resident*. In a core-resident system, all active programs are kept in main storage. This method reduces system overhead and I/O activity but is obviously limited by the size of core storage. Large-capacity storage (LCS) is frequently used in a hierarchical sense with main storage and provides a cost-effective means of increasing the number of potential users. Large-capacity storage is sufficiently fast to satisfy the operational needs of a user at a remote terminal. *Swapping* is the most frequently used method of storage management in time sharing. At the end of a time slice, user A's program is written out to auxiliary storage and user B's is brought in for execution. All necessary control information is saved between invocations. In the above case, the system would have to wait while user B's program was brought in for execution. Thus, two or more partitions can be used for swapping to reduce the I/O wait. The use of several partitions permits other user programs to be on their way in or on their way out while one user's program is executing. This method reduces *wait* time but increases the amount of system housekeeping and overhead. A variation to the single-partition approach is the *onionskin* method used with the CTSS system at M.I.T.[8] With this method, only enough of user A's program is written out to accommodate user B. In a sense, user A's program is peeled back for user B's program. If user C requires still more space than B, then A is peeled back even more. In a *paging* system, main storage is divided into fixed-size blocks called pages. Pages are allocated to users as needed, and a single user's program need not occupy consecutive pages, as implied in Figure 8.6. Thus a translation is required between a user's virtual storage, which is contiguous, and real storage, which is not. A technique called *dynamic address translation* is employed that uses a table look-up, implemented in hardware, to perform the translation. First, the address field is segmented to permit a hierarchical set of look-up tables (Figure 8.7). Then, each

Segment	Page	Byte

Fig. 8.7 Segmentation.

effective computer address goes through an address translation process (Figure 8.8) before operands are fetched from storage. The process is usually speeded up with a small associative memory (Figure 8.9). When a user program references a page that is not in main storage, a hardware interrupt is generated. The interrupt is fielded by the supervisor program which brings the needed page in for execution. Meanwhile, another user can use the processor. Look-up tables (Figure 8.8) are maintained such that when a page is brought into main storage, an entry is made to correspond to its relative location in the user's virtual storage.

The methods vary, obviously, in complexity. An eventual choice on

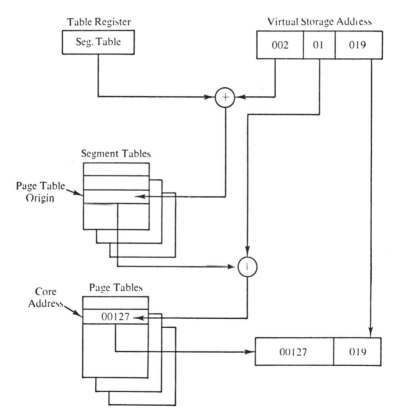

Fig. 8.8 Dynamic address translation.

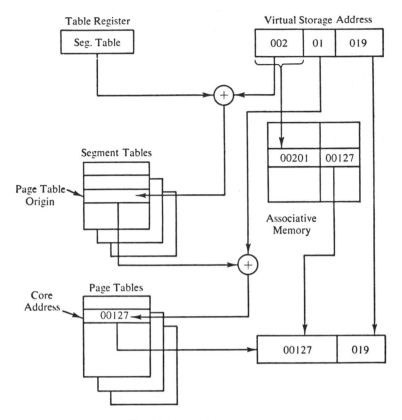

Fig. 8.9 Associative memory.

which technique to employ depends solely on the sophistication of the operating system, the access, performance, and utilization required, and the underlying hardware.

Scheduling

In modern operating systems, the supervisor program assumes the highest priority and essentially processes and does the housekeeping for interrupts generated by problem programs and external and I/O devices. In this sense, the supervisor (or the system) is interrupt-driven. It is generally hoped that the processing done by the supervisor is kept to a minimum. When the supervisor has completed all of its tasks, it must decide to whom the processor should be allocated. In a single-job system, the running program simply retains control of the processor. In a multi-job batch environment, where the system is performance-oriented but not response-oriented, the processor is usually given to the highest-priority job that demands it. This philosophy is generally termed multiprogramming as discussed previously.

In a time-sharing environment, performance is measured in terms of terminal response, and processor scheduling is oriented towards that end. Thus, a user is given a slice of processor time on a periodic basis—frequently enough to give him the operational advantage of having a machine to himself. The scheduling philosophy is influenced by the user environment (i.e., compute-bound jobs, small jobs, response-oriented jobs) and the method of storage management. Three strategies have been used frequently enough to warrant consideration. The most straightforward method is *round robin*. Jobs are ordered in a list on a first-in–first-out basis. Whenever a job reaches the end of a time slice or it can no longer use the processor for some reason, it is placed on the end of the list and the next job in line is given a slice of processor time. A strict round robin strategy favors "compute" jobs and "terminal response" jobs equally and tends to be best suited to a core-resident storage management system. With an *exponential scheduling* strategy, several first-in–first-out lists are maintained, each with a given priority. As a job enters the system, it is assigned to a list on the basis of its storage requirements—with lower storage requirements being assigned a higher priority since they facilitate storage management. The scheduling lists are satisfied on a priority basis, no list is serviced unless higher-priority lists have been completed. Terminal (or response) oriented jobs are kept in the highest-priority list—thus assuring rapid terminal response. If a job is computing at the end of its time slice, then it is placed at the end of the next lowest-priority list. However, lower-priority lists are given longer time slices, of the order $2t, 4t,$ $8t, \ldots$, so that once in execution, a compute-bound job stays in execution longer. Exponential scheduling has "human factors" appeal in that a terminal-oriented user, who gets frequent time slices, is very aware of his program behavior whereas the program behavior of a compute-bound user is generally transparent to him. One of the biggest problems in processor scheduling is the difficulty in developing an algorithm to satisfy all users. The *schedule table* strategy is an attempt to do that. Each user is given a profile in a schedule table. When a job enters the system, it is assigned default values. As the job develops a history, however, the table values are modified according to the dynamic nature of the program. The scheduler is programmed to use the schedule table in allocating the processor while satisfying both user and installation objectives. The schedule table approach is particularly useful in a paging environment where certain programs require an excess of pages for execution. Once the required pages have been brought into main storage, then the job can be given an appropriate slice of processor time.

Scheduling strategies differ to the extent that a different one probably exists for each installation that is developing one. As such, scheduling algorithms continue to be the object of mathematical description and analysis by simulation.

In summary, an operating system facilitates the process of running a job on the computer—that is, when not using a terminal system such as APL —and also provides a multitude of valuable services. The next question is, "If a user doesn't program in a language like APL, what does he use?" The answer is that he uses a procedure-oriented language such as FORTRAN, which is presented in the next section.

8.3 THE FORTRAN LANGUAGE

The purpose of FORTRAN is to provide a programming language with which the scientific community can prepare programs for execution on a digital computer with a minimum of involvement. The language closely resembles the notation of ordinary mathematics, and built-in functions are available for executing most basic mathematical functions, such as the square root and the trigonometric functions. Additional facilities are available which permit the programmer to define his own functions and subroutines as well. Because of its mathematical nature, the language is computation-oriented, deals with words of data, and possesses a limited number of data types. As a result, FORTRAN is not generally amenable to applications that involve character or file operations.

Program Elements

A program in FORTRAN is comprised of a series of statements each recorded on a source document (usually taken to be a punched card). A statement may be one of two types: an executable statement or a non-executable statement. An executable statement may specify computation, input/output, looping, or program control. Nonexecutable statements usually provide the compiler with information necessary for compiling* the computer program.

The basic unit of information in FORTRAN is the character (see Table 8.1) from which operators, constants, variables, and statements are formed. The *FORTRAN operators* are given in Table 8.2 and are of two types: single symbols, such as + or *, and composite symbols such as .GE.

---

*The subject of compiling was discussed earlier.

TABLE 8.1   FORTRAN CHARACTER SET

Alphabetic Characters

A B C D E F G H I J K L M N O P Q R S T U V W X Y Z $

Digits

0 1 2 3 4 5 6 7 8 9

Special Characters

+ − * / ( ) = . , ' ƀ

TABLE 8.2   FORTRAN OPERATORS

Arithmetic Operators

+	addition or identity
−	subtraction or negation
*	multiplication
/	division
**	exponentiation

Comparison Operators

.LT.	less than ($<$)
.LE.	less than or equal to ($\leq$)
.EQ.	equal to ($=$)
.NE.	not equal to ($\neq$)
.GE.	greater than or equal to ($\geq$)
.GT.	greater than ($>$)

Logical Operators

.NOT.	.NOT. X is true if X is false and false if X is true.
.AND.	X .AND. Y is true if both X and Y are true and false, otherwise.
.OR.	X .OR. Y is true if either X or Y is true.

or .EQ.. Operators are used in arithmetic and logical expressions and in subscripts. Names are called identifiers and serve to denote variables and statements. A *statement identifier*, such as GOTO, specifies a particular statement in the language. A *variable identifier* is composed of from one to six alphabetic or numeric characters, the first of which must be alphabetic. The following examples give valid and invalid variable identifiers and several statement identifiers:

Valid Variable Identifiers	Invalid Variable Identifiers	Statement Identifiers
ABI2	1AB2	GOTO
ZETA	K123456T	DO
I	A−CD	REAL
DO	C.D.E	IF

There are no reserved words in FORTRAN and spaces are ignored except in character literals. Thus the following DO statements are equivalent:

DO10 I=1,10
DO 10 I=1,10

Statements may be numbered by the programmer for reference purposes as indicated in the following statement format:

Columns 1 through 5:   statement number (may be omitted)
Column 6:   continuation
Columns 7 through 72: FORTRAN statement

A C or an * in column one denotes a comment line, and a nonblank character in column six indicates a continuation of the preceding line. The general form of a statement in FORTRAN is as follows:

[*statement number*] ƀ [*statement identifier*] *statement-body*

where the brackets indicate that the enclosed constituent is optional. If the statement identifier is omitted, then the statement is an assignment statement. For example:

1	7	
138	READ(N,9000)B,C,D	(1)
	A=B+C*D	(2)
	WRITE(N,9001) A	(3)
	GO TO 138	(4)

Statements (1), (3), and (4) have statement identifiers which are READ, WRITE, and GOTO, respectively. Statement (2) has no statement identifier and is an arithmetic assignment statement. Statement (1) has a statement number of 138.

Data

Five types of data are permitted in FORTRAN: integer, real, double precision, complex, and logical. In addition, character data are permitted in certain I/O statements and as subprogram arguments. The data may be organized as scalars or as arrays. The size of all arrays must be declared with a specification statement; for example:

REAL A(10,10),B(10),XZP1(500)

Fortran assigns default-type attributes in the absence of a specific declaration. Variables whose initial letter is I,J,K,L,M, or N are defaulted to type INTEGER. All others are given the type REAL. The user may override these default attributes whenever appropriate.

Constants may be integer, real, double precision, complex, logical, and character. *Integer constants*, such as -1, 2397, $+34$, are written with an optional sign and without a decimal point. *Real constants* require a decimal point and may optionally have an exponent of the form: $E \pm i$, where i is an integer. Sample real constants are: 0.0, -2.5, .1E-13. A *double precision constant* can be specified in the exponential form by replacing the E with a D. For example: .12345678910111213D-3. A *complex constant* is written in the form (a,b) which corresponds to the complex number $a + bi$. *Logical constants* are the composite symbols: .TRUE. and .FALSE.. *Character literals* may be enclosed in quote symbols or be of the form:

$$nHc_1c_2...c_n$$

where n is the number of characters in the literal.

An element of an array is selected with a subscript(s) which is enclosed in parentheses following the variable name. A subscript must exist for each dimension of the array and multiple subscripts are separated by commas. Up to seven subscripts are permitted and each must be one of the following forms: $v, c', v+c', v-c', c*v, c*v+c'$, and $c*v-c'$, where v is an unsigned integer variable, without a subscript, and c and c' are unsigned integer constants. For example:

```
AB(10)
I(3*J−1, 4)
X(K+4,M,N,2*N−1)
```

Expressions

Operators and operands are combined in the usual fashion to form expressions, with the following conditions:

1. Two operators may not appear in succession.
2. Mixing integer and real quantities in the same expression is not permitted in some implementations of the language.*
3. It is not permitted to raise a negative quantity to a real power or raise zero to a zero power.

A hierarchy exists among operators, and those with the greatest priority are executed first. Parentheses may be used for grouping to override the order of execution. For example:

```
3*4+2=14
3*(4+2)=18
3*2 .GT. 4 .OR. 3−2 .EQ. 2=.TRUE.
```

The hierarchy of FORTRAN operators is given in Table 8.3.

*Except for exponentiation; see Table 8.4.

TABLE 8.3 HIERARCHY OF FORTRAN OPERATIONS

Operation	Hierarchy
Evaluation of functions	1st (highest)
Exponentiation (**)	2nd
Multiplication and division (* and /)	3rd
Addition and subtraction (+ and −)	4th
.LT., .LE., .EQ., .NE., .GE., .GT.	5th
.NOT.	6th
.AND.	7th
.OR.	8th

Assignment Statements

In FORTRAN, data manipulation is performed with the assignment statement. Three forms exist: arithmetic, logical, and the ASSIGN. The form of arithmetic and logical assignment statements is:

$$v = e$$

where v is a scalar or subscripted variable and e is an expression. v may be a logical variable if and only if e is a logical expression. Thus, the assignment statement can be used to convert values from one type to another. For example:

$$A = 2.5$$
$$B = 3.5$$
$$I = A*B + 1.0$$

After the last statement I would have the integer value 9. (Note here that the partial result 9.75 is truncated to 9 since I is an integer variable). Other examples are:

```
ZTL = X+P(3)*(SQRT(Y)+1.0)
T(I+1,K,13) = (A(1,2)+13.2*MAX(X,Y))/6.789
U = .NOT.V.AND.W
```

TABLE 8.4 VALID TYPE COMBINATIONS FOR THE EXPONENTIATION OPERATOR (**)

Base	Exponent	Result
Integer	Integer	Integer
Real	Integer, Real	Real
Real	Double precision	Double precision
Double precision	Real, Double precision	Double precision

The ASSIGN statement is used with the assigned GOTO statement and is classed as an assignment statement for consistency. Its form is:

ASSIGN i TO n

where i is a statement number and n is an integer variable. For example:

ASSIGN 925 TO LOOP

Control Statements

Control statements determine the sequence of control in a program. Statements are executed sequentially until a control statement is reached. Then one of three actions is taken depending upon the statement:

1. Execution of the program is suspended or terminated.
2. Control is directed to another statement on a conditional or unconditional basis.
3. A statement is executed conditionally.
4. Looping is performed.

The GO TO statements transfer control to a specified statement and has the form:

GO TO n

where n is the statement number of an executable statement in the program. The statement numbered n may precede or follow the GO TO statement, that is:

```
10...                    GO TO 20
  :                         :
  :                         :
GO TO 10                 20...
```

The arithmetic IF statement permits control to be transferred to one of three statements depending upon the value of an expression. It has the form:

$$\text{IF } (e)\, n_1, n_2, n_3$$

where e is an arithmetic expression and n_1, n_2, and n_3 are statement numbers. Control is transferred to n_1, n_2, or n_3 depending upon whether $e < 0$, $e = 0$, or $e > 0$ respectively. For example, the step function:

$$y = 0, \quad \text{if } x \leq 0$$
$$y = 13.2, \quad \text{if } 0 < x < 131.4$$
$$y = 50, \quad \text{if } x \geq 131.4$$

would be computed as:

```
        Y = 0.0
        IF(X)100,100,200
    200 IF(X − 131.4)57,300,300
     57 Y = 13.2
        GO TO 100
    300 Y = 50.0
    100
```

The computed GO TO statement permits control to be transferred to one of several statements depending upon the value of an index variable. It has the form:

$$GOTO \ (n_1, n_2, n_3, \ldots, n_m), i$$

where the n_j's are statement numbers, which do not have to be in sequence, and i is an integer variable. Control is transferred to n_1 if i is 1, n_2 if i is 2, etc. The following example transfers control to statements 533, 41, or 290 depending upon KL:

$$GOTO(533,41,290),KL$$

The logical IF statement allows another statement to be executed conditionally depending upon the truth value of a logical expression. It has the general form:

$$IF \ (l) \ S$$

where l is an expression which reduces to a *true* or *false* value and S is an executable statement other than another logical IF or a DO statement. The statement S is executed if l has the value *true*. For example,

```
IF(X.LT.0.0) X = 0.0
IF(A + B.GT.SQRT(BL)) GO TO 600
```

The assigned GO TO statement has the form:

$$GO \ TO \ k, (n_1, n_2, n_3 \ldots, n_m)$$

where the integer variable k has been assigned one of the statement numbers n_1 through n_m with the ASSIGN statement. For example:

```
ASSIGN 7050 TO NLOOP
       ⋮
GO TO NLOOP, (600,75,7050,9000,310)
```

The DO statement permits a series of statements, called the *range* of the DO, to be executed repeatedly while an induction variable assumes successive values. The general form of the DO statement is:

$$\text{DO } n\ i = m_1, m_2, m_3$$

where n is the statement number of the end of the range; i is an integer scalar variable; m_1 is the initial value for i; m_2 is the limit value for i; and m_3, which may be omitted, is the amount that i is incremented for each iteration. If m_3 is omitted, then it is assumed to be one. The m's may be positive integer constants or positive integer variables. The following statements sum the elements of the vector V, which has a size of N:

$$\text{SUM} = 0.0$$
$$\text{DO } 100\ I = 1, N$$
$$100 \quad \text{SUM} = \text{SUM} + V(I)$$

The last statement in a DO loop cannot be an IF statement. Therefore, the CONTINUE statement can be used as a dummy statement terminating a loop.

Three miscellaneous control statements are also contained in the language. The PAUSE statement, that is,

$$\text{PAUSE}$$
$$or \quad \text{PAUSE} \quad n$$
$$or \quad \text{PAUSE} \quad \textit{'message'}$$

temporarily halts execution and prints the integer value n or the *message* on the operator's console. The STOP statement, that is,

$$\text{STOP}$$
$$or \quad \text{STOP} \quad n$$

terminates execution of the program and prints n on the operator's console. The END statement signifies the end of the program or subprogram being processed.

Input/Output Statements

Data can be read from or written to an external device in one of two forms: formatted and unformatted. Formatted processing uses a FORMAT statement which describes the data on the external media. The general form of formatted READ and WRITE statements are:

$$\text{READ } (n, f)\ \textit{list}$$
$$\text{WRITE } (n, f)\ \textit{list}$$

where n is the number of an external device and f is the statement number of a FORMAT statement. The *list* is a series of variables or implied DOs separated by commas. An implied DO has the form:

$$(v(s), i=m_1, m_2, m_3)$$

where v is an array variable and s is a subscript, with the remainder of the skeleton being similar to the DO statement. The subscripted variable in an implied DO may be interpreted as though each occurrence of the subscripted variable were in the list. For example:

```
      READ(5,9000) A,B,K
9000  FORMAT(F10.5,F5.2,I8)

      WRITE(6,500)C,(A(I), I=1,10)
 500  FORMAT(E5.1,10F6.3)
```

The format number is omitted for unformatted processing and data are read or written in a form related to the internal coding structure of the computer. Unformatted READ and WRITE statements have the general form:

READ(n) *list*

WRITE(n) *list*

where n is an external device number and *list* is a list as discussed previously.

The FORMAT statement provides a format code for each of the data types of the language. The general form of the FORMAT statement is:

$$m \ \text{FORMAT} \ (q_1 t_1 z_1 t_2 z_2 \ldots t_n z_n q_2)$$

where: 1. m is a statement number.
2. $(q_1 t_1 z_1 t_2 z_2 \ldots t_n z_n q_2)$ is the format specification.
3. Each q is a series of slashes or is empty.
4. Each t is a field descriptor or group of field descriptors.
5. Each z is a field separator (comma, slash, series of slashes, or parentheses)
6. n may be zero.

The format field descriptors are of the forms:

srFw.d

srEw.d

srGw.d

srDw.d

rIw

rLw

rAw

$nHc_1 c_2 \ldots c_n$

nX

where:
1. The letters F,E,G,D,I,L,A,H, and X indicate the manner of conversion and editing between the internal and external representations and are called the conversion codes. They may be used as follows:

F —to transfer real data without an exponent;
E —to transfer real data with an *E* exponent;
G—to transfer integer, real, complex, or logical data;
D—to transfer real data with a *D* exponent;
I —to transfer integer data;
L —to transfer logical data;
A—to transfer alphanumeric data;
H—to transfer Hollerith (literal) data;
X —to either skip data when reading or insert blanks when writing.

2. *w* and *n* are nonzero integer constants representing the width of the field in the external character string.
3. *d* is an integer constant representing the number of digits in the fractional part of the external character string (except for G conversion code).
4. *r*, the repeat count, is an optional nonzero integer constant indicating the number of times to repeat the succeeding field descriptor.
5. *s* is optional and represents a scale factor designator.
6. Each *c* is one of the characters in the FORTRAN character set.

Field designators or field separators may be grouped by enclosing them in parentheses. Repetition of a group is accomplished by preceding the left parenthesis by an integer constant representing the repeat count.

A scale factor designator is defined for use with the F,E,G, and D conversions and is of the form:

$$nP$$

where *n*, the scale factor, is an integer constant or minus followed by an integer constant. A data format may also be read into the computer during execution of a program using the A format code. In that case, the format statement number in the READ or WRITE statement is replaced by the name of the array variable containing the format.

Three utility statements for input/output are included in the language. The ENDFILE statement, written as:

$$ENDFILE \; n$$

defines the end of a set of data on an external device *n*. The BACK-SPACE statement, defined as:

$$BACKSPACE \; n$$

backspaces the indicated device one data record. The REWIND statement, written:

$$REWIND \ n$$

positions the indicated device to the beginning of the set of data.

Specification Statements

Specification statements indicate the type and size of variables and determine the manner in which storage is allocated.

The general form of the type statements is:

$$type \ x_1(t_1)/v_1/,x_2(t_2)/v_2/,\ldots x_n(t_n)/v_n/$$

where: 1. *type* can be INTEGER, REAL, DOUBLE PRECISION, LOGICAL, or
COMPLEX.

2. x_i is the name of a variable.

3. (t_i) gives the dimension of a variable where t_i is from one to
seven integer constants separated by commas indicating the
maximum bound for a dimension—this entry is optional.

4. $/v_i/$, which is also optional, represents initial data values.

For example:

```
REAL A,B,MTOT(10,5,8),
REAL MTOT, A(10,5), C1(3)/1.0,2.0,3.0/
INTEGER COUNT
LOGICAL U,V,W(10,10)/100*.TRUE./
```

For variables whose type is declared implicitly, the DIMENSION
statement can be used to specify array bounds. The general form of
the DIMENSION statement is:

$$DIMENSION \ x_1(t_1),x_2(t_2)\ldots$$

where x_i and t_i are described above. For example:

$$DIMENSION \ IAREA(100)$$

The COMMON statement allows different programs to share the same
storage and has the form:

$$COMMON \ /l_1/y_1,/l_2/y_2,\ldots$$

where l_i is an optical label and y_i is a list of variables. Common blocks
with the same label from different programs share the same main storage
in the computer. For example:

$$COMMON \ A,B/STAT/M,S,TOT$$

The EQUIVALENCE statement has the form:

$$\text{EQUIVALENCE } (x_1,x_2,x_3\ldots),(z_1,z_2,z_3\ldots),\ldots$$

where the x_i and z_i denote variables, arrays, or parts of arrays which are to share the same storage. For example:

```
REAL A(100),B(50)
EQUIVALENCE (A(51),B)
```

The DATA statement assigns initial values to specified variables. It has the general form:

$$\text{DATA } v_1,v_2,\ldots/i{*}d_1,i{*}d_2,\ldots/,\ldots$$

where v_i are variables, i is an optional repetition count, and d_i are data values of the correct type. v_i may be an array or a subscripted variable provided that the data count agrees with the constituent being initialized. For example:

```
REAL A(100)
DATA A/100*1.0/B/34.1/,I/13/
```

Subprogram Statements

The benefits to be derived from structuring a computer program into mainline programming and separate functions are well known.* The needs are particularly obvious in a language like FORTRAN which contains a limited number of operations that are defined primarily on scalar operands. Four types of subprograms are available in FORTRAN:

1. Built-in functions.
2. Statement functions.
3. FUNCTION subprograms.
4. SUBROUTINE subprograms.

Built-in functions are part of the language and are either *open* or *closed*. Table 8.5 contains a representative list of functions of this type. As shown in the following example, built-in functions are invoked through their use as a constituent of an expression:

$$X = -25.0 \qquad (1)$$
$$Y = SQRT(ABS(X))+2.0 \qquad (2)$$

After statement (2) is executed, Y contains the value 7. Built-in functions always produce a scalar result although as many arguments as are necessary may be used. Arguments always follow the function name, enclosed

*See Chapter 2.

TABLE 8.5   FORTRAN FUNCTIONS

Function	Definition	Symbolic Names
Absolute value	$\|a\|$	ABS, IABS, or DABS
Truncation	Sign of a times largest integer $\leq a$	AINT, INT, or IDINT
Remaindering	$a_1 (\bmod \ a_2)$	AMOD, MOD, or DMOD
Largest value	$\text{Max}(a_1, a_2, \ldots)$	AMAX0, AMAX1, MAX0, MAX1, or DMAX1
Smallest value	$\text{Min}(a_1, a_2, \ldots)$	AMIN0, AMIN1, MIN0, MIN1, or DMIN1
Float	Conversion from integer to real	FLOAT
Fix	Conversion from real to integer	IFIX
Transfer of sign	Sign of a_2 times $\|a_1\|$	SIGN, ISIGN, or DSIGN
Positive difference	$a_1 - \text{Min}(a_1, a_2)$	DIM or IDIM
Obtain most significant part of double precision argument		SNGL
Obtain real part of complex argument		REAL
Obtain imaginary part of complex argument		AIMAG
Express single precision argument in double precision form		DBLE
Express two real arguments in complex form	$a_1 + a_2 i$	CMPLX
Obtain conjugate of a complex argument		CONJG
Exponential	e^a	EXP, CEXP, or CEXP
Natural logarithm	$\log_e(a)$	ALOG, DLOG, or CLOG
Common logarithm	$\log_{10}(a)$	ALOG10 or DLOG10
Trigonometric sine	$\sin(a)$	SIN, DSIN, or CSIN
Trigonometric cosine	$\cos(a)$	COS, DCOS, or CCOS
Hyperbolic tangent	$\tanh(a)$	TANH
Square root	$(a)^{1/2}$	SQRT, DSQRT, or CSQRT
Arctangent	$\arctan(a)$	ATAN or DATAN
Arctangent	$\arctan(a_1/a_2)$	ATAN2 or DATAN2
Modulus		CABS

in parentheses and separated by commas. Arguments may be expressions containing other function references.

Statement functions are defined by the user and consist of one FORTRAN statement. Ordinarily, the definitions of statement functions come first in a program and have the following form:

$$name(x,y,\ldots) = e$$

where: *name* is a function name determined by the user.

$x,y,\ldots$ are unsubscripted variables in e.

e is an expression without subscripted values.

For example:

$$CROOT(X) = X**(1.0/3.0)$$
$$\vdots$$
$$Z = CROOT(27.0)$$

After the last statement, Z contains the value 3.

FUNCTION subprograms allow functions to be defined which are **not** among the built-in functions and are more complicated than those that can be defined in one statement. A FUNCTION subprogram is compiled independently of the mainline program. Data are passed between the two modules via an argument list or COMMON storage. A FUNCTION subprogram returns a value so it can be used in an expression. The general form of a FUNCTION definition is:

$$type \text{ FUNCTION } name (x_1, x_2, \ldots)$$

specification statements (if any)

$$\vdots$$

FORTRAN statements

$$\vdots$$

END

where: *type* is optionally INTEGER, REAL, DOUBLE PRECISION, COMPLEX, or LOGICAL (*name* may also appear in a type statement).

name is the identifier with which the function will be invoked.

x_i are dummy parameters which can be scalar or array variables.

The function name must appear to the left of an assignment statement at least one place in the function. Control is returned to the calling program with the return statement. The following function adds the elements of a vector:

```
        FUNCTION VADD (A,N)
        REAL A(N)
        VADD = 0.0
        DO 50 I = 1,N
    50  VADD = VADD + A(I)
        RETURN
        END
```

Note here that the dimension of A is a variable quantity; this facility is permitted in subprograms. VADD would be used somewhat as follows:

```
        REAL VECTOR (100)/100*5.0/
            .
            .
            .
        MEAN = VADD(VECTOR,100)/100
            .
            .
            .
```

A SUBROUTINE subprogram is similar to a FUNCTION subprogram except that it does not return an explicit result and it is invoked with the CALL statement. The general form is:

$$\text{SUBROUTINE } name (x_1, x_2, \ldots)$$

where *name* and x_i are defined above. The following subroutine transposes the given matrix (A) and assigns it to B:

```
        SUBROUTINE TRANS (A,B,M,N)
        REAL A(M,N), B(N,M)
        DO 7 I = 1,M
        DO 7 J = 1,N
    7   B(J,I) = A(I,J)
        RETURN
        END
```

It is used as follows:

```
        REAL A(3,2)/1.0,2.0,3.0,4.0,5.0,6.0/,B(2,3)
            .
            .
            .
        CALL TRANS(A,B,3,2)
```

After the last statement, B contains:

$$\begin{pmatrix} 1 & 2 & 3 \\ 4 & 5 & 6 \end{pmatrix}$$

Evident here is the fact that arrays are stored in column-wise order with the first subscript varying most rapidly.

Two final subprogram statements remain. The RETURN statement, mentioned previously, causes control to be returned to the calling program. The EXTERNAL statement specifies that a specific name is a subprogram allowing function names to be passed among programs.

A Final Note

Many versions of the FORTRAN language are in existence and several implementations contain statements that have not been mentioned. Some contain READ, PRINT, and PUNCH statements which are carry-overs from initial versions of the language. Others contain statements, such as ACCEPT and TYPE, which refer to a particular mode of operation. Lastly, many statements reflect new concepts to facilitate the art of programming. A discussion of these topics is beyond the scope of this section; the reader is directed to one of the bibliographical references or to a FORTRAN manual provided by one of the computer manufacturers.

FORTRAN has its limitations, as do most computer languages, and may even be inappropriate for some applications which are generally classed as being scientific in nature. The reader is urged to explore some of the other languages in widespread use today:*

ALGOL 60   The international algorithmic language.
BASIC   An easy-to-use time-sharing language.
COBOL   The common business-oriented language.
PL/I   A multipurpose programming language.

*For a comprehensive treatment of programming languages, see: J. E. Sammet, *Programming Languages: History and Fundamentals*, Englewood Cliffs, N.J., Prentice-Hall, Inc., 1969.

BIBLIOGRAPHICAL
REFERENCES

1. Berry, P. C., *APL/360 Primer* (Student Text), White Plains, N.Y., IBM Corporation, Form C20-1702, 1969.
2. Brooks, F. P., Jr., and K. E. Iverson, *Automatic Data Processing: System/360 Edition*, New York, John Wiley & Sons, Inc., 1969.
3. Calingaert, P., *Principles of Computation*, Reading, Mass., Addison-Wesley Publishing Company, Inc., 1965.
4. Cole, R. W., *Introduction to Computing*, New York, McGraw-Hill Book Company, 1969.
5. Comfort, W. T., "A Computing System Design for User Service," *Proceedings of the Fall Joint Computer Conference*, 1965.
6. Corbato, F. J., and V. A. Vyssotsky, "Introduction and Overview of the MULTICS System," *Proceedings of the Fall Joint Computer Conference*, 1965.
7. Davis, G. B., *Computer Data Processing*, New York, McGraw-Hill Book Company, 1969.
8. Corbato, F. J., *et al.*, *The Compatible Time-Sharing System*, Cambridge, Mass., The M.I.T. Press, 1963.
9. Falkoff, A. D., and K. E. Iverson, *APL/360: User's Manual*, Yorktown Heights, N.Y., IBM Corporation, Thomas J. Watson Research Center, 1968.
10. Foster, G. H., "APL: A Perspicuous Language," *Computers and Automation*, November, 1969, pp. 24 28.
11. Gibson, C. T., "Time-Sharing in the IBM System/360: Model 67," *Proceedings of the Spring Joint Computer Conference*, 1966.
12. Golde, H., *FORTRAN II and IV for Scientists and Engineers*, New York, The Macmillan Company, 1966.
13. Gschwind, H. W., *Design of Digital Computers*, New York, Springer-Verlag, 1967.
14. Hellerman, H., *Digital Computer System Principles*, New York, McGraw-Hill Book Company, 1967.

15. Iverson, K. E., *A Programming Language*, New York, John Wiley & Sons, Inc., 1962.
16. Iverson, K. E., *Elementary Functions: An Algorithmic Treatment*, Chicago, Science Research Associates, Inc., 1966.
17. Iverson, K. E., *The Use of APL in Teaching*, Yorktown Heights, N.Y., IBM Corporation, Thomas J. Watson Research Center, Form 320-0996, 1969.
18. Katzan, H., Jr., *Advanced Programming: Programming and Operating Systems*, New York, Van Nostrand Reinhold Company, 1970.
19. Knuth, D. E., *The Art of Computer Programming, Vol. 1, Fundamental Algorithms*, Reading, Mass., Addison-Wesley Publishing Company, 1968.
20. McCracken, D. D., *Digital Computer Programming*, New York, John Wiley & Sons, Inc., 1957.
21. McCracken, D. D., *FORTRAN with Engineering Applications*, New York, John Wiley & Sons, Inc., 1967.
22. McDaniel H., *An Introduction to Decision Logic Tables*, New York, John Wiley & Sons, Inc., 1968.
23. Pakin, S., *APL\360 Reference Manual*, Chicago, Science Research Associates, Inc., 1968.
24. Smillie, K. W., *STATPACK2: An APL Statistical Package*, Edmonton, Alberta, Canada, Department of Computing Science, The University of Alberta, Publication No. 17, 1969.
25. Stein, M. L., and W. D. Munro, *A FORTRAN Introduction to Programming and Computers*, New York, Academic Press, 1966.
26. Trakhtenbrot, B. A., *Algorithms and Automatic Computing Machines*, Boston, D. C. Heath and Company, 1963.
27. Weiss, E. (editor), *Computer Usage Fundamentals*, New York, McGraw-Hill Book Company, 1969.
28. *An Introduction to CP-67/CMS*, Cambridge, Mass., IBM Cambridge Scientific Center, Report 320-2032, 1969.

APPENDICES

APPENDIX A
APL PROGRAMS

The purposes of this appendix are twofold: (1) to give the reader an idea of the form and structure of programs written in APL; and (2) to present a collection of useful programs which, perhaps, are representative of the many already developed in APL and which are available from companies offering APL service. The source of the programs given here is APL-MANHATTAN, a division of Industrial Computer Systems, Inc. Individual authors are acknowledged, whenever appropriate.

The nature of the programs varies. Some are short and straightforward and the algorithms used are readily apparent. Others are more sophisticated and fully utilize the power of APL. One of the programs interacts with the user in such a manner that a programming knowledge of APL is not required. The more mathematical functions are intended for use in more comprehensive functions that a user might be developing.

The programs are grouped into four categories and organized as follows:

A.1 *Graph Plotting*
Graph

A.2 *Statistics*
Descriptive statistics
Probability and correlation
Regression
Analysis of variance
Critical path

A.3 *Mathematics*
Matrix algebra
Curve fitting

Calculus programs
Utility programs

A.4 *Business*
Compound interest
Investment

Each program listing is given the caption *Program*. Similarly, an application program is titled *Application*. The numbers agree so that Program 1 corresponds to Application 1, etc.

A.1   GRAPH PLOTTING*

The *GRAPH* program, listed as Program 1, plots on one coordinate axis any number of functions of a single variable. The independent variable extends vertically and the dependent variable is plotted horizontally. Scaling is applied automatically to keep the range of the dependent variable (ordinate of the curve) as large as possible but less than a given width, which may be changed by the user. *GRAPH* is a one operand implicit result function, used as follows:

$$GRAPH \ A$$

where A is an array of rank 1, 2, 3, or 4. If A is a vector, then it is plotted against its own indices and the number of points is equal to ρA. If A is of rank 2, then the $(\rho A)[2]$ columns are taken as equally spaced abscissa points. The first row is the set of abscissa labels and remaining rows represent functions, which are plotted with different symbols (that may be modified). If several points have the same value, the symbol corresponding to the lowest row number is plotted. Rank-3 arrays are plotted as successive matrices on the same graph. The first row for planes, after the first one, is ignored. Rank-4 arrays may be plotted if the first coordinate has an extent of 2. The first coordinate of a rank-4 array is used as a logic structure to delete elements of the other coordinate (which amounts to a rank-3 array).

Several global variables govern execution of the function:

$QSIZE$—sets the maximum length (in typewriter spaces) of the ordinate axis.
$ACON$—controls the printing of abscissa labels. $ACON$ is expanded cyclically to the number of abscissa points. For example, 1 0 0 would label every third point.
$SSWITCH$—scaling switch: if 1, scaling is computed from the data; if 0, scaling is determined by the global variable $SDATA$
$SDATA$—contains ordinate scaling information. $SDATA$ is respecified each time. *GRAPH* is invoked with $SSWITCH$ set to 1. One typewriter

*The *GRAPH* program is listed with permission from W.R. Newman, APL-MANHATTAN, a division of Industrial Computer Systems, Inc.

```
                  ∇GRAPH[[]]∇
         ∇ G←GRAPH X;A;AL;B;C;I;J;K;L;M;OR;RA;SE;SF;T;W;XL
    [1]     →((ρρX)=ι4)/ 3 4 5 7
    [2]     →0,ρ[]←'INCORRECT DATA FORMAT'
    [3]     X←(2,ρX)ρ(ιρX),X
    [4]     X←(1,ρX)ρX
    [5]     XL←(ρX)ρ1
    [6]     →9
    [7]     XL←X[2;;;]∧1
    [8]     X←X[1;;;]
    [9]     RA←ρA←X[1;1;]
   [10]     AL←RAρACON,(0=ρ,ACON)/XL[1;1;]
   [11]     X[;J+1;]←X[;2;]
   [12]     XL←XL∧(X≥L/CLIP)∧X≤⌈/CLIP
   [13]     →(0=SSWITCH)ρ4+ι26
   [14]     SE←⌊10⊛(I=0)+I+2×((SE=0)+SE←(⌈/(,XL)/,X)-C←⌊/(,XL)/,X)÷
            QSIZE
   [15]     SF←((I< 2 4 10 ×10*SE)/ 1 2 5)[1]
   [16]     SDATA←SF,SE,OR←C-(SF×10*SE+1)|C
   [17]     X←(X÷I)-OR+SDATA[3]÷I+(SF÷SDATA[1])×10*SE÷SDATA[2]
   [18]     X←⌊X+0.5
   [19]     X←⌽[1] 2 1 3 ⍉⍉[1] 0 1 0 ÷X
   [20]     M←10×⌈0.1×⌈/⌈/⌈/X÷X×XL←(⌽[1] 2 1 3 ⍉⍉[1] 0 1 0 ÷XL)×Y;≥0
   [21]     A←A-(10*I)|A←A+0.5×10*I+1+(⌊10⊛|A+A=0)-J+3+⌊10⊛⌈/1,|A÷⌈/A-
            ⌊/A
   [22]     B←AL\[1] AL/[1](0⌈J-3|I) DFT(RA,1)ρA÷10*L+3×⌊(I+1+⌊
            10⊛⌊/|A+A=0)÷3
   [23]     B[;1]←RAρATITLE,RAρ' '
   [24]     B←(0,2×0=ρ,ATITLE)↓B
   [25]     L←(L≠0)/'(×10*',((L<0)/'-'),'0123456789'[1+((1+10≤|L)ρ
            10)⊤|L],')'
   [26]     A←(SF×(OR÷10)+0,ιM÷10)×10*¯1+3|SE÷2
   [27]     A←A-(10*I)|A←A+0.5×10*I+(⌊10⊛|A+A=0)-J+1+⌊10⊛⌈/1,|A÷⌈/A-⌊/
            A
   [28]     A←(⌈/0,J-⌊10⊛|A+1E¯8>|A) DFT((1+M÷10),1)ρA
   [29]     B←1⌽(((⌈/(-(ρB)[2])+ ¯3 1 2 +W←(ρA)[2],(ρB)[2],ρL)ρ0),(ρB)
            [2]ρ1)\B
   [30]     G←TITLE,C∆R,((⌈/W- 5 1 0 +W[3])ρ' '),L,' \',(6ρ' '),QTITLE
            ,5ρ' '
   [31]     G←G,(C≠0)/'(×10*',((C<0)/'-'),'0123456789'[1+((1+
            10≤|C)ρ10)⊤|C+3×⌊(2+SE)÷3],')'
   [32]     G←G,C∆R,((⌈/W+ 0 4 5 -W[1])ρ' '),,((W[1]ρ1),(10-W[1])ρ0)\
            2⌽A
   [33]     W←' |',(ρX)[1]ρSYMBOLS
   [34]     A←,(ρX)[2 1]ρ⌽ι(ρX)[C+1]
   [35]     →(ρJ←RSWITCHρC∆R)ρ2+ι26
   [36]     G←0ρ[]←G
   [37]     L←2,(⌈/(M×C=1,RA),⌈/X[;;C])ρ1
   [38]     L[1+(Cν.=1,RA)×10×ιM÷10]←2
   [39]     L[1+I/,X[;;C]]←2+(I+,XL[;;C])/A
   [40]     G←G,J,B[C;],W[L]
   [41]     →(RA≥C←C+1)ρRSWITCH+¯5+ι26
   [42]     G←G,C∆R
   [43]     →((I←0)=ρL←LEGEND)ρ5+ι26
   [44]     G←G,C∆R,(' ',(ρX)[1]ρSYMBOLS)[I←I+1],'  ',(¯1+B+L\C∆R)ρL
   [45]     L←(B⌊ρL)↓L
   [46]     →((ρX)[1]≥I)ρ¯2+ι26
   [47]     G←G,C∆R
   [48]     →RSWITCHρ0
   [49]     G←0ρ[]←G
         ∇
```

Program 1. Graph plotting (GRAPH).

```
        ∇DFT[⎕]∇
    ∇ Z←W DFT X;D;E;F;G;H;I;J;K;L;Y
[1]     D←' 0123456789.¯'
[2]     →(∨/W≠⌊W←,W+(H←0)×L←1<ρρX)/DFTERR+0×F←2
[3]     →(3 2 1 <ρρX)/(DFTERR+F←0), 2 3 +I26
[4]     →(ρρρX←((∨/ 1 2 =ρW)⌽ 1 2)⍉(1,ρ,X)ρX)/2+I26
[5]     X←(0 1 1 /ρX)ρX
[6]     →((∧/(ρW)≠ 1 2 ,2×E←1ρϕρX),1≠ρW)/(DFTERR×F←1),3+I
        26
[7]     I←1+⌈/0,,⌊100|X+1>|X
[8]     W←(2+I+W+(W≠0)+∨/,X<0),W
[9]     →(∨/2>-/[1] W←⍉(E,2)ρW)/DFTERR+0×F←2
[10]    Z←((K←1ρρX),+/W[1;])ρ' '
[11]    X←J-1|J←0.5+X×10*(ρX)ρW[2;]
[12]    DFTLP:→(E<H←H+1)/DFTEND
[13]    J←1+10|J-1|J←(|Y←X[;H])∘.÷10*¯1+ϕιI+W[1;H]
[14]    J←(,J)×G←,⍉(ϕρJ)ρ(,⍉(J≠1)∨.∧(ιI)∘.≤ιI-F+1),(K×1+F+W[
        2;H])ρ1
[15]    →(∧/0≤Y)/2+I26
[16]    J[(I-+/(K,I)ρG)+I×¯1+ιK]←12×Y<0
[17]    J←(K,I)ρJ
[18]    →(0=F)/3+I26
[19]    J←J[;(1ϕιG),(G←-/W[;H])+ιF]
[20]    J[;G]←11
[21]    →DFTLP×ρρρZ[;(+/W[1;ιH-1])+ιI]←D[1+J]
[22]    DFTEND:→L/0
[23]    →0×ρZ←,Z
[24]    DFTERR:'DFT ',(3 6 ρ' RANK LENGTHDOMAIN')[F+1;],' PROBLEM.'
    ∇
```

Program 1. (Continued)*

space is equal to $\underline{S}DATA[1]\times 10*\underline{S}DATA[2]$ and the left edge starts
   at $\underline{S}DATA[3]$.

$\underline{R}SWITCH$—controls the result returned: if 1, the entire graph is returned as a
   literal vector; if 0, $\iota 0$ is returned and the graph is printed as it is
   computed.

$\underline{T}ITLE$—printed above the graph. $TITLE$ may contain carriage returns.

$\underline{A}TITLE$—abscissa title.

$\underline{O}TITLE$—ordinate title.

$\underline{S}YMBOLS$—symbols used to plot the functions. They are assigned to the
   rows of data in order.

$\underline{C}LIP$—specifies upper and lower clipping levels for ordinate values. Data outside the range are ignored and data inside are scaled to fill the graph.

$\underline{L}EGEND$—a legend printed at the bottom of the graph. If $LEGEND$ is null, no
   legend is printed. Otherwise, $LEGEND$ is printed as a legend title.

Application 1 plots a series of points, a straight line, and a step function against
a coordinate axis.

*A. D. Falkoff of IBM is credited with being the originator of *DFT*, which is used as
a subprogram by *GRAPH*. It is listed here with his permission.

```
X←ι20
Y←ι20
Z←(.5×X)+6
W←1  1  1  1  3  3  3  3  5  5  5  5  7  7  7  7  9  9  9  9

GRAPH 4 20ρX,Y,Z,W
```

GRAPH

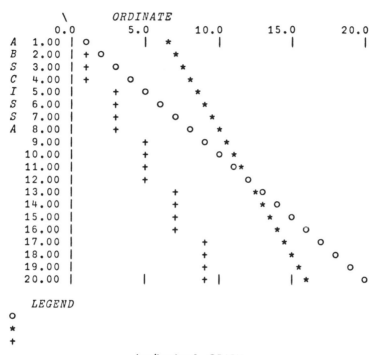

```
            \          ORDINATE
            0.0        5.0         10.0        15.0        20.0
A    1.00  |  o         |    *        |           |          |
B    2.00  |  +  o           *
S    3.00  |  +     o            *
C    4.00  |  +        o          *
I    5.00  |        +     o          *
S    6.00  |        +       o         *
S    7.00  |        +          o        *
A    8.00  |        +             o      *
     9.00  |           +             o    *
    10.00  |           +               o  *
    11.00  |           +                o*
    12.00  |           +                  o
    13.00  |              +              *o
    14.00  |              +            *   o
    15.00  |              +             *    o
    16.00  |              +              *      o
    17.00  |                 +            *        o
    18.00  |                 +              *        o
    19.00  |                 +               *         o
    20.00  |              |      +  |           |  *       o
```

LEGEND
```
o
*
+
```

Application 1. GRAPH.

A.2 STATISTICS*

Descriptive Statistics

Program 2 lists *DSTAT*, a function which computes, prints, and labels the following statistics for a vector of ungrouped data: sample size, maximum value, minimum value, range, mean, variance, standard deviation, mean deviation, median, and mode. If all values are distinct, no mode is listed. The syntax of *DSTAT* is:

$$DSTAT\ X$$

*Statistical programs are reprinted with permission from Smillie, K. W., *STATPACK2: An APL Statistical Package* (24).

```
       ∇DSTAT[□]∇
     ∇ DSTAT X;R;MAX;MIN;N;MEAN;VAR;SD;MD;MED;MODE;V;M
[1]    R←(MAX←X[ρX])-MIN←(X←X[⍋X])[1]
[2]    SD←(VAR←(+/(X-MEAN←(+/X)÷N)*2)÷(N←ρX)-1)*0.5
[3]    MD←(+/|X-MEAN)÷N
[4]    MED←0.5×+/X[(⌈N÷2),1+⌊N÷2]
[5]    →(N>ρMODE←((ρV)ρ(⍳M)≤1)/V←X[((V=M←⌈/V←+/X∘.=X)/⍳ρX])/7
[6]    MODE←⍳0
[7]    ('SAMPLE SIZE         ';N)
[8]    ('MAXIMUM             ';MAX)
[9]    ('MINIMUM             ';MIN)
[10]   ('RANGE               ';R)
[11]   ('MEAN                ';MEAN)
[12]   ('VARIANCE            ';VAR)
[13]   ('STANDARD DEVIATION  ';SD)
[14]   ('MEAN DEVIATION      ';MD)
[15]   ('MEDIAN              ';MED)
[16]   ('MODE                ';MODE)
     ∇
```

Program 2. Descriptive Statistics (DSTAT).

where X is a vector. *DSTAT* is applied to some sample data values in Application 2.

Program 3 lists *MVSD*, a function which computes the means, variances, and standard deviations for a matrix of variates and observations. The syntax of

```
           DATA←1 3 5 6 7 7 8 9 11 13
           DSTAT DATA
     SAMPLE SIZE          10
     MAXIMUM              13
     MINIMUM              1
     RANGE                12
     MEAN                 7
     VARIANCE             12.66666667
     STANDARD DEVIATION   3.559026084
     MEAN DEVIATION       2.6
     MEDIAN               7
     MODE                 7

           DSTAT 1 3 5 6 7 7 6 5 3 1
     SAMPLE SIZE          10
     MAXIMUM              7
     MINIMUM              1
     RANGE                6
     MEAN                 4.4
     VARIANCE             5.155555556
     STANDARD DEVIATION   2.270584849
     MEAN DEVIATION       1.92
     MEDIAN               5
     MODE                 1   3   5   6   7
```

Application 2. DSTAT.

```
      ∇MVSD[□]∇
   ∇ T←MVSD X;N;M;VAR;SD
[1]   SD←(VAR←(+/[1](X-(ρX)ρM←(+/[1] X)÷N)*2)÷(N←(ρX)[1])-1)*
      0.5
[2]   T←⍉(3,ρM,10)ρM,VAR,SD
   ∇
```

Program 3. Mean, Variance, and Standard Deviation (MVSD)

MVSD is:

$$T← MVSD X$$

where T is an explicit result and X is a matrix. The rows of X correspond to observations and the columns of X correspond to variates. An example of *MVSD* is given in Application 3.

```
      DATA←1 3 5 6 7 7 8 9 11 13
      MVSD DATA

7                 12.66666667          3.559026084

      MVSD 1 3 5 6 7 7 6 5 3 1

4.4               5.155555556          2.270584849

      MVSD ι10

5.5               9.166666667          3.027650354
```
Application 3. MVSD.

Program 4 lists *HIST*, a function which plots a histogram of frequencies. The syntax of *HIST* is:

$$G← W HIST F$$

where G is an explicit result and F is a vector of frequencies. Each component of F is divided by W and rounded before plotting. Application 4 plots a simple histogram.

```
      ∇HIST[□]∇
   ∇ G←W HIST F;MAX;K
[1]   MAX←⌈/F←⌊0.5+F÷W
[2]   G←('.'),(⌈/K←(F≥MAX)/ιρF)ρ' '
[3]   G[K+1]←'т'
[4]   G
[5]   →(0<MAX←MAX-1)/2
[6]   (1+ρF)ρ'.'
[7]   G←ι0
   ∇
```
Program 4. Histogram Plotting (HIST).

```
DATA←1 4 8 13 10 8 12 17 24 30 31 20 24 21 15 9 6 4 2 1
1 HIST DATA
```

```
•            T
•           TT
•           TT
•           TT
•           TT
•           TT
•           TT
•          TTT T
•          TTT T
•          TTT T
•          TTT TT
•          TTTTT
•          TTTTT
•          TTTTT
•         TTTTTT
•         TTTTTT
•        TTTTTTT
•        TTTTTTT
•    T    TTTTTTT
•    T   TTTTTTTT
•    T   TTTTTTTT
•   TT   TTTTTTTT
•   TT  TTTTTTTTT
•  TTTTTTTTTTTTTT
•  TTTTTTTTTTTTTT
•  TTTTTTTTTTTTTTT
•  TTTTTTTTTTTTTTT
• TTTTTTTTTTTTTTTT
• TTTTTTTTTTTTTTTT
• TTTTTTTTTTTTTTTTT
•TTTTTTTTTTTTTTTTTTTT
•••••••••••••••••••••
```

Application 4. HIST.

Probability and Correlation

Program 5 lists $BINOM$, a function which calculates a vector of probabilities in N binomial trials with probability P of success in a single trial. The syntax of $BINOM$ is:

$$B \leftarrow N \ BINOM \ P$$

```
    ∇BINOM[□]∇
  ∇ B←N BINOM P
[1]   B←(R!N)×(P*R)×(1-P)*N-R←0,ιN
  ∇
```

Program 5. Binomial Distribution (BINOM).

```
      2 BINOM .1
0.81  0.18  0.01

      2 BINOM .5
0.25  0.5  0.25

      2 BINOM .9
0.01  0.18  0.81

      5 BINOM .1
0.59049  0.32805  0.0729  0.0081  0.00045  1E⁻5

      5 BINOM .9
1E⁻5  0.00045  0.0081  0.0729  0.32805  0.59049

      GRAPH 20 BINOM .5
```

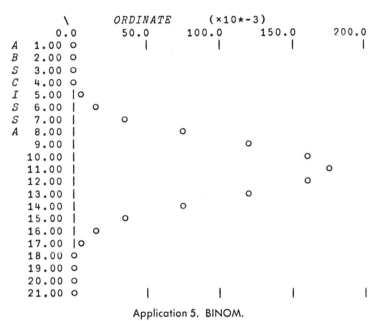

```
GRAPH

               \      ORDINATE    (×10*-3)
             0.0       50.0    100.0     150.0      200.0
A   1.00  ○        |         |         |          |
B   2.00  ○
S   3.00  ○
C   4.00  ○
I   5.00  |○
S   6.00  |   ○
S   7.00  |      ○
A   8.00  |          ○
    9.00  |              ○
   10.00  |                  ○
   11.00  |                    ○
   12.00  |                   ○
   13.00  |              ○
   14.00  |          ○
   15.00  |      ○
   16.00  |   ○
   17.00  |○
   18.00  ○
   19.00  ○
   20.00  ○
   21.00  ○        |         |         |          |
```

Application 5. BINOM.

where the scalars N and P satisfy the following conditions:

$$N > 0 \text{ and } (1 \mid N) = 0$$
$$0 \leq P \leq 1$$

and B is an explicit result. $BINOM$ is applied to sample values in Application 5.

Program 6 lists $POISSON$, a function which calculates a vector of the first $N+1$ probabilities for a Poisson distribution with parameter K. The syntax of

```
        ∇POISSON[□]∇
     ∇ P←N POISSON K
 [1]    P←(*-K)×(K*X)÷!X←0,⍳N
     ∇
```

Program 6. Poisson Distribution (POISSON).

POISSON is: $P ← N \; POISSON \; K$

where *P* is an explicit vector result and *N* and *K* are scalars greater than zero. *K* is interpreted as $r×p$, where *r* is the number of items in the sample and *p* is the probability of success. An example of *POISSON* is given in Application 6.

```
     2 POISSON .1
0.904837418   0.0904837418   0.00452418709

     2 POISSON .5
0.6065306597   0.3032653299   0.07581633246

     2 POISSON .9
0.4065696597   0.3659126938   0.1646607122

     5 POISSON 4
0.01831563889   0.07326255555   0.1465251111   0.1953668148
     0.1953668148   0.1562934519

     GRAPH 20 POISSON 9

GRAPH
```

```
              \        ORDINATE      (×10*-3)
         0.0        50.0      100.0        150.0
A   1.00  o          |          |            |
B   2.00  o
S   3.00  |o
C   4.00  |    o
I   5.00  |        o
S   6.00  |            o
S   7.00  |                o
A   8.00  |                    o
    9.00  |                        o
   10.00  |                        o
   11.00  |                    o
   12.00  |                o
   13.00  |            o
   14.00  |        o
   15.00  |     o
   16.00  |   o
   17.00  | o
   18.00  |o
   19.00  |o
   20.00  o
   21.00  o          |          |            |
```

Application 6. POISSON.

```
      ∇CM[□]∇
    ∇ R←CM X;V
[1]   R←R÷(V∘.×V←(1 1)⌽R←(⌽R)+.×R←X-(ρX)ρ(+/[1] X)÷(ρX)[1])*
      0.5
    ∇
```

Program 7. Coefficient of Correlation (CM).

Program 7 lists *CM*, a function which computes a matrix of correlation co-efficients from a matrix whose rows correspond to observations and whose columns correspond to variates. The syntax of *CM* is:

$$R \leftarrow CM \ X$$

where *X* is a matrix and *R* is an explicit result. If $(\rho X)=(m,n)$, then $(\rho R)=(n,n)$. *CM* is applied in Application 7.

```
        DATA←20 2ρ0
        DATA[;1]←ι20
        DATA[;2]←20?20

        CM DATA

     1                 ¯0.1233082707
   ¯0.1233082707           1

        GRAPH DATA[;2]

   GRAPH

                 \      ORDINATE
             0.0        5.0         10.0        15.0        20.0
    A    1.00 |  o       |           |           |           |
    B    2.00 |                    o
    S    3.00 |                                 o
    C    4.00 |                                            o
    I    5.00 |                           o
    S    6.00 |                              o
    S    7.00 |              o
    A    8.00 |                                       o
         9.00 |                                 o
        10.00 |            o
        11.00 |                                     o
        12.00 |                 o
        13.00 |                       o
        14.00 |           o
        15.00 |        o
        16.00 |                                           o
        17.00 |    o
        18.00 |         o
        19.00 |                                  o
        20.00 |         |           | o         |           |
```

Application 7. CM.

```
∇SR[□]∇
∇ T←X SR Y;N;MX;SX;MY;SY;B1;B0;R;RSQ;TV;SE;A;B
[1]  SX←((A←+/(X-MX←(+/X)÷N)*2)÷(N←(ρX))-1)*
     0.5
[2]  SY←((B←+/(Y-MY←(+/Y)÷N)*2)÷N-1)*0.5
[3]  B0←MY-MX×B1←(+/(X-MX)×(Y-MY))÷A
[4]  SE←((B×1-RSQ←(R←B1×SX÷SY)*2)÷N-2)*0.5
[5]  TV←B1÷SB1←(SY÷SX)÷((N-2)÷(1-RSQ))*0.5
[6]  T←(5 3)ρMX,SX,0,MY,SY,0,B0, 0 0 ,B1,SB1,TV,SE,R,RSQ
∇
```

Program 8. Regression (SR).

Regression

Program 8 lists SR, a simple regression function applied to operands X (independent variable) and Y (dependent variable). The syntax of SR is:

$$T \leftarrow X\ SR\ Y$$

where T is a matrix of five rows and three columns containing the results of fitting the straight line $Y = A + B \times X$ by the method of least squares. T is interpreted as follows:

Row 1: mean of X; standard deviation of X, 0
Row 2: mean of Y; standard deviation of Y; 0
Row 3: A; 0; 0
Row 4: B; standard error of B; T-value
Row 5: standard error estimate; R = simple correlation coefficient; $R*2$

X and Y are vectors such that $(\rho X) = (\rho Y)$. SR is applied to sample data in Application 8.

Analysis of Variance

Program 9, $ANOVA$, does an analysis of variance on a complete factorial design with arbitrary numbers of replications and factors. The syntax of $ANOVA$ is:

$$T \leftarrow ANOVA\ D$$

where the explicit result T is a matrix with four columns giving: identification, degrees of freedom, sums of squares, and mean squares; and whose rows represent: replications, main effects and interactions, error, and total. The first coordinate of D represents replications. The other coordinates of D represent factors. Application 9 applies $ANOVA$ to some sample data.*

Critical Path

Program 10, $CPM1$, is a set of functions for performing a critical path analysis of an activity network. The program interacts with the user to obtain the necessary

---

*For a complete analysis and interpretation of this problem, see P. G. Hoel, *Introduction to Mathematical Statistics* (2nd edition), New York, John Wiley & Sons, Inc., 1954, p. 254.

```
        X←ι20
        Y←1.5+.75×X

        X SR Y

    1.050000000E1      5.916079783E0      0.000000000E0
    9.375000000E0      4.437059837E0      0.000000000E0
    1.500000000E0      0.000000000E0      0.000000000E0
    7.500000000E⁻1     1.862645149E⁻9     4.026531840E8
    4.803313672E⁻8     1.000000000E0      1.000000000E0

        Y←3 4 1 5 7 9 4 8 11 9 8 13 16 17 13 14 18 16 19 20
        Z←X SR Y
        Z

    10.5               5.916079783        0
    10.75              5.784507439        0
     1.110526316       0                  0
     0.9180451128      0.07930539021      11.57607459
     2.045095198       0.9389266396       0.8815832345

        W←Z[3;1]+Z[4;1]×X

        GRAPH 3 20ρX,Y,W

GRAPH

           \        ORDINATE
         0.0         5.0         10.0        15.0        20.0
A   1.00 |     * o   |           |           |           |
B   2.00 |       * o |           |           |           |
S   3.00 | o       * |           |           |           |
C   4.00 |         o |           |           |           |
I   5.00 |        *  o           |           |           |
S   6.00 |         * o   o       |           |           |
S   7.00 |     o      *          |           |           |
A   8.00 |          o*           |           |           |
    9.00 |           *   o       |           |           |
   10.00 |          o   *        |           |           |
   11.00 |         o     *       |           |           |
   12.00 |               * o     |           |           |
   13.00 |               *    o  |           |           |
   14.00 |              *      o  |          |           |
   15.00 |             o    *    |           |           |
   16.00 |              o     *  |           |           |
   17.00 |                *    o |           |           |
   18.00 |               o    *  |           |           |
   19.00 |                     *o |          |           |
   20.00 |         |           |           |        *o  |

    LEGEND
o
*
```

Application 8. SR.

```
      ∇ANOVA[□]∇
    ∇ T←ANOVA D;DIM;N;REPS;K;R;CT;V;I;S
[1]   N←(ρDIM←ρD)-1
[2]   T←((R←(2*N)+2×K←(REPS←DIM[1])≥2),4)ρ0
[3]   CT←((N+1)ρ0) SS D
[4]   T[R; 2 3]←((×/DIM)-1),((N+1)ρ1) SS D
[5]   →(REPS=1)/7
[6]   T[1; 2 3]←(REPS-1),((ι(N+1))≤1) SS D
[7]   D←+/[1] D
[8]   DIM←1↓DIM
[9]   V←⌊((2*(N+1)-ιN)∘.|ιS)↑(2*N-ιN)∘.×(S←(2*N)-1)ρ1
[10]  V[;ι(2*N)-1]←V[;(+/(X∘.>X)+((ιρX)∘.≥ιρX)∧X∘.=X)ιιρX←+/[1]
      V]
[11]  I←1
[12]  T[I+K; 2 3]←(×/(((V[;I]=1)/DIM)-1)),(V[;I] SS D)÷REPS
[13]  →((2*N)>I←I+1)/12
[14]  T[;3]←T[;3]-CT
[15]  →(N=1)/20
[16]  I←2
[17]  DV←(KρO),(X←(~(~CT)∨.∧S)∧(CT←V[;I])∨.∧S←V[;ιI-1]),(R-(I+K-
      1))ρ0
[18]  T[I+K;3]←T[I+K;3]-+/T[;3]×DV
[19]  →((2*N)>I←I+1)/17
[20]  →(REPS=1)/23
[21]  T[R-1;2]←T[R;2]-+/[1] T[ι(R-2);2]
[22]  T[R-1;3]←T[R;3]-+/[1] T[ι(R-2);3]
[23]  T[ι(R-1);4]←T[ι(R-1);3]÷T[ι(R-1);2]
[24]  I←1
[25]  T[I+K;1]←10⊥V[;I]
[26]  →((2*N)>I←I+1)/25
    ∇


      ∇SS[□]∇
    ∇ S←Y SS R;DIM;K;ZEROS;ONES
[1]   →(K=ONES←K-ρZEROS←(Y=0)/ιK←ρDIM←ρR)/4
[2]   R←+/[((ι0)ρZEROS[ρZEROS]]] R
[3]   →(0≠ρZEROS←¯1↓ZEROS)/2
[4]   R←R*2
[5]   R←+/R
[6]   →(0<ONES←ONES-1)/5
[7]   S←R÷×/(Y=0)/DIM
    ∇
```

Program 9. Analysis of Variance (ANOVA).

input consisting of: node number, node duration, and successor nodes. If there are *n* nodes, then they should be numbered 1 through *n*. Output includes:

> length of the critical path
> critical activities
> node numbers
> durations
> early start and early finish times

late start and late finish times
total and free slack

$CPM1$ is applied to a sample network* in Application 10.

A.3   MATHEMATICS

Matrix Algebra

Program 11 and 12 list functions for computing the inverse and determinant of a matrix, respectively. The syntax of the functions are:

$$R \leftarrow INV \ X$$
$$R \leftarrow DET \ X$$

INV uses the Gauss-Jordon method with pivoting. Examples of INV and DET are given in Applications 11 and 12.

Curve Fitting

Program 13 lists PCF,† a function which fits a polynomial to a set of data points. The syntax of PCF is:

$$R \leftarrow N \ PCF \ X$$

where R is a vector of polynomial coefficients in descending order; N is the degree of the polynomial; and X is a $2 \times K$ matrix of K data points. The first row of X represents the independent variable and the second row represents the dependent variable. PCF is applied to sample data in Application 13.

```
PLOT1←310 353 366 299 367
PLOT2←284 293 335 264 314
PLOT3←307 306 339 311 377
PLOT4←267 308 312 266 342
DATA←4 5ρPLOT1,PLOT2,PLOT3,PLOT4

ANOVA DATA
```

0	3	6430
2143.333333		
1	4	12712
3178		
0	12	2388
199		
0	19	21530
0		

Application 9. ANOVA.

*For a complete analysis and interpretation of this network see: P. G. Carlson, *Quantitative Methods for Managers*, New York, Harper and Row, Publishers, 1967, p. 99.

†The *PCF* program is listed with permission from W. R. Newman, APL-MANHATTAN, a division of Industrial Computer Systems, Inc.

```
        ∇CPM1[☐]∇
    ∇ CPM1
[1]    INPUT
[2]    NETWORKCHECK
[3]    →ERRORREPORT
[4]    TOPOLOGICALSORT
[5]    CPMALGORITHM
[6]    PREOUTPUTSORT
[7]    OUTPUT
    ∇


        ∇BASICDATA[☐]∇
    ∇ BASICDATA;V
[1]    'IS THIS A NEW PROBLEM?'
[2]    →(∧/'NO'=☐[ι2])/0
[3]    'ENTER PROBLEM NUMBER'
[4]    PROBNO←☐
[5]    'ENTER NODE NUMBER,DURATION AND SUCCESSOR NODES,ONE NODE A
       T A'
[6]    'TIME IN ANY NODE ORDER.AFTER ALL DATA HAVE BEEN ENTERED,E
       NTER'
[7]    'A NODE NUMBER OF 0.'
[8]    DATA←ι0
[9]    →((V←,☐)[1]=0)/11
[10]   →9,ρDATA←DATA,V,(10-ρV)ρ0
[11]   DATA←(0≠+/[1] DATA)/DATA←(((ρDATA)÷10),10)ρDATA
    ∇


        ∇CONSISTENCY[☐]∇
    ∇ CONSISTENCY;I;J
[1]    I←Nρ1
[2]    →((∧/I=J)∨∧/~J←(∨/I/PM)∧∨/[1] I/[1] PM)/4
[3]    →2,ρI←J
[4]    ERROR←ERROR,∨/J
[5]    LOOPS←J/NODES
    ∇


        ∇CPMALGORITHM[☐]∇
    ∇ CPMALGORITHM
[1]    EARLYSTART
[2]    EARLYFINISH
[3]    LATEFINISH
[4]    LATESTART
[5]    TOTALSLACK
[6]    CRITICALPATH
[7]    FREESLACK
    ∇


        ∇CRITICALPATH[☐]∇
    ∇ CRITICALPATH
[1]    CRPATH←(TS=0)/NODES
    ∇
```

Program 10. Critical Path Method (CPM1).

```
      ∇DURATIONVECTOR[□]∇
   ∇ DURATIONVECTOR
[1]   DURATIONS←DATA[DATA[;1]ιNODES;2]
   ∇

      ∇EARLYFINISH[□]∇
   ∇ EARLYFINISH
[1]   EF←ES+DURATIONS
   ∇

      ∇EARLYSTART[□]∇
   ∇ EARLYSTART;J
[1]   ES←1ρ0
[2]   →(N>ρES←ES,⌈/ES[J]+DURATIONS[J←(,PM[;1+ρES]=1)/ιN])/
      2
   ∇

      ∇ERRORREPORT[□]∇
   ∇ EXIT←ERRORREPORT
[1]   EXIT←(∨/ERROR)/0
[2]   →(~∨/ERROR)/0
[3]   ('PROBLEM NUMBER  ';PROBNO;'    DATE  ';ι25;□←' ';□←' ')
[4]   ERROR1:→(~ERROR[1])/ERROR2
[5]   ('NODES NOT NUMBERED CORRECTLY';□←' ')
[6]   NODES[⍋NODES]
[7]   ERROR2:→(~ERROR[2])/ERROR3
[8]   ('INCORRECT NUMBER OF INITIAL NODES';□←' ')
[9]   INODES
[10]  ERROR3:→(~ERROR[3])/ERROR4
[11]  ('INCORRECT NUMBER OF TERMINAL NODES';□←' ')
[12]  TNODES
[13]  ERROR4:→(~ERROR[4])/0
[14]  ('INCONSISTENT PRECEDENCE MATRIX';□←' ')
[15]  LOOPS
   ∇

      ∇FREESLACK[□]∇
   ∇ FREESLACK;I
[1]   FS←ι0
[2]   →((N-1)>ρFS←FS,⌊/ES[(,PM[I;]=1)/ιN]-EF[I+1+ρFS])/
      2
[3]   FS←FS,0
   ∇
```

Program 10 (Continued)

```
      ∇INITIALNODES[□]∇
    ∇ INITIALNODES
[1]   ERROR←ERROR,1≠ρINODES←(0=∨/[1] PM)/NODES
    ∇


      ∇INPUT[□]∇
    ∇ INPUT
[1]   BASICDATA
[2]   NODEVECTOR
[3]   NUMBEROFNODES
[4]   DURATIONVECTOR
[5]   PRECEDENCEMATRIX
    ∇


      ∇LATEFINISH[□]∇
    ∇ LATEFINISH;I
[1]   LF←1ρEF[N]
[2]   →(N>ρLF←(⌊/LF[I+(ρLF)-N]-DURATIONS[I+(,PM[N-ρLF;]=1)/ιN]),
      LF)/2
    ∇


      ∇LATESTART[□]∇
    ∇ LATESTART
[1]   LS←LF-DURATIONS
    ∇


      ∇NETWORKCHECK[□]∇
    ∇ NETWORKCHECK
[1]   ERROR←ι0
[2]   NODENUMBERING
[3]   INITIALNODES
[4]   TERMINALNODES
[5]   CONSISTENCY
    ∇


      ∇NODENUMBERING[□]∇
    ∇ NODENUMBERING
[1]   ERROR←ERROR,~∧/∨/(ιN)∘.=NODES
    ∇


      ∇NODEVECTOR[□]∇
    ∇ NODEVECTOR
[1]   NODES←(DATA[;1])[⍋DATA[;1]]
    ∇


      ∇NUMBEROFNODES[□]∇
    ∇ NUMBEROFNODES
[1]   N←⌈/NODES
    ∇
```

Program 10 (Continued)

```
      ∇OUTPUT[□]∇
   ∇ OUTPUT
[1]   ('PROBLEM NUMBER ';PROBNO;'     DATE ';ɪ25;□←' ';□←    )
[2]   ('LENGTH OF CRITICAL PATH: ';+/DURATIONS[CRPATH];□←' ')
[3]   ('CRITICAL ACTIVITIES:  ';CRPATH;□←' ')
[4]   ('NODES:';□←' ')
[5]   NODES
[6]   ('DURATIONS:';□←' ')
[7]   DURATIONS
[8]   ('EARLY START TIMES:';□←' ')
[9]   ES
[10]  ('EARLY FINISH TIMES:';□←' ')
[11]  EF
[12]  ('LATE START TIMES:';□←' ')
[13]  LS
[14]  ('LATE FINISH TIMES:';□←' ')
[15]  LF
[16]  ('TOTAL SLACK:';□←' ')
[17]  TS
[18]  ('FREE SLACK:';□←' ')
[19]  FS
   ∇


      ∇PRECEDENCEMATRIX[□]∇
   ∇ PRECEDENCEMATRIX;I;ROW;COLS;V
[1]   PM←(N,N)ρ0
[2]   I←1
[3]   ROW←DATA[I;1]
[4]   COLS←(V>0)/V←DATA[I;2+ι¯2+(ρDATA)[2]]
[5]   PM[ROW;COLS]←1
[6]   →(N≥I←I+1)/3
   ∇


      ∇PREOUTPUTSORT[□]∇
   ∇ PREOUTPUTSORT;I
[1]   PM←PM[I;I←NODEORDERιιN]
[2]   DURATIONS←DURATIONS[I]
[3]   ES←ES[I]
[4]   EF←EF[I]
[5]   LF←LF[I]
[6]   LS←LS[I]
[7]   TS←TS[I]
[8]   CRPATH←IιCRPATH
[9]   FS←FS[I]
   ∇


      ∇TERMINALNODES[□]∇
   ∇ TERMINALNODES
[1]   ERROR←ERROR,1≠ρTNODES←(0=∨/PM)/NODES
   ∇
```

Program 10 (Continued)

```
                    ∇TOPOLOGICALSORT[□]∇
               ∇   TOPOLOGICALSORT;V;I
        [1]      NODEORDER←ι0
        [2]      V←Nρ1
        [3]      V[I←(V\~∨/[1] V/V/[1] PM)ι1]←0
        [4]      →(N>ρNODEORDER←NODEORDER,I)/3
        [5]      PM←PM[NODEORDER;NODEORDER]
        [6]      DURATIONS←DURATIONS[NODEORDER]
               ∇

                    ∇TOTALSLACK[□]∇
               ∇   TOTALSLACK
        [1]      TS←LS-ES
               ∇
```

Program 10 (Continued)

```
        CPM1
IS THIS A NEW PROBLEM?
YES
ENTER PROBLEM NUMBER
□:
        10
ENTER NODE NUMBER,DURATION AND SUCCESSOR NODES,ONE NODE AT A
TIME IN ANY NODE ORDER.AFTER ALL DATA HAVE BEEN ENTERED,ENTER
A NODE NUMBER OF 0.
□:
        1 5 2
□:
        2 6 3 4 5
□:
        3 10 9
□:
        4 5 6 7
□:
        5 19 11
□:
        6 2 8
□:
        7 1 8
□:
        8 2 9
□:
        9 2 10
□:
        10 3 11
□:
        11 1 12
□:
        12 2
□:
```

Application 10. CPM1.

```
        0
```

PROBLEM NUMBER 10   *DATE* 13070

LENGTH OF CRITICAL PATH: 33

CRITICAL ACTIVITIES: 1   2   5   11   12

NODES:
1   2   3   4   5   6   7   8   9   10   11   12

DURATIONS:
5   6   10   5   19   2   1   2   2   3   1   2

EARLY START TIMES:
0   5   11   11   11   16   16   18   21   23   30   31

EARLY FINISH TIMES:
5   11   21   16   30   18   17   20   23   26   31   33

LATE START TIMES:
0   5   15   16   11   21   22   23   25   27   30   31

LATE FINISH TIMES:
5   11   25   21   30   23   23   25   27   30   31   33

TOTAL SLACK:
0   0   4   5   0   5   6   5   4   4   0   0

FREE SLACK:
0   0   0   0   0   0   1   1   0   4   0   0

Application 10. (Continued)

```
        ∇INV[□]∇
     ∇ RB←INV RA;RK;RS;RP;RI
[1]    →((2=ρρRA)∧=/1,ρRA)ρ4
[2]    'NO INVERSE!'
[3]    →~RB←1
[4]    RK←⌊/ρRA
[5]    RS←RK
[6]    RP←ιRK
[7]    RA←RA[;(ιRS),1]
[8]    RA[;1+RS]←(ιRS)≤1
[9]    RI←(|RA[ιRK;1])ι⌈/|RA[ιRK;1]
[10]   RP[1,RI]←RP[RI,1]
[11]   RA[1,RI;ιRS]←RA[RI,1;ιRS]
[12]   →(1E¯30>|RA[1;1])ρ2
[13]   RA[1;]←RA[1;]÷RA[1;1]
[14]   RA←RA-((~(ιRS)≤1)×RA[;1])∘.×RA[1;]
[15]   RA←RA[1+RS|ιRS;(1+ιRS),1]
[16]   RP←RP[1+RS|ιRS]
[17]   →(0<RK←RK-1)/8
[18]   RB←RA[;RPιιRS]
     ∇
```

Program 11. Matrix Inverse (INV).

```
        A←4 4ρ3 2 1 ¯1 ¯3 ¯1 2 1 6 1 7 ¯3 9 ¯1 ¯2 2
        A
  ¯3   2   1  ¯1
  ¯3  ¯1   2   1
   6  ¯1   7  ¯3
   9  ¯1 ¯2   2

        B←3  2  2  5

        AINV←INV A

        X←AINV+.×B
        X
0.33333   2   1   3
        A[1;]+.×X
3
        A[2;]+.×X
2
        A[3;]+.×X
2
        A[4;]+.×X
5
```
Application 11. INV.

Calculus Programs*

Program 14 lists the function *INTEGRAL*1, which computes the area under a curve by trapezoidal integration or by Simpson's rule. The syntax of *INTEGRAL*1 is:

$$R \leftarrow INTEGRAL1\ X$$

where X is a matrix whose first row gives values of the independent variable and whose subsequent rows give values of the dependent variables. The result R gives an area for each curve represented. If an odd number of points is given, Simpson's

```
        ∇DET[□]∇
      ∇ C←DET Z;J;Q
  [1]     →(1=ρ,Z)ρ0,C←,Z
  [2]     →L2×ι(2=ρρZ)∧=/ρZ
  [3]     →0,ρ□←'ILLEGAL  STRUCTURE'
  [4]   L2:→0×ι(1↑ρZ)<J←(Z[1;]=0)ιC←,0
  [5]     Z←(J-1)⌽Z
  [6]   L6:Z←Z-Z[;1]∘.×Z[1;]÷C←Z[1;1]
  [7]     C←(¯1*J-1)×C×DET 1 1 ↓Z
      ∇
```
Program 12. Determinant of Matrix (DET).

*The programs *INTEGRAL*2 and *MAX*, as well as the utility functions, are listed with permission from E. M. Edwards, Department of Electrical Engineering, University of Alberta.

```
        A←2 2ρ1 3 2 4
        A

   1    3
   2    4

        DET A
  ¯2

        B←3 3ρ1 1 1 2 3 1 4 9
        B

   1    1    1
   1    2    3
   1    4    9

        DET B
   2

        C←4 4ρ2 4 6 8 3 1 2 1 1 2 ¯2 2 2 3 4 1
        C

   2    4    6    8
   3    1    2    1
   1    2   ¯2    2
   2    3    4    1

        DET C
  ¯228
```

Application 12. DET.

rule is used. If an even number is given, trapezoidal integration is used for the last interval and Simpson's rule is used for the remainder. Application 14 uses *INTEGRAL1* to find the area under three standard deviations of the normal curve.

Program 15 lists *MAX*, a function which locates the maximum of a defined function over a specified interval. The function uses a monadic APL function named *FCN*, which returns a vector result from a vector operand. *FCN* is a definition of the curve under study by the user. The syntax of *MAX* is:

$$XM← MAX\ I$$

```
        ∇PCF[□]∇
     ∇ R←N PCF X;A
[1]    R←(INV(⍉A)+.×A)+.×X[2;]+.×A←X[1;]∘.*⌽0,ιN←0⌈⌊
       0.5+1ρN⌊¯1+(ρX)[2]
[2]    X[2;]←X[2;]-A+.×R
[3]    A←ι0
[4]    DEV←(((+/X[2;]*2)÷(ρX)[2])*0.5),φ,⍉((|X[2;])=⌈/|X[
       2;])/X
     ∇
```

Program 13. Polynomial Curve Fit (PCF).

```
      X←ι10
      Y←(3×X)+2
      1 PCF 2 10ρX,Y
3 2
      Y←((5×X*2)-(10×X))+7
      2 PCF 2 10ρX,Y
5  ⁻10  7

      X←ι20
      Y←?20ρ20
```

```
      GRAPH Y

GRAPH

             \        ORDINATE
           0.0         5.0        10.0        15.0        20.0
A    1.00 |           |     o     |           |           |
B    2.00 |                             o                o
S    3.00 |                       o
C    4.00 |            o
I    5.00 |                             o
S    6.00 |               o
S    7.00 |              o
A    8.00 |                  o
     9.00 |         o
    10.00 |                     o
    11.00 |                              o
    12.00 |                     o
    13.00 |                                         o
    14.00 |                     o
    15.00 |         o
    16.00 |                                         o
    17.00 |               o
    18.00 |         o
    19.00 |                     o
    20.00 |           |  o      |           |           |


      LEGEND

o
```

```
      C←4 PCF 2 20ρX,Y
      C
⁻5.47480798E⁻5  ⁻0.007272677985  0.2427199075  ⁻1.934862398
   14.1002322
```

Application 13. PCF.

```
Z←(C[1]×X*4)+(C[2]×X*3)+(C[3]×X*2)+(C[4]×X)+C[5]
GRAPH 3 20ρX,Y,Z
```

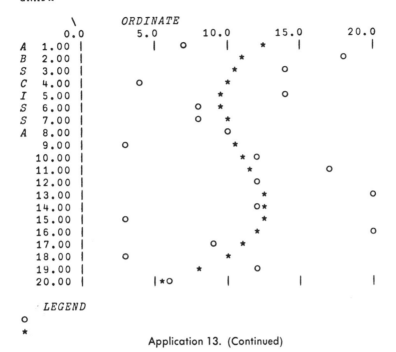

```
GRAPH

              \        ORDINATE
            0.0        5.0       10.0       15.0       20.0
   A   1.00  |          |    o     |    *     |          |
   B   2.00  |                          *          o
   S   3.00  |                         *       o
   C   4.00  |          o             *
   I   5.00  |                       *         o
   S   6.00  |                  o  *
   S   7.00  |                  o   *
   A   8.00  |                     o
       9.00  |          o           *
      10.00  |                         * o
      11.00  |                        *        o
      12.00  |                         o
      13.00  |                          *          o
      14.00  |                         o*
      15.00  |          o              *
      16.00  |                         *           o
      17.00  |                 o     *
      18.00  |          o            *
      19.00  |                  *      o
      20.00  |          |*o     |          |          |

    LEGEND
  o
  *
```

Application 13. (Continued)

where $I[1]$ is the lower bound; $I[2]$ is the upper bound; and $I[3]$ is the tolerance value used as + or $-I[3]× | I[1]-I[2]|$. If $(\rho I)=2$, then an $I[3]=1E^{-}6$ is supplied. XM is the abscissa value for the maximum point. The minimum value may be computed using $-F(X)$. Application 15 finds the maximum value of the normal curve with a mean of 10 and a standard deviation of 3.

```
        ∇INTEGRAL1[□]∇
      ∇ R←INTEGRAL1 X;T;O
  [1]    →3×ι2=ρρX
  [2]    →0,ρ□←'REQUIRE MATRIX ARGUMENT'
  [3]    T←X[1;]
  [4]    X← 1 0 ↓X
  [5]    →8×ι(2≤ρT)∧∧/T=H←1↑T←1↓T-¯1ϕT
  [6]    R←(0 1 ↓X+¯1ϕX)+.×T÷2
  [7]    →0
  [8]    R←(H÷6)×X+.×2,((¯1-O-ρT)ρ 8 4),(1+O)ρ 2 0 +3×O÷2|ρT
      ∇
```

Program 14. Numerical Integration (INTEGRAL1).

```
        ∇P←NORM X
[1]     M←10
[2]     S←3
[3]     P←(*-((X-M)*2)÷2×S*2)÷S×(○2)*.5
[4]     ∇

        GRAPH NORM ι19

GRAPH
```

```
           \           ORDINATE      (×10*-3)
               0.0         50.0       100.0         150.0
    A   1.00  o             |           |             |
    B   2.00  |o
    S   3.00  |  o
    C   4.00  |     o
    I   5.00  |        o
    S   6.00  |           o
    S   7.00  |              o
    A   8.00  |                 o
        9.00  |                    o
       10.00  |                      o
       11.00  |                   o
       12.00  |                o
       13.00  |             o
       14.00  |          o
       15.00  |       o
       16.00  |    o
       17.00  |  o
       18.00  |o
       19.00  o             |           |             |
```

```
        INTEGRAL1 2 19ρ(ι19),NORMι19
0.9972894445
```

Application 14. INTEGRAL1.


```
    ∇MAX[□]∇
  ∇ XM←MAX I;M;D;E;L;XQ II
[1]     E←(I,1E⁻6)[2+MAX+1]
[2]     →13×ι1≠ρρFCN II←I+I[1 2]
[3]     XQ←II[1]-(-/II)×0.05×0,ι20
[4]     →9×ι1≠+/L←M=⌈/M←FCN XQ
[5]     II←M+(D←0.05×-/II)× 1 ⁻1 ×II≠M←L/XQ
[6]     →3×ιE<D÷-/I
[7]     →0×ιΛ/I≠XM←M
[8]     →0,ρ□←'MAXIMUM IS AT AN END POINT'
[9]     →12×ι1=-/L[1,ρL],ρL←L/ιρL
[10]    'MULTIPLE MAXIMUM AT ';XQ[L]
[11]    →0
[12]    →7,M←+/XQ[L]÷MAX←ρL
[13]    'YOUR FCN DOES NOT RETURN A VECTOR RESULT FOR A VECTOR ARG
    UEMENT'
  ∇
```

Program 15. Maximum of a Function (MAX).

```
         ∇R←FCN X
[1]      M←10
[2]      S←3
[3]      R←(*-((X-M)*2)÷2×S*2)÷S×(○2)*.5
[4]      ∇

         CURVE←FCNι19
         MAXΔX←MAX 1 19
         MAXΔY←FCN MAXΔX

         GRAPH 3 19ρ(ι19),CURVE,19ρMAXΔY
```

GRAPH

```
                 \     ORDINATE      (×10*-3)
                 0.0      50.0      100.0      150.0
     A    1.00  o          |          |       *   |
     B    2.00  |o                            *
     S    3.00  |   o                         *
     C    4.00  |       o                     *
     I    5.00  |          o                  *
     S    6.00  |             o               *
     S    7.00  |                o            *
     A    8.00  |                   o         *
          9.00  |                          o  *
         10.00  |                             o
         11.00  |                          o  *
         12.00  |                      o      *
         13.00  |                 o           *
         14.00  |            o                *
         15.00  |        o                    *
         16.00  |    o                        *
         17.00  | o                           *
         18.00  |o                            *
         19.00  o          |          |       *   |

         LEGEND
     o
     *
```

Application 15. MAX.

Utility Programs

Program 16 lists four utility functions: *DEG* converts radians to degrees: *RAD* converts degrees to radians; *RND* rounds to *N* decimal places; and *SIG* rounds to *N* significant figures. The syntax of these functions is:

$$R←DEG\ X$$
$$R←RAD\ X$$
$$R←N\ RND\ X$$
$$R←N\ SIG\ X$$

Some simple examples are given as Application 16.

```
        ∇DEG[□]∇
     ∇  R←DEG X
[1]     R←57.29577951308232×X
     ∇
```

```
        ∇RAD[□]∇
     ∇  R←RAD X
[1]     R←0.0174532925199433×X
     ∇
```

```
        ∇RND[□]∇
     ∇  R←N RND X
[1]     →4×ι∧/(N≤0),,(2*31)≥X
[2]     R←X-N|X←X+0.5×N←10*-N
[3]     →0
[4]     R←⌊0.5+N×⌊0.5+X÷N←10*-N
     ∇
```

```
        ∇SIG[□]∇
     ∇  R←N SIG X
[1]     R←X-N|X←X+0.5×N←10*1-N-⌊10⊕|X÷X=0
     ∇
```

Program 16. Utility Programs (DEG, RAD, RND, SIG).

A.4 BUSINESS

Program 17 lists two functions: compound interest ($COMPINT$) and invest ($INVEST$). Compound interest computes the future value of an amount if compounded periodically at a given interest. The syntax of $COMPINT$ is:

$$V \leftarrow COMPINT\ D$$

```
        DEG 1
57.29577951

        DEG o1
180

        RAD 180
3.141592654

        (RAD 180)=o1
1

      5 RND o1
3.14159

      5 SIG o1
3.1416
```

Application 16. DEG, RAD, RND, SIG.

```
      ∇COMPINT[□]∇
    ∇ V←COMPINT D
[1]   V←2 RND D[1]×((1+(D[2]÷100)÷D[4])*D[3]×D[4])
    ∇


      ∇INVEST[□]∇
    ∇ V←INVEST D
[1]   V←2 RND D[1]÷((1+(D[2]÷100)÷D[4])*D[3]×D[4])
    ∇
```

Program 17. Business (COMPINT, INVEST).

```
          COMPINT 1000 5 10 1
    1628.89
          COMPINT 1000 5 10 2
    1638.62

          INVEST 1000 5 10 1
    613.91
          INVEST 1000 5 10 2
    610.27
```

Application 17. COMPINT, INVEST.

where $(\rho D)=4$ and V is a scalar result. $D[1]$ is the amount to be invested; $D[2]$ is the interest rate in percent; $D[3]$ is the number of years; and $D[4]$ is the number of times a year that interest is compounded.

INVEST computes the present value that must be invested at a given interest to be worth a given amount in the future. The syntax of *INVEST* is:

$$V \leftarrow INVEST\ D$$

where $(\rho D)=4$ and V is a scalar result. $D[1]$ is the future value; $D[2]$ is the interest rate in percent; $D[3]$ is the number of years; and $D[4]$ is the number of times a year that interest is compounded.

Application 17 applies *COMPINT* and *INVEST* to some sample values.

APPENDIX B
APL\360

This appendix contains information pertinent to the implementation of APL on the IBM System/360 computers (See Falkoff and Iverson[9]). Additional facts which are outside of the scope of earlier chapters are also presented here.

B.1 SPECIFICATIONS

Names

Variables, function names, groups, and labels can be of any length up to 77 characters. Workspace names, theoretically, may be of any length but only 11 characters are retained.

Line Width

In a clean workspace, the width of a line of output is set nominally at 120 spaces. It may be changed with the system command:

$$)WIDTH\ n$$

where n can be from 30 to 130.

Number of Digits

In a clean workspace, the maximum number of digits displayed is set at 10. It may be changed to $1 \leq n \leq 16$ with the digits command, that is

$$)DIGITS\ n$$

Indexing Origin

The indexing origin is set to 1 in a clean workspace. It can be changed to 0, and back to 1, with the)ORIGIN command.

System Information

A set of functions denoted by the monadic operator I (formed by overstriking $\top$ with $\bot$) provides information from the APL\360 system. The operand to I must be a scalar. They are listed as follows:

I19—The time the keyboard has been unlocked during the current session.
I20—The time of day in 60ths of a second.
I21—Processor time used since sign-on in 60ths of a second.
I22—Unused storage in the active workspace in bytes. Storage can be estimated using the following equivalences:

  1 character = 1 byte
  1 integer = 2 bytes
  1 mixed number = 4 bytes
  8 logical numbers = 1 byte

I23—The number of users currently signed on.
I24—Time since sign-on in 60ths of a second.
I25—Today's date as MMDDYY to the base ten.
I26—Current value of the line counter during function execution.
I27—Vector of line numbers in the state indicator.

Sign-On Information

A session begins with a dialog of the form:

```
              )123456:    PASSWORD
     005      01.02.03      01/01/70      JSMITH
              A P L   \      3 6 0
     SAVED 01.01.01        12/31/69
```

The items are identified as follows:

  123456 is the user's sign-on number.
  PASSWORD is the user's password.
  005 is the user's port number.
  01.02.03 is the sign-on time in hours, minutes, and seconds.
  01/01/70 is today's date.
  JSMITH is the user's identification.
  SAVED 01.01.01 12/31/69 is the date and time when the last CONTINUE workspace was saved.

Passwords

The user can protect his user's identification by signing off with a password. It takes the form:

$$)OFF: n$$

where *n* is a password containing from one to eight characters. The password must be used the next time the user signs on. The password may be discontinued by signing off with the colon but with no password.

B.2 WORKSPACE MANAGEMENT

Libraries

Each user is assigned a private library in which he may save workspaces. The)*LIB* command lists the saved workspaces in the user's private library.

Public libraries are denoted by numbers 1 through 99. A list of workspaces in public library *n* are displayed with the command)*LIB n*.

Continue Workspace

Each user is assigned an additional workspace name *CONTINUE*. It is stored when the following system commands are entered:

$$)SAVE\ CONTINUE$$
$$)CONTINUE$$
$$)CONTINUE\ HOLD$$

or when a line disconnect occurs during execution. The continue workspace may be saved or loaded, as required.

Loading, Saving, and Dropping Workspaces

A workspace can be saved with the save command:

$$)SAVE\ n$$

where *n* is a workspace name, and can be subsequently loaded with the same name, that is,

$$)LOAD\ n$$

The save and load commands may be optionally followed by a key, which provides another level of protection. A key may be up to eight characters in length. For example:

$$)SAVE\ ASPACE{:}JS$$
$$\vdots$$
$$)LOAD\ ASPACE{:}JS$$

A workspace may be dropped from the user's library with the drop command:

$$)DROP\ n$$

when n is a workspace that has previously been saved.

Groups

Function and variable names may be combined to form a *group* of names with the group command:

$$)GROUP\ n\ r...$$

where n is a name and r is a list of referents. Groups are used with the copy command for moving several items from a library to the active workspace.

Copy Command

The copy command is used to copy one item—variable, function, or group—from a saved workspace to the active workspace. It has the form:

$$)COPY\ name:\ key\ x$$

where *name* is the name of the saved workspace, *key* is the optional key, and x is the variable, function, or group.

Locked Functions

Functions can be locked during function definition (or editing) by overstriking the opening or closing del with a tilde, that is, $\nabla\!\!\!\sim$. A locked function can be copied, executed, or erased. It cannot be modified or displayed.

B.3   EDITING

Line Editing

During function definition, a single line can be edited by overriding the statement number with $[N \square K]$, where N is a statement number and K is a position in the statement. The Nth statement is printed, the paper is moved up one line, and the carriage stops under the Kth position. Editing proceeds as follows:

1. To *delete* a character, type a / beneath it.
2. To *insert* spaces, type the number of spaces under the character to the right of where spaces should be inserted.

In the latter case, the line is retyped and the user can enter the characters desired. When editing lines, a good rule to follow is that a line is entered as it looks on the page. Editing can be discontinued with the ATTN key.

Correcting a Line Before It Is Entered

Errors can be corrected before a line is entered by backspacing to the error and then pressing ATTN, INDEX, or LINEFEED. Characters to the right of the carriage are deleted.

B.4   ERROR REPORTS

Error	Cause
CHARACTER	Illegal overstrike
DEPTH	Limit of nested functions exceeded
DEFN	Ill-formed function definition or locked function
DOMAIN	Function or operation not defined for operand(s)
INDEX	Attempt to select nonexistent component of array
LABEL	Illegal use of colon or illegal statement label
LENGTH	Arrays not comformable
RANK	Ranks not conformable
SI DAMAGE	Modifying a pendent function
SYMBOL TABLE FULL	Too many names
SYNTAX	Illegal construction
SYSTEM	*APL\360* system failure
VALUE	Undefined variable
WS FULL	Workspace overloaded

B.5   SYSTEM COMMANDS

Terminal Control

Command[a]	Function
)*NUMBER* [:KEY]	Sign-on
)*OFF* [:LOCK]	End work session
)*OFF HOLD* [:LOCK]	End work session and hold line connection
)*CONTINUE* [:LOCK]	End work session and save active workspace
)*CONTINUE HOLD* [:LOCK]	End work session, save workspaces, and hold line connection

[a] Items enclosed in brackets are optional.

Workspace Control

Command	Function
)CLEAR	Clear workspace
)LOAD WSID[:KEY]	Load saved workspace
)COPY WSID[:KEY] NAME	Copy referent from saved workspace
)COPY WSID[:KEY]	Copy all objects (functions, variables) from saved workspace
)PCOPY WSID[:KEY] NAME	Same as COPY but protect objects in active workspace
)PCOPY WSID[:KEY]	Same as COPY but protect objects in active workspace
)GROUP NAME(S)	Group objects
)ERASE NAME	Erase named object
)ORIGIN I	Set index origin where I = 0 or 1
)DIGITS I	Specify significant digits for output; $1 \leq I \leq 16$
)WIDTH I	Set page width; $30 \leq I \leq 130$
)WSID NAME	Change name of active workspace
)WSID	Gives name of active workspace

Library Control

Command	Function
)SAVE	Save active workspaces with name WSID
)SAVE WSID [:LOCK]	Save active workspace
)DROP WSID	Drop workspace from library

Inquiry

Command	Function
)FNS	Lists names of defined functions
)FNS LETTER	Lists names of defined functions beginning with the given letter
)VARS	Lists global variables
)VARS LETTER	Lists global variables beginning with the given letter
)GRPS	Lists names of groups
)GRPS LETTER	Lists names of groups beginning with the given letter
)GRP NAME	Lists members of named group
)SI	Lists halted functions
)SIV	Lists halted functions and local variables
)WSID	Lists identification of active workspace
)LIB [NUMBER]	Lists workspaces in library
)PORTS	Lists ports in use by user
)PORTS CODE	Lists ports for a designated user

Communications

Command	Function
)*MSGN* PORT [TEXT]	Send message to designated port
)*MSG* PORT [TEXT]	Send message to designated port and lock keyboard
)*OPRN* [TEXT]	Send message to APL operator
)*OPR* [TEXT]	Send message to APL operator and lock keyboard

APPENDIX C
APL FUNCTIONS

APL FUNCTION SYMBOLS

Symbol	Monadic Name	Dyadic Name
+	Identity	Addition
−	Negation	Subtraction
×	Signum	Multiplication
÷	Reciprocal	Division
*	Exponential	Exponentiation
∧		And
∨		Or
~	Not	
⍲		Nand
⍱		Nor
<		Less than
≤		Less than or equal to
=		Equal to
≥		Greater than or equal to
>		Greater than
≠		Not equal to
⌈	Ceiling	Maximum
⌊	Floor	Minimum
|	Absolute value	Residue

Symbol	Monadic Name	Dyadic Name
○	Pi times	Circular functions
⊛	Natural log	Common log
!	Factorial	Combination
?	Roll	Deal
ι	Index generator	Index of
ρ	Dimension (size)	Reshape (restructure)
,	Ravel	Catenation
∊		Membership
↑		Take
↓		Drop
⌽	Reversal	Rotation
⍉	Monadic transpose	Dyadic transpose
⍋		Grade up
⍒		Grade down
⊥		Base value
⊤		Representation
\		Compression
/		Expansion
∘.ƒ		Outer product
ƒ.g		Inner product
ƒ/	Reduction	
[ ]		Indexing (subscripting)
←		Specification
→	Branch	
I	I beam	
TΔ...	Trace control	
SΔ...	Stop control	
▯	Quad	
▯	Quote-quad	
( )	Grouping	
:	Delimits statement labels	
;	Separates subscripts, precedes local variables, and separates mixed output	
‾	Denotes negative constant	
E	Denotes exponent	
∇	Delimits function definition	
⍝	Comment	
'	Delimits literal	
⍫	Locks function	

CONSTANTS

$\pi = 3.141592653589793$
$e = 2.718281828459045l$
$SEED = 16807 = 7*5$
$FUZZ = 1.0E^-13$

PRIMITIVE OPERATIONS AND MATHEMATICAL FUNCTIONS

Primitive operations and mathematical functions produce a scalar result when their operands are scalars and produce array results when extended on an element-by-element basis. If one operand is a scalar, then it is extended to all components of the other operand. If both operands are arrays, then they must be of the same size. Some operators are formed from composite symbols. Appendix D describes how they are formed.

$A + B$	A plus B
$+ B$	B (identity operation)
$A - B$	A minus B
$- B$	Minus B
$A \times B$	A times B
$\times B$	Signum of $B(-1, 0, +1$ if $B<0$, $B=0$, or $B>0$ respectively)
$A \div B$	A divided by B
$\div B$	Reciprocal of B (i.e., $1 \div B$)
$A*B$	A raised to the power B (A^B)
$*B$	e raised to the power B (e^B)
$A \lceil B$	Maximum of A and B
$\lceil B$	Ceiling of B (smallest integer not exceeded by B)
$A \lfloor B$	Minimum of A and B
$\lfloor B$	Floor of B (largest integer not exceeding B)
$A \mid B$	Residue of B modulus A (always gives a positive result)
$\mid B$	Absolute value of B
$A < B$	Is A less than B?
$A \leq B$	Is A less than or equal to B?
$A = B$	Is A equal to B?
$A \geq B$	Is A greater than or equal to B?
$A > B$	Is A greater than B?
$A \neq B$	Is A not equal to B?
$A \wedge B$	A *and* B
$A \vee B$	A *or* B
$\sim B$	*Not* B
$A \barwedge B$	A *nand* B equivalent to $\sim (A \vee B)$
$A \veebar B$	A *nor* B equivalent to $\sim (A \wedge B)$
$A!B$	Combinations of B things taken A at a time ($\binom{B}{A}$)
$!B$	B factorial or the gamma function of $(B-1)$
$?B$	Random selection from the first B positive integers

$A \circledast B$ $\mathrm{Log}_A B$

$\circledast B$ $\mathrm{Ln}\ B\ (\log_e B)$

$A \bigcirc B$ Circular functions (e.g., $\sin B \equiv 1\bigcirc B$)

$\bigcirc B$ Pi times B

COMPOSITE FUNCTIONS

Composite functions include reduction, inner product, and outer product; they are the extensions of the scalar dyadic operations to arrays.

f/B Reduction along the last coordinate of B

$f \neq B$ Reduction along the first coordinate of B

$f/[I]B$ Reduction along the Ith coordinate of B

$Af.gB$ Inner product of A and B ($A + . \times B$ denotes ordinary matrix multiplication)

$A \circ .fB$ Outer product of A and B

MIXED FUNCTIONS

Mixed functions extend the primitive operations to arrays in such a manner that they do not always produce a uniform result. A mixed function always involves an array—either as an operand or as a result.

ιB Generates the first B positive integers (uses the index origin)

$A \iota B$ Index of the first occurrence of B in A

ρB Size of B

$A \rho B$ Reshape (restructure) B as determined by A

$A \phi B$ Rotation of B by A along the last coordinate

$A \ominus B$ Rotation of B by A along the first coordinate

$A \phi [I] B$ Rotation of B by A along the Ith coordinate

ϕB Reversal along the last coordinate of B

$\ominus B$ Reversal along the first coordinate of B

$\phi [I] B$ Reversal along the Ith coordinate of B

$A \lozenge B$ Transpose (interchange coordinates of B as determined by A)

$\lozenge B$ Monadic transpose (interchange last two coordinates of B)

A,B Concatenation of A and B

$,B$ Ravel of B

$A \uparrow B$ Take the first A (or last if A is negative) components of B

$A \downarrow B$ Drop the first A (or last if A is negative) components of B

$\upharpoonleft B$ Grade up of B (permutation of indices that would order B in ascending sequence)

ψB Grade down of B (indices that would order B in descending sequence)

$A \top B$ Representation of scalar B to the base A

$A \perp B$ Value of the vector B to the base A

$A \epsilon B$ Membership (Is A an element of B?)

$A?B$	Select A components of B at random without replacement.
$A \leftarrow B$	A specified by B (assignment of B to A)
$A[B]$	Select the components of A with indices B
U/B	Compress B by U (logical) along the last coordinate
$U\not/B$	Compress B by U (logical) along the first coordinate
$U/[I]B$	Compress B by U (logical) along the Ith coordinate
$U\backslash B$	Expand B by U (logical) along the last coordinate
$U\not\backslash B$	Expand B by U (logical) along the first coordinate
$U\backslash[I]B$	Expand B by U (logical) along the Ith coordinate

APPENDIX D
APL ALPHABET

KEYBOARD ARRANGEMENT

APL KEYBOARD SYMBOLS

Symbol	Name	Symbol	Name
$A \ldots Z$	Letters	⌈ ⌊	Angle beams
$0 \ldots 9$	Digits	—	Underscore
−	Negative sign	∇	Del
$< \leq = \geq > \neq$	Comparison operators	Δ	Delta
∧ ∨ ~	Logical operators	○	Small circle
$+ - \times \div *$	Arithmetic operators	'	Quote
?	Question mark	▢	Quad
ϵ	Epsilon	( )	Parentheses
ρ	Rho	[ ]	Brackets
↑	Up arrow	⊥ ⊤	T beams
↓	Down arrow	|	Vertical stroke
ι	Iota	;	Semicolon
○	Circle symbol	:	Colon
→	Branch arrow	.	Period
←	Specification arrow	,	Comma
∩	Cap	/	Solidus
		\\	Reverse solidus

311

COMPOSITE SYMBOLS

A composite symbol is formed in APL by striking one key, backspacing, and then striking the other key. The order in which the keys are struck is not significant.

Composite Symbol	Used for	Formed with	
!	Combination, factorial	'	.
Ꮪ	Comment	∩	○
⍒	Grade down	∇	|
⍋	Grade up	△	|
⌶	⌶ beam	⊤	⊥
⊛	Logarithm	○	*
⍲	Nand	∧	~
⍱	Nor	∨	~
⍫	Protected function	∇	~
⍞	Quote-quad	☐	'
⌽	Reversal, rotation	○	|
⍉	Transpose	○	\

FUNCTION SYMBOLS

The APL function symbols are summarized in Appendix C.

APPENDIX E

PROSE GLOSSARY OF APL

1   The **APL terminal system** approaches the state of the art in computer tech-
2   nology by combining the concept of time sharing and the power and rele-
3   vance of Iverson's language* into a single programming system. APL is
4   accessed with a remote terminal device, which may use a **dataset** or an
5   **acoustical coupler** to prepare information for transmission over ordinary
6   telephone lines.
7   The user instructs the computer in two ways: by system commands and
8   with APL statements. A **system command**, such as)$ERASE\ ABC$, is used to
9   have a function performed by the computer which is outside of the scope of
10   the language. A **system command** always begins with a right parenthesis.
11   Two system commands are used to **initiate** and **terminate** a work session and
12   are especially important; they are:)XXXXXXX and)OFF, respectively.
13   (Here XXXXXXX is an installation-defined account number.) A user in-
14   dicates the processing that he wants performed by entering a statement,
15   which is executed immediately or is stored as part of a defined function. A
16   **statement** can be either of two types: specification or branching. A **specifica-**
17   **tion statement** is of the form $X \leftarrow EXP$ where X is a scalar variable, array
18   variable, or a subscripted array variable and EXP is a mathematical ex-
19   pression. The value of X is replaced by the value of EXP. Example: $T \leftarrow 5*2$.
20   If the specification operator $\leftarrow$ is not the last operation in the statement,
21   then the result is printed at the terminal. The **branch statement**, which uses
22   the operator $\rightarrow$, is normally used in defined functions to depart from the
23   sequential order of execution. The operand to the branch operator $\rightarrow$ is the

*K. E. Iverson, *A Programming Language*, New York, John Wiley and Sons, Inc., 1962.

24   number of a statement. If it is zero or does not exist, then an exit is made
25   from the function.
26   **Numeric constants** are of two forms: decimal and exponential. The deci-
27   mal form uses the characters 0 1 2 3 4 5 6 7 8 9. and ¯; a number expressed in
28   decimal form may be negative and possess integral or fractional parts as re-
29   quired. Examples ¯1 173 45.678 ¯.3. The exponential form involves a
30   power of 10 and uses the character E to indicate a positive or negative ex-
31   ponent. Examples: 13 E7 ¯13.638 E17 25.1E¯4. Numeric constants may
32   not contain embedded spaces. Data may be organized as scalars or arrays
33   and be named. A scalar has a rank of 0; a vector has a rank of 1; a matrix has
34   a rank of 2; etc. A **name** is a sequence of letters, digits, or the character Δ.
35   Moreover, a letter of a name may be underlined for clarity. The first char-
36   acter of a name must not be a digit; the initial sequences SΔ and TΔ and
37   embedded spaces are not permitted. Sample names are I AB12 $XPRIME$
38   ALLΔ$DONE$. A variable associates a name and a value in an active work-
39   space, which may be saved and loaded by the user. A **workspace** contains
40   variables, functions, and control information for a terminal session.
41   The ordinary dyadic arithmetic **operators** are: **addition** (+), **subtraction**
42   (−), **Multiplication** (×), **division** (÷), and **exponentiation** (∗). The monadic
43   counterparts of the above operators are: − for **negation** so that $-B \equiv 0-B$;
44   + for **identity** so that $+B \equiv 0+B$; × for the **signum** function so that $\times B \equiv -1$,
45   0, or +1 if $B<0$, $B=0$ or $B>0$ respectively; ÷ for **reciprocal** so that $\div B \equiv$
46    $1 \div B$; and ∗ for **exponential** so that $\ast B \equiv e^B$ where $e = 2.718281828459045$.
47   Other primitive arithmetic operators are a part of the language and are mo-
48   nadic or dyadic as indicated. For all operations, operands may be constants,
49   variables, or expressions. **Maximum,** $A\lceil B$, selects the algebraic largest of
50   its operands: $5 = 3\lceil 5$. **Minimum,** $A\lfloor B$, selects the algebraic smallest of its
51   operands: $3 = 3\lfloor 5$. **Floor,** $\lfloor A$, gives the largest integer not exceeding the
52   operand: $3 = \lfloor 3.14$. **Ceiling,** $\lceil A$, gives the smallest integer not exceeded by the
53   operand: $4 = \lceil 3.14$. **Absolute value,** $|A$, produces the magnitude of the
54   operand: $5 = |{-5}$. **Residue,** $A|B$, provides the remainder after dividing B
55   by A and is always positive: $1 = 3 | 7$, $1.6 = 5 | {-13.4}$. **Comparison operations**
56   assume their normal meaning and use the following symbols: **less than** (<),
57   **less than or equal to** (≤), **equal to** (=), **greater than or equal to** (≥), **greater**
58   **than** (>), and **not equal to** (≠). How close is equal is of importance, and a
59   tolerance of approximately $1.0E^-13$ is used and is termed **fuzz.** Fuzz is used
60   with all of the comparison operations, which produce the result 1 for true
61   and 0 for false. Thus, the result of a comparison operation can be used in an
62   arithmetic or logical expression. The APL language contains five primitive
63   **connectives** whose domain and range is the set {0,1}. **And,** $U \wedge V$, returns the
64   value 1 if both operands are 1. **Or,** $U \vee V$, returns the value 1 if either or both
65   of the operands is 1. **Not,** $\sim U$, returns the value 0 if its operand is 1 and
66   returns 1 if its operand is 0. **Nand,** $U \tilde{\wedge} V$, returns the value 0 if both operands
67   are 0 and returns 1 otherwise. **Nor,** $U \tilde{\vee} V$, returns the value 1 if both
68   operands are 0 and returns a 0 otherwise.
69   Several basic mathematical functions are also included in the language.

70   The **generalized combination**, $K!N$, gives the number of combinations of N
71   things taken K at a time: $3 = 2!3$. **Factorial**, $!N$, gives the number of distinct
72   arrangements of N things: $24 = !4$. **Roll**, $?N$, selects an integer pseudo-
73   randomly from the first N positive integers: $1 = ?5$. Roll uses a starting
74   number termed the **seed** which is set initially to 16807 or $7*5$ and is stored
75   with a workspace. The **natural logarithm**, $\circledast N$, computes $\log_e N$. The **com-**
76   **mon logarithm**, $M \circledast N$, computes $\log_M N : 10 \circledast 2 = 0.3010299957$. **Pi times**,
77    $\bigcirc N$, computes the mathematical value π times the operand: $3.141592654 = \bigcirc 1$.
78   The **circular functions** are expressed as $I \bigcirc X$ where: $\sin X \equiv 1 \bigcirc X$; $\cos X \equiv 2 \bigcirc X$;
79    $\tan X \equiv 3 \bigcirc X$; $\arcsin X \equiv {}^-1 \bigcirc X$; $\arccos X \equiv {}^-2 \bigcirc X$; and $\arctan X \equiv {}^-3 \bigcirc X$. For
80   example: $0.5 = 1 \bigcirc 0 \div 6$.
81   Operators and operands can be combined to form **compound expressions**,
82   such as $2+3\times4$, which has the value 14. Because of the multiplicity of
83   operators in APL, a strict right-to-left order of execution is adopted. For
84   example, $3 \times 4 + 5$ produces the value 27. **Parentheses** can be used to depart
85   from the normal order of execution so that $(3 \times 4) + 5$ would produce a result
86   of 17.
87   Most operator symbols have monadic and dyadic counterparts. An oper-
88   ator is assumed to be **monadic** if the symbol to its immediate left is another
89   operator symbol. The operand to the left of a **dyadic** operator can be a
90   variable, a constant, or an expression in parentheses. The **right operand** to
91   either type of operator is the value of the entire expression to its right.
92   **Arrays** can have numeric or character components that cannot be mixed
93   within any one array. A **numeric vector** is specified as $V \leftarrow v_1\ v_2\ v_3\ \dots\ v_n$,
94   where the v_i are numeric constants: $A \leftarrow {}^-7\ 3\ 9\ 6$. The monadic form of the
95   **iota** symbol, ιN, is called the **index generator** and generates a vector of the
96   integers 1 through N (in 1-origin indexing) and 0 through $N-1$ (in 0-origin
97   indexing). A **character vector** is specified as $C \leftarrow {}'c_1 c_2 \dots c_n{}'$, where the c_i are
98   characters from the APL alphabet including composite symbols:
99    $C \leftarrow {}'ABC - 12\phi{}'$. Each character is one component of a character array and
100   a series of characters in quote symbols is termed a **literal**. A quote within
101   a literal is denoted by **two quote marks**. **Arrays of higher dimension** are gen-
102   erated with the **reshape function**, $M \rho N$, where M specifies the size of the
103   result and N specifies the components. If N contains less than the required
104   number of components, it is used cyclically. If it contains more, only the
105   required number are used. For example, $M \leftarrow 3\ 4 \rho 1$ specifies a matrix with 3
106   rows and 4 columns, all components of which are 1. A component of an
107   array may be selected or specified with a subscript. A **subscript** is enclosed
108   in brackets and follows the array name. A **single component** is indicated by
109   an **index** for each coordinate of an array; indices, which may be scalars or
110   arrays, are separated by a semicolon. If $A \leftarrow 2\ 3 \rho \iota 6$, then $A[1;2] = 2$ and
111    $A[2;\ \iota 3] = 4\ 5\ 6$. If an index is omitted, then an entire coordinate is selected:
112    $A[;2] = 2\ 5$. Thus, $A[1\ 2;2] = A[;2]$.
113   Primitive operations and mathematical functions, defined on scalars, are
114   extended to arrays on an **element-by-element basis.** If $V \leftarrow \iota 6$ and $W \leftarrow 6\rho 2$,
115   then $(V*W) = 1\ 4\ 9\ 16\ 25\ 36$. If either operand is a scalar, then it is ex-

116   tended to apply to all components of the other operand: $(V+1)=2\ 3\ 4\ 5\ 6\ 7$.
117   The monadic form of ρ gives the **size** of an array and always produces a
118   vector result. Applied to a vector, ρN produces a vector with one com-
119   ponent—the magnitude of which is the **dimension** of N. Applied to a **matrix**,
120   ρN produces a vector where each component gives the dimension of one of
121   the coordinates of the array. The concept is extended to higher-dimensioned
122   arrays systematically. Thus, if $V \leftarrow ^-7\ 3\ 9\ 6\ 5\ 4$, then $(\rho V)=6$. Also, if
123    $A \leftarrow 2\ 3\rho\ \iota 6$, then $(\rho A)=2\ 3$.
124   The vectors can be catenated with the **catenation operation**: V,W where
125    $(\rho(V.W))=(\rho V)+\rho W$.
126   When arrays are generated from a vector using the **reshape function**, the
127   array is formed by lexicographic order of its subscripts. Similarly, an array
128   is **raveled** with the monadic form of the operator (,). If $A \leftarrow 2\ 3\rho\ \iota 6$, then
129    $(,A)=1\ 2\ 3\ 4\ 5\ 6$. Also, if $X \leftarrow 5$, then ρX produces a null value. However,
130    $(\rho,X)=1$. Thus, **ravel** produces a vector result.
131   Dyadic operations are applied to the components of a single array with
132   the **reduction** operator: $\oplus/X=X[1]\oplus X[2]\oplus\ldots\oplus X[(\rho X)-1]\oplus X[\rho X]$. For
133   example: $(+/\iota 6)=21$. Here, the **right-to-left rule** is also applied. Reduction
134   is also applied to the Ith coordinate of an array A as follows: $\oplus/[I]A$. The
135   ordinary **matrix multiplication** is a special case of the **inner product** expressed
136   as: $C[I;J]=f/A[I;]gB[;J]$, where f and g are scalar dyadic operators. It is de-
137   noted in APL as $Af.gB$ so that a matrix multiply of matrices A and B is
138   specified as $A+.\times B$. A and B can be vectors, matrices, or higher-dimen-
139   sioned arrays. The familiar **cartesian product** is termed the **outer product** in
140   APL and expressed as: $A\circ.fB$, where A and B are arrays and f is a scalar dy-
141   adic operation. **Transposition** exists in two forms. Monadic transposition,
142    $\lozenge M$, interchanges the last two coordinates of the operand. Dyadic trans-
143   position, $N\lozenge M$, utilizes a left operand which specifies the coordinates that
144   are to be interchanged.
145   Components of a vector V are **reversed** with the monadic operation ϕV;
146   the operation is extended to higher-dimensioned arrays by specifying a co-
147   ordinate index: $\phi[I]V$. The operation $K\phi V$ rotates the vector left K places
148   if K is positive and right K places if K is negative. Applied to higher-dimen-
149   sioned arrays, $K\phi[I]A$ also specifies the coordinate index; K may be a scalar
150   (and is extended to all dimensions or A) or an array (where each component
151   of K specifies the rotation to be applied to the respective coordinate of A).
152   **Compression**, U/V, uses a logical vector U and suppresses from V those
153   components that correspond to 0 components in U. When applied to a
154   higher-dimensioned array, an index, $U/[I]A$, specifies along which coordi-
155   nate compression is applied. **Expansion** provides the converse of compres-
156   sion and is expressed as $U\backslash V$ and $U\backslash[I]A$ to correspond with the forms of
157   compression.
158   The function $T\uparrow V$, called **take**, selects the first T components of V if T is
159   positive and the last T if T is negative. Similarly, **drop**, $T\downarrow V$, drops the first
160   T components or the last T components of V if T is positive or negative,
161   respectively.

162   The **index of** the first occurrence of a scalar S in a vector V is expressed
163   as $V \iota S$. The concept is extended to right operands which are arrays and the
164   result assumes the size of the right operand. The **membership** function, $S \epsilon V$,
165   produces a value 1 if a scalar S is an element of a vector V and produces 0
166   otherwise. The left operand, in this case, is extended to arrays and produces
167   a result of the same size.
168   The permutation of indices necessary to order a vector in ascending or
169   descending sequence is provided with the grade up and grade down func-
170   tions. **Grade up** is expressed as ΔV so that $V[\Delta V]$ produces V in ascending
171   order. Similarly, **grade down**, ∇V, applied to V, that is $V[\nabla V]$, produces V
172   in descending order. The **deal** function, expressed as $A?B$, produces a
173   vector of A components selected pseudo-randomly from B without
174   replacement.
175   **Encode**, written $B \perp A$, produces the base ten value of the vector A to the
176   base B. Similarly, **decode**, written $B \top A$, produces the vector of coefficients
177   to the base B necessary to decode the value A.
178   In addition to primitive arithmetic operations, mathematical functions,
179   and functions on arrays, APL permits the user to define functions which are
180   not a part of the language and effectively to develop programs in the usual
181   sense. **Function definition** requires that the APL system leave the **execution**
182   **mode**, which is the normal mode of operation, and enter the definition mode.
183   In the **definition mode**, statements are not executed as they are entered but are
184   stored as part of a **defined function**. The syntax of a function is determined
185   by the **function header**, which is the opening statement and which gives a
186   prototype of the function. Defined functions can be: **dyadic**, $A \ FCN \ B$;
187   **monadic**, $FCN \ A$; or **niladic**, FCN—where FCN is the function name and
188   A and B are arguments. Moreover, a function can produce an **explicit result**,
189   so that it can be used in a mathematical expression, or provide an **implicit**
190   **result** so that it must be invoked in a statement by itself. A **function definition**
191   consists of four kinds of constructs: (1) an opening ∇ (del) symbol; (2) a
192   **function header**, such as $R \leftarrow X \ PLUS \ Y$; (3) a **function body** containing the
193   statements that comprise the function; and (4) a final del symbol. Variables
194   may be specified as being **local** to a function by including them in the func-
195   tion header, each preceded by a semicolon.
196   Within a defined function, statements are numbered so that they may be
197   used as an operand to the monadic **branch** operation, written as $\rightarrow E$. If E
198   is a scalar constant or variable, then the next statement executed is the one
199   with that number—if it exists. Otherwise, an **exit** is made from the function.
200   If E is a vector, then the statement with the number $1 \uparrow E$ is executed next.
201   If E is an empty (null) vector, then the next statement in sequence is executed
202   —that is, control drops through the branch statement. Given variables X
203   and Y and relation r, the following statements branch to S or drop through
204   if X r Y *are true or false respectively:* $\rightarrow(X \text{r} Y)/S$, $\rightarrow(X \text{r} Y)\rho S$, and $\rightarrow S \times \iota X \text{r} Y$.
205   Branching is facilitated through use of **statement labels**, which precede the
206   body of a statement and are separated from it with a colon and which are
207   local to the function definition.

208   **Function modification** is achieved in a variety of ways. Statements can be
209   **deleted, inserted,** and **replaced.** The function header may be modified and
210   an entire function or parts of it can be displayed with one of several display
211   operations.
212   **Program checkout** is enhanced by a trace function and a stop control func-
213   tion. The **trace function** is invoked by a statement of the form: $T\Delta FCN \leftarrow V$
214   where FCN is the function to be traced and V is a vector of statement num-
215   bers in FCN. The explicit value of designated statements is displayed and
216   identified as they are executed. The **stop control function** is invoked by:
217    $S\Delta FCN \leftarrow V$, where the FCN and V are defined above. Execution of an in-
218   voked function is stopped prior to the execution of designated statements.
219   When a function is stopped, facilities ordinarily available in the execution
220   mode are available to the user.
221   **Halted functions** arise in three ways: (1) as a result of a statement error
222   detected by the computer; (2) by pressing the ATTN key to halt execution;
223   and (3) by the stop control function. Execution may be resumed by branch-
224   ing, $\rightarrow S$, to the next statement to be executed. Defined functions can invoke
225   other defined functions and the process is extended to as many levels as
226   required. A halted (or stopped) function is said to be a **suspended function**
227   and the functions that invoked the suspended function are termed **pendent**
228   **functions.** Pendent functions may not be modified. Suspended functions can
229   be modified and execution may proceed with the statement that was
230   modified.
231   The **input** operation can take two forms: evaluated input and character
232   input. **Evaluated input** is denoted by the **quad symbol,** $\square$, and may be used
233   in any context that a constant or variable can be used. The input provided
234   by the user is evaluated as though it were a part of the expression containing
235   the quad symbol. **Character input** uses the **quote-quad symbol,** $\square$, and allows
236   a **literal** to be entered without the enclosing quote symbols. A quad or
237   quote-quad immediately to the left of a specification operator denotes **output**
238   and is frequently used to display partial results of a complex expression.
239   APL achieves its greatest utility in three ways: (1) as an interactive desk
240   calculator; (2) as a programming system; and (3) as a means of describing
241   complex discrete systems. In the last case, the system description can be
242   verified with the APL system.

INDEX

INDEX